®

THE INSTITUTE FOR

INTEGRATIVE NUTRITION WORKBOOK

YOUR GUIDE TO A SUCCESSFUL HEALTH COACHING CAREER

SECOND EDITION

Published by Integrative Nutrition
3 East 28th St. 12th Floor, New York, NY 10016
integrativenutrition.com

For ordering information or special discounts for bulk purchases, please contact
Integrative Nutrition, 3 East 28th St. 12th Floor, New York, NY 10016, 877-730-5444

Design and composition by Greenleaf Book Group LLC.

This book has been published to support the success of our students.
We are committed to educating our students to lead healthy, fulfilling lives in
a desired career, and we are happy to provide the latest, most accurate information
at the time of publication. Please note that information changes rapidly in our fast paced world,
and students should consult the website for the most up-to-date curriculum content.

Publisher's Cataloging-In-Publication Data
(Prepared by The Donohue Group, Inc.)
The Institute for Integrative Nutrition workbook : your guide to a successful
health coaching career. -- 2nd ed.

p. ; cm.

ISBN: 978-0-9795264-4-2 (pbk.)

1. Health coaches--Vocational guidance--Textbooks. 2. Nutrition counseling--Vocational guidance--Textbooks. 3. Entrepreneurship--Textbooks. 4. Health coaches--Vocational guidance--Problems, exercises, etc. 5. Nutrition counseling--Vocational guidance--Problems, exercises, etc. 6. Entrepreneurship--Problems, exercises, etc. I. Integrative Nutrition (Firm)

R727.415 .I578 2013
610.737/069 2012954317

Part of the Tree Neutral® program that offsets the number of trees consumed
in printing this book by taking proactive steps such as planting trees in direct
proportion to the number of trees used. www.treeneutral.com.

Printed in the United States of America on acid-free paper.

14 15 16 17 10 9 8 7 6 5 4 3

Second Edition

ACKNOWLEDGMENTS

Joshua Rosenthal for his visionary leadership, commitment, and unending support of Integrative Nutrition students, alumni, and staff.

Integrative Nutrition Staff for being the most intelligent and committed group of people around.

Integrative Nutrition Students for inspiring us with their passion for learning and desire to help others.

Integrative Nutrition Alumni for blazing the trail to a new future of health and happiness in America and the world.

Current and Future Health Coaching Clients for their commitment to personal growth and their trust in the 6-month program.

Our mission is to play a crucial role in improving health and happiness, and through that process, create a ripple effect that transforms the world.

CONTENTS

Never doubt that a small group of thoughtful, committed citizens can change the world; indeed, it's the only thing that ever has.

—Margaret Mead

INTRODUCTION

Our current healthcare system is not getting people healthy. Food-related disease is one of the leading causes of preventable death in the United States. Poor diet is linked to certain types of cancer, obesity, diabetes, and heart disease. Other health conditions, such as headaches, ADD, IBS, asthma, and allergies are rapidly increasing in the United States and spreading around the world as other countries adopt our way of life and our eating habits. As a result, more people depend on prescriptions, medication costs are soaring, health insurance prices are higher than ever before, and doctors spend less time with their patients. Increasing medications and operations is not the answer to our current health dilemma. Prevention through diet and lifestyle is the answer. People are still gaining weight and getting sick despite abundant advice to eat more fruits and vegetables, exercise, and cut out junk food. We desperately need straightforward, honest advice on how to become healthier.

As a student at the Institute for Integrative Nutrition (IIN), you will gain fundamental and practical knowledge of nutrition and how to live a balanced life. This information will help you find a new level of health and happiness in your life and positively influence other people. Step out and use this education to influence a world that desperately needs your help. You may fear this work and want to procrastinate getting started. We encourage you to take action and move beyond being only a consumer of information. Get out there and educate people about your beliefs.

If you are passionate about health and want a life and career that you love, this is a great career for you. We are here to teach you and guide you through the process. Our curriculum will show you how to develop a successful practice as a Health Coach, step by step. As a student at Integrative Nutrition, you will learn how to share your education with friends, family, and the general public, and those people you touch will influence the people they encounter. As Health Coaches, we have the ability to create a ripple effect that will improve the lives of countless people around the globe.

Our school's mission is to play a crucial role in improving health and happiness, and through that process, create a ripple effect that transforms the world. With your dedication and hard work, we can make this happen. Thank you for choosing our school and thank you for following your heart. Let's get started!

You can't just sit there and wait for people to give you that golden dream; you've got to get out there and make it happen for yourself.

—Diana Ross

HOW TO USE THIS BOOK

FOLLOW OUR SIMPLE INSTRUCTIONS

Building a business does not have to be complicated, but it does take hard work. This book, along with the curriculum and a guideline of basic steps that we call the Golden Path, outlines our simple, time-tested process for starting your practice. Along the way you may find yourself distracted by details or tempted to overcomplicate things. Relax and stay focused. Follow our simple instructions and you will experience success.

MAKE IT YOUR OWN

Just as there is no one diet that is right for everyone, there is no one business plan that is best for every Health Coach. The information in this book reflects our years of experience helping coaches build successful businesses. Not every suggestion will be right for you, so use your intuition and intelligence to personalize these business strategies.

GET SUPPORT

Starting your own business will be a new, challenging experience for many of you. Our community provides tremendous support to make this happen. Ask your Accountability Coach, and fellow students for help along the way. Hold study groups related to business topics. Enlist your friends and family to cheer you on or to provide expert advice from their fields. Having a support team increases your chances of success.

DO THE EXERCISES

Even though they may seem simple, the exercises in this book are carefully designed to walk you through the process of starting your business. We have created sections for notes throughout this workbook, so make a mess of it. When in doubt, refer back to the Golden Path to help keep you on track.

USE YOUR WHOLE EDUCATION

Don't rely only on this book to teach you how to start a practice as a Health Coach. All the course components provide critical information about how to be successful. This book is just one part of your curriculum. It supplements all of the other tools that we provide to help increase your knowledge base.

GO AT YOUR OWN PACE (BUT DON'T PROCRASTINATE)

This book contains a lot of information, and you don't have to do everything all at once. Some of these steps will be easy and fun for you. Others will be more challenging. Build your business at your own pace.

THE INSTITUTE FOR

INTEGRATIVE NUTRITION WORKBOOK

YOUR GUIDE TO A SUCCESSFUL HEALTH COACHING CAREER

SECOND EDITION

If one advances confidently in the direction of his dreams, and endeavors to live the life which he has imagined, he will meet with success unexpected in common hours.

—Henry David Thoreau

CHAPTER 1:

YOUR ROAD TO SUCCESS

Congratulations! You are on your way to transforming yourself and having a career and life you love. The key to having success in this endeavor is to maintain a deep level of focus. Treat this year at Integrative Nutrition as if you were in Harvard Medical School. Work hard, pay attention, make your education a priority, and follow our guidelines, and you will experience success.

CAREER OPPORTUNITIES

So many opportunities are available for working in the health coaching field. Your Integrative Nutrition education will open many doors for you. Your personal and professional interests can help shape the design of your business. You can choose the path you most enjoy. Doing this work gives you the ability to help many people in ways you may not have previously imagined.

Some of you will want to build a practice as a full-time Health Coach. You have the entrepreneurial spirit! You will be able to work with clients one-on-one and in groups. If you want to address large groups, you will receive training on how to give lectures and other public speaking engagements.

Some of you will want to be Health Coaches but would like to work in a setting such as a spa, a yoga studio, or doctor's office instead of setting up your own practice. You can work in corporate wellness and help organizations change the health of their employees. Many of our graduates choose holistic occupations other than health coaching, and we'll cover more career possibilities throughout the program and in this book. You may find yourself inspired to write a book, create healthy products, design customized health programs, or even be on television or the radio. You may also want

Notes:

WHAT IS HEALTH COACHING?

Health coaching is a process in which a Health Coach guides a client to reach his or her health and life goals by making step-by-step changes to his or her diet and lifestyle. The client learns about new, healthy foods and the concept of primary foods: relationships, physical activity, career, and spirituality. The Health Coach works with the client to set goals to gradually incorporate improved primary and secondary foods into the client's life. Health coaching is completely focused on the client—where the client is and where he or she wants to go with his or her health and life. The Health Coach acts as a guide, helping the client to gain control of and take responsibility for his or her health.

to become involved in advocacy and outreach work. And finally, some of you are here to learn how to make healthier food choices for yourself and your families. Whichever path you choose, you have the opportunity to do work you love and be an instrument of change in your community and for the world.

You are at the very beginning of your Integrative Nutrition journey. We will guide you step-by-step throughout the program and this book to have a career you love. You may know now what you want to do with this work. Or, you may not know. For some of you, your vision will change over time. For others it will stay the same. That's okay! As you go through the first part of the program, you'll experience a personal transformation and learn more about yourself. You'll be asked to consider if entrepreneurship is right for you. Many of you will be surprised with the results! You'll also be asked to consider things like how much time you have to commit toward building your practice. It takes a lot of work and dedication to be an entrepreneur—so being realistic about your vision is important. If you have less time to dedicate to this program and to building a health coaching practice, that doesn't mean you can't do this work. It just may take you longer before you will be able to do this work full-time. Know that we are here to support you and guide you to achieve your dreams and have a career you love.

CAREER ASSESSMENT

At this time, we ask that you reflect on your reasons for wanting to become a Health Coach or for enrolling at Integrative Nutrition. Maybe it is to help other people, or maybe you want to learn how to best care for yourself. Perhaps you want to leave your current job and create a new career that you are passionate about. Whatever your reasons, please consider the following questions:

What are you doing in your current career?

On a scale of 1–10, how much do you enjoy your career?

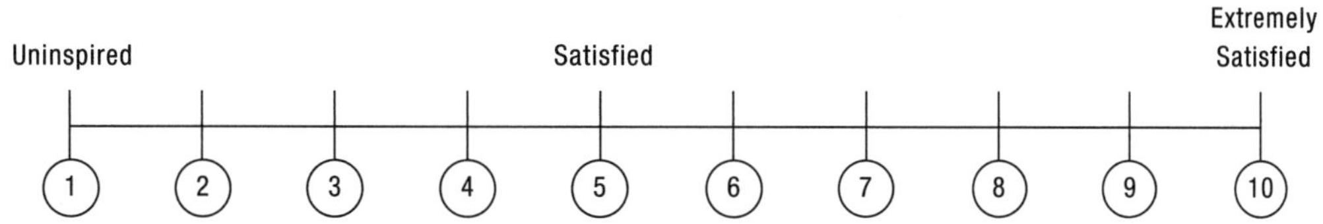

What are five things you like about your current career?

1.
2.
3.
4.
5.

What are five things you wish you could change about your current career?

1.
2.
3.
4.
5.

Notes:

Notes:

Please list your top five reasons for wanting to launch a new career:

1. ....

2. ....

3. ....

4. ....

5. ....

CREATING YOUR VISION

You are ultimately in charge of your business and the direction you would like to go. The clearer your intentions and vision for your practice become, the more likely it is that you will be successful. Your vision, or internal mission, is simply what you would like to accomplish. It is the compass for your business and gives you direction on how to move forward with purpose and clarity. This vision will keep you going every day, even when things are not going so well or according to your plan. It will help give you a road map to follow. Focus on your vision every day. Let it inspire and guide you to reach your goals and be successful.

To develop your vision, it is important to consider why you want to do this work and your higher goals for your business. Take a moment to think about why you are here. What are your intentions for the school year and beyond? Why are you attending Integrative Nutrition? What do you want to do with your Institute of Integrative Nutrition (IIN) experience? Slow down your mind and go back to the conversations you had when you first heard of IIN. Recall your visions of success and freedom. What did your life look like as a result of making the decision to enroll? What problems did you see dissolve? What situation was improved?

Did you envision what your life would look like one year from now? Five years from now? Did you see yourself sitting across from a client experiencing a massive breakthrough? Were you in a kitchen experimenting with new recipes? Did you see your product in a store, sitting on a shelf in Whole Foods?

Your vision may be less specific right now, but think about the larger feeling behind it all. What sort of impact do you want to have? Do you want to teach, guide, and support others? Perhaps you would like to feel the joy of changing another's life or your own. Everyone's vision will be different, but when paired with a strong intention, it can be very powerful. The clearer your vision, the clearer your path toward reaching your goals.

Here is a quick exercise that will help you define your vision. You may even want to cut these pages out of the workbook and put them on your wall or someplace where you will see them frequently or, copy your intention onto a Post-it and carry it with you. It's important not to lose sight of your vision!

Why do you want to do this work?

What motivates you?

What type of person do you want to help?

What difference do you want to make in the world?

Notes:

Notes:

When are you inspired?

Do you want to build a practice as a Health Coach and do this work full-time?

Do you want to use your Integrative Nutrition education to launch a business or product other than health coaching?

What is your life's purpose?

Put all that together and complete these sentences:

Notes:

My intention for being at Integrative Nutrition and doing this work is:

....

....

....

....

....

....

My vision for myself and my life is to:

....

....

....

....

....

....

Now think about living your ideal life and map out that feeling in your mind. What words come to mind? Keep those words around you constantly. Change them until you get them right. Engage in business opportunities and activities that bring out those feelings!

Your intentions and your vision are vital to your success. That's why having a deep, clear vision is an important step of the Golden Path! Without it, you would be all over the map, confused about what to do and what direction to take. So when you are feeling like you have lost your way, come back to your vision. Refocus. Dedicate your energy and resources to tasks, people, and activities that light your fire. This workbook will help you to define your goals, prioritize, delegate, and challenge yourself in new ways. But it is up to you to see your vision clearly, so include details and specifics! Brace yourself for the wave of energy as success comes your way.

Never leave that till tomorrow which you can do today.

—Benjamin Franklin

CHAPTER 2:

A PERSONAL TRANSFORMATION

The main challenge that prevents some students from starting a business as a Health Coach is thinking that they don't know enough. This thought process causes people to get stuck in what we call "paralyzed and procrastination mode." You put everything ahead of health coaching, saying that your life is too busy or you have more important things to do, but underlying all of this is the belief that you may not be good enough. We do not want this to happen to you! Chances are you are an incredibly intelligent and gifted person who has a knack for helping others. It is important for you to recognize that not everyone has these gifts.

To become a successful Health Coach and entrepreneur, you must work to increase your level of self-esteem, confidence, and self-trust. You are a unique person with a lot to offer the world. It is essential that you become familiar with your strengths, and that you are able to communicate them to other people.

FACING YOUR FEARS

We've designed this workbook and the business and marketing curriculum to provide all of the necessary tools to build your practice. However, marketing knowledge will not be enough if your fears get in your way. The following thoughts and feelings can hold us back: self-doubt, lack of confidence, confusion, jealousy, comparison to others, anger, fear, and unworthiness. We are all human; it's normal to have a fear of the unknown, especially if you have never done this work before. Ultimately, fear is behind everything that holds us back. We wonder if we will be successful, if people will like us, if we know enough, if we will succeed financially, and so on. The good thing is that fear is only in your mind and you have the power to choose how you respond to it. Fear can paralyze

Notes:

you or you can use the energy to push yourself forward. Our fears sometimes give us a false sense of safety, but in the long run they keep us stuck. If you take steps to get support to face your fears and build your confidence, you can achieve the success you truly desire.

Try the following exercise to help you work on the fears you may have about doing this work.

What is one fear you have around doing this work (e.g., knowing enough, public speaking, financial success)?

....

....

....

....

....

When you really examine this fear, do you believe it is true or will come true?

....

....

What is it costing you to hold on to this fear (e.g., peace of mind)?

....

....

....

....

....

What are the benefits of letting go of this thought (e.g., you'd be able to focus on your goals and passions)?

....

....

....

....

....

What are three to five actions you can take now to reduce this fear and move forward?

1. ....

2. ....

3. ....

4. ....

5. ....

Notes:

CREATING SELF-TRUST

Self-trust is one of the most powerful abilities we have, yet many of us overlook it, don't know how to harness it, or are unaware it even exists. In order to succeed, we must know and trust our own opinions, instincts, and desires.

This is often difficult to do because many of us live in a constant state of fear, worry, or overwhelm. All of your actions and decisions come from a reaction to these feelings, not from a place of power and certainty. It is important to understand that the things into which you put your energy, how you react to life's surprises and curveballs, and the daily choices you make, all shape your life. If all of these actions and thought processes stem from fear, you are giving up your personal power.

When you trust in yourself to handle what life brings your way, challenges big or small, you begin to take an active role in your life. You begin to let go of what the experts have to say, what the latest self-help book tells you to do, and the conflicting advice from friends and family, and you learn how to rely on yourself.

Self-trust grows when you slow down and notice your thoughts or feelings. Choose not to dismiss them right away, but ask yourself why they are there. Make it a learning experience. Practice self-kindness and curiosity. Finally, make self-trust a continued practice. You will consistently build self-trust by making promises to yourself and then keeping them. Be clear with your agreements, make sure you are fully able to commit, and then acknowledge when you have kept your promise.

It's a very rewarding exercise to cultivate and nurture your self-trust. It is most needed when you are experiencing personal and professional growth, and see your life changing around you. Self-trust will give you the energy and direction to confidently move forward and survive whatever comes your way.

Notes:

TIPS TO CULTIVATE SELF-CONFIDENCE

1. **Dress for success.** How you dress can have a big impact on how you perceive yourself. When you feel confident about how you look, it changes the way you carry yourself and encourages you to interact with others confidently. This doesn't mean that you have to spend a lot of money. Consider spending a bit more on a few high-quality items instead of buying a bunch of lesser-quality items.

   ACTION STEP: Clean out your closet. Donate all of the clothing that no longer suits you and mindfully choose some new pieces that make you feel great.

2. **Walk this way.** Walk with energy and purpose. Allow your body to invigorate your mind.

   ACTION STEP: Practice! Make a conscious effort to STRUT.

3. **Stand tall.** The way you carry yourself paints a picture of who you are. Sit up straight, stand up tall, hold your head up, and look people in the eye. Empower yourself to empower others.

   ACTION STEP: Check in with yourself while you're sitting at your desk. Are you sitting up straight, shoulders back, abdominals in? Is your head in alignment with your spine?

4. **Get moving.** Exercising energizes your body and mind, improves physical appearance, and encourages positive momentum to move forward to reach your goals.

   ACTION STEP: Schedule a time to get moving in your planner, so that you're sure to follow through. Perhaps it's time to try a fun new exercise that interests you.

5. **Speak up.** Challenge yourself to speak up in every group discussion. This will help you organize your thoughts and refine your public speaking skills. It will also help others to perceive you as a leader.

   ACTION STEP: Practice! Next time you're in a group, either in a personal or professional setting, make a point to contribute.

6. **Be thankful.** Having gratitude for all the positive components of your life will help you to focus on what you have rather than what you don't. List everything that you are grateful for: loving relationships, personal successes, your health, your unique impact on the world. Let this list encourage you to move forward with confidence.

   ACTION STEP: Write a list once a week. Let it guide you through to the following week.

Please take a moment now to evaluate what you believe are your greatest qualities.

List your top eight qualities:

1. ....

2. ....

3. ....

4. ....

5. ....

6. ....

7. ....

8. ....

Notes:

FACING YOUR STRENGTHS AND WEAKNESSES

We all have strengths and weaknesses. The SWOT analysis on the next page allows you to pinpoint your strengths and weaknesses and recognize the obstacles that may come your way. This exercise also highlights the opportunities in your life and helps you realize your full potential as a Health Coach and entrepreneur. Your SWOT analysis will change as you change, so it's helpful to revisit this exercise periodically.

TAKING CARE OF YOU

Starting a new career is exciting and rewarding. For most of you, it's an opportunity to do what you love while simultaneously helping others. However, starting a new business can be challenging at first. For this reason, we want you to take incredibly good care of yourself this year. In order to be a successful Health Coach and entrepreneur, you have to be healthy, happy, well rested, and in balance. To support you in taking care of yourself while building your business, we will continuously offer exercises to help you stay in balance. In addition, you will have the support of your classmates throughout the program to help you stay on track with self-care. We want you to be healthy and happy throughout the process and graduate from Integrative Nutrition feeling better than ever.

TOP SELF-CARE TIPS

1. Take one step at a time.
2. Schedule primary food activities.
3. Eat healthy foods.
4. Use a coach for support.
5. Take breaks.
6. Move your body.
7. Take slow, deep breaths frequently.
8. Don't compare yourself to others.
9. Spend time with supportive people.
10. Keep a gratitude journal.

Notes:

SWOT ANALYSIS

SWOT is an acronym for strengths, weaknesses, opportunities, and threats. Using this chart enables you to clarify what direction to move in by being aware of where you are and where you have the potential to go. The reason some coaches fail to grow their businesses and improve isn't necessarily because they lack the ability. Instead, they lack awareness of their skills, skill deficiencies, and opportunities that could propel them forward. Once you identify these areas and take responsibility for each, you can then focus on what will help you progress.

Strengths: Things you do well, areas in which you excel, your resources
Weaknesses: What you do poorly, what you lack, what is not working well
Opportunities: What opportunities are coming your way, where you see potential
Threats: What could get in the way, obstacles or problems you foresee

Here are some examples of strengths and weaknesses to get you started:

- Written communication
- Speaking/presentation skills
- Interpersonal skills
- Computer and technical skills
- Coaching skills
- Conceptual skills (ability to see the big picture)
- Ability to confront others constructively
- Organizational skills, including the ability to set priorities
- Listening skills
- Sales skills
- Ability to delegate
- Relationship-development abilities

INTERNAL	**STRENGTHS:**	**WEAKNESSES:**
EXTERNAL	**OPPORTUNITIES:**	**THREATS:**

PRIMARY FOOD

Notes:

At Integrative Nutrition, we have coined the phrase "primary food." Primary food feeds us, but doesn't come on a plate. When our primary foods are balanced and fulfilling, our lives feed us, making what we eat secondary.

We group primary foods into four categories: healthy relationships, regular physical activity, a desired career, and a spiritual practice. We invite you to look at these areas of your life from a new perspective—as a form of nutrition. This is especially important when starting this new career, because being at your best will encourage other people to want to work with you.

Consider these four areas of your life: relationships, physical activity, career, and spirituality. Write a few sentences about each, describing any imbalances you may have in these areas and any actions you would like to take to create more balance.

How are your relationships?

How is your physical activity?

Notes:

How is your career?

....

....

....

....

....

....

How are you in the area of spirituality?

....

....

....

....

....

....

POSITIVE THINKING

Henry Ford once said, "Whether you think that you can, or that you can't, you are usually right." When it comes to health coaching and being an entrepreneur, this is definitely true. Believing in yourself is a key to success.

Start to envision yourself as a Health Coach or in your new career. What does your life look like? What do your days look like? When do you work? What other types of services might you offer? What do you do in your free time? Who are the key support people in your life? What health concerns have you cleared up? What else is going on in your life?

Unfortunately, we seldom have an abundance of positive thoughts in our heads. Most of us have a tendency to focus on the things in our life that are not working. At Integrative Nutrition we like to ask, "What is new and good?" This question breaks the habit of focusing on negative thoughts and retrains your brain to focus on what is going well. The study of positive psychology tells us that focusing on positive thoughts rewires our brains to think in terms of accomplishment, opportunity, and possibility. You will attract more good into your life because what you put your attention on will grow.

Notes:

What are three things that are going well in your life now?

1. ....

2. ....

3. ....

What are three things that are going well for you so far at Integrative Nutrition?

1. ....

2. ....

3. ....

What are three things you are looking forward to about health coaching or about your new career?

1. ....

2. ....

3. ....

Start to pay attention to where your mind goes most of the time. How much of your attention is on what is not going well in your life? How much attention is on what is going well?

You can incorporate positive thinking into your life in many different ways. Some simple ways are to ask people what is new and good, brag to others about what is going well with you (and then let them brag back), consciously put your mind on positive thoughts, or write everything for which you are grateful in a journal. Practice different ways to increase positive thinking in your life and see what works best for you. Keeping a journal is a great tool. You can write about the positive food and lifestyle changes you're exploring, jot down what you're grateful for each day, and write down the goals that you have for your life. We recommend you use the Integrative Nutrition Journal that you received in your welcome box, and after three months you can continue your own journal. Also, use your classmates for support by sharing with them what is going well in your life. Notice how you create your own reality. When you practice positive thinking, your world begins to look brighter.

Begin somewhere;
you cannot build a reputation
on what you intend to do.

—Liz Smith

CHAPTER 3:

ENTREPRENEURSHIP BASICS

Welcome to entrepreneurship! As a small business owner, you have stepped into a whole new world that operates very differently from most corporate environments. While you will be afforded new freedoms, working for yourself requires using a different skill set that you may not be accustomed to using.

First, ask yourself: are you right for entrepreneurship? Is entrepreneurship right for you? Entrepreneurs are self-motivated, organized, and take responsibility. Staying motivated requires a mindset of constant focus on your goals, deciding moment to moment to move forward, creating momentum in actions that directly build your progress toward a completed goal, and a little bit of sacrifice.

Note that even though you get to make your own hours and decide when to take your lunch break or vacation without asking for permission from a boss, you are still controlled by other people like clients, vendors, and yourself. Starting a business is about the customer, not you.

Starting a business is also stressful and time consuming, especially in the beginning. You may experience a transition period of instability and uncertainty while establishing your practice or business. Honoring your structure and respecting your strengths and weaknesses will help make this stage smoother.

On the other side of this stage is the freedom you seek from nine-to-five monotony, the flexibility for location freedom, instituting work hours that support your personal interests, working to live rather than living to work, and the unbeatable satisfaction of contributing to the betterment of someone else's life.

Second, evaluate your experience. Passion is not a substitute for the skills to grow and sustain a business. What skills do you need to develop? Which ones need dusting off? Where are you already strong? Where will you need support? Acknowledging your strengths and weaknesses early on will keep you focused during your training.

Notes:

Third, how comfortable are you with risk? How comfortable are you operating without knowing everything? Are you flexible? Spontaneous? Creative? How do you view potential obstacles? Do you shut down or do you dig in and find value in the challenge? What is your relationship with failure? Fear? Does it paralyze you or reveal new information to you?

Getting answers to all of the above is not pertinent to starting a business, but prepare to evaluate yourself from that perspective throughout the process. Because you answer to yourself, getting stuck is an easy trap to slow your momentum. Remember you have the support of the school and fellow students to help you uncover nuggets of truth that will reinvigorate the pursuit of your vision.

Often, it is very easy for us to think about how we are "not good enough," and we wonder if we have what it takes to be successful in business. Our inner critic likes to tell us that we have faults or that other people know more than we do. It's important to recognize this inner voice, and take steps to lessen its potential effect on you. If you listen to your doubts, or if you let your fears get in the way, you may not take the steps needed to attain the success you truly desire. If you are able to catch the negative thought patterns and then recognize that they truly have no power over you, you can move forward more easily.

When you really stop to think about it, you will understand that you have a lot to offer your friends, family, clients, and yourself by being a Health Coach. Use these steps to help minimize any potential self-limiting beliefs before they sabotage your efforts:

- When a fear or negative thought comes up, stop and recognize that the thought is there. Take a deep breath, and notice how you feel.
- Check in with yourself, and notice that the thought only has power over you if you allow it.
- Ask yourself, "Do I know for sure that this thought is true?" or, "What is the worst that can happen if I take this action or do this marketing step?"
- Focus on turning your negative thought around and choose a different thought that causes you less anxiety or fear.
- Figure out how to keep your mind focused on your goals, and believe in yourself.
- Take step-by-step actions toward your goals and don't let your fears hold you back.
- Keep practicing, continue this process, and trust yourself.

Again, entrepreneurship is living moment-to-moment in action, driven by an insatiable appetite for seeing dreams come to life, whatever those dreams look like.

CREATING A BUSINESS MIND

As you begin your education and learn the skills needed to build your practice, it's important to cultivate your mindset. Believe it or not, once you become immersed in

Notes:

this work, you are a business owner, whether you end up health coaching full-time or part-time or launching a product or program. As such, you will need to start thinking like a business person. Consider what it will take for you to be successful, how you will talk about your work, the confidence you will project, the structure of your time, and in general the ways you can present a professional image to the world. Start practicing what it is like to be more professional and concise in your emails and in conversations, especially when you talk about your training at the school. Ask yourself, "How would a successful business person behave in this situation?" Focus on building your confidence, and trust that you know enough to try the marketing tips you will learn in this workbook and in the program. And most importantly, take action every week toward building your business.

BALANCING HOME AND WORK LIFE

Dedicating yourself to this work means reaching deep to stay aware and in tune with your clients. Although giving of yourself comes to you naturally as a holistic health professional, your gift has its limits. Honor those limits by caring for yourself along the way. Your energy to give to others is powered by your own wellness, so guard your self-care carefully. It is the foundation for successful clients.

Starting a new career as a Health Coach is exciting and rewarding. For most of you, it's an opportunity to do what you love while simultaneously helping others. However, starting a new business can be challenging at first. For this reason, we want you to take incredibly good care of yourself this year. In order to be a successful Health Coach, you have to be healthy, happy, well rested, and in balance. To support you in taking care of yourself while building your business, we will do exercises to help you stay in balance. In addition, you will have the support of your classmates throughout the program to help you stay on track with self-care. We want you to be healthy and happy throughout the process, and graduate from Integrative Nutrition feeling better than ever.

When seeking balance between your home and work life, allow for the ebb and flow of life. We have busy seasons and not-as-busy seasons, but some seasons are more predictable than others. Take a bird's eye view of your year and plan within that rhythm.

Time management will greatly contribute to a manageable workload and stress level. Create dedicated work and study hours—then stick to that commitment. When your time is up, walk away from the project until your next dedicated time. Time away is just as important as the time spent focusing on a particular task. Relax, focus on family, care for yourself, and be present. When you're away from work or study, be very away from it. This allows for deeper relaxation, more effective recharging, and better work efficiency. Your set hours can change with the availability of your seasons, too. To get others (like family members) on board with your set hours, you have to honor your word about when you work or study and when you don't.

Notes:

This separation between family or personal life and work or study also applies to conversation. Those closest to you can be your best support resources, but establish boundaries about when and where you talk shop. This may also mean you find a professional support group, a study group, or even an online support community to reserve your personal conversations for personal matters.

We believe in working smarter, not harder, so batch similar activities together. The energy spent jumping from one task to another can slow you down, but staying on one mental track for several activities can free up time as well as energy. For instance, cooking several meals at once, running all errands at the same time, and seeing clients only on certain days are examples of batching similar activities.

To be successful in doing this work and building your business, it's important to develop an initial structure so that you consistently have time for study or work. Do the exercises, follow the recommendations in class, and start putting yourself out there to set up, organize, and develop your practice. If you have consistent time in your schedule each week to learn, practice, and reach out for support, you will be more likely to succeed. Take a moment now and think about when you will find time for your business.

Which day(s) of the week do you have time to devote toward your business?

What time on that day(s) will you spend on these activities?

What day(s) of the week will you dedicate to yourself and self-care?

What will you do to take care of yourself?

Notes:

The trouble with not having a goal is that you can spend your life running up and down the field and never score.

—Bill Copeland

CHAPTER 4:

GOAL SETTING AND TIME MANAGEMENT

Keeping your energy focused is futile without direction. Where are you headed? What are you working toward? How will you know once you've arrived?

Now we would like you to think about what you want to do with your education at Integrative Nutrition. What are your goals for building your health coaching practice? How do they fit in with goals you have for other aspects of your life? This process will help clarify what you want to accomplish. In each section, please be sure to list at least one goal related to health coaching and your career, the number of clients you want to have, when you want to leave your current job, what kind of clients you would like to work with, or how much money you would like to make from doing work that makes a difference. During the coming months, you will be taking consistent action to make these goals a reality.

What are three goals you have for the next week?

1. ....

2. ....

3. ....

What are three goals you have for the next month?

1. ....

2. ....

3. ....

Notes:

What are three goals you have for the next six months?

1. ...

2. ...

3. ...

What are three goals you have for the next year?

1. ...

2. ...

3. ...

What are three goals you have for the next two years?

1. ...

2. ...

3. ...

What are three goals you have for the next five years?

1. ...

2. ...

3. ...

What are three goals you have for the next ten years?

1. ...

2. ...

3. ...

BE YOUR OWN BEST MANAGER

Here are some tips to be your own best manager. Incorporate a few into your week and see how it goes. Add more as you feel more comfortable and get ready to feel accomplished!

- Identify your values and operate from them.
- Clarify your purpose, priorities, and goals.
- Design and implement an effective business plan.

Notes:

- Create strategic plans of action.
- Learn to work smarter—not harder.
- Eliminate time wasters.
- Plan your days.
- Set a schedule and keep it.
- Take a stretch break every 20 minutes.
- Be dressed for "work."
- Get feedback from colleagues and experts.
- Collect information: quotes, articles, statistics.
- Keep your workspace organized.
- Enhance telephone skills.
- Follow through with clients.
- Market your business consistently.
- Join at least one professional association.
- Develop powerful networking abilities.
- Keep accurate records.
- Be a calculated risk taker.
- Be willing to move on.
- Make sure your needs are being met.
- Exercise regularly.
- Create a support system.
- Continue your education.
- Get out of the house/office EVERY DAY!!!
- Take responsibility for yourself.
- Choose appropriate advisors.
- Keep things in perspective.
- Delegate the tasks you don't like.
- Respect your mind's and body's cycles.
- Balance your personal and professional life.
- Remember, we're all human—we all make mistakes.
- Acknowledge your accomplishments every day.

Excerpted from *Business Mastery: A Guide for Creating a Fulfilling, Thriving Business and Keeping It Successful*, 4th ed., by Cherie M. Sohnen-Moe, Tucson, Arizona: Sohnen-Moe Associates, Inc., 2008.

TIME MANAGEMENT

Time management is an important skill to have in life, and it is especially critical when you own and operate your own business. Everyone has a different idea of time management. Whatever way you choose to look at it, we all have the same 24 hours in a day. The secret to managing your time effectively is to know how much it is worth and put your time toward the things that are most important to you.

Notes:

What are your current beliefs about time? Not enough time in a day? Time goes by too quickly?

What were your parents' beliefs and relationships to time?

Where does the majority of your time go?

What are three things you spend time on that aren't important to you?

1.
2.
3.

Notes:

If you had more time, what would you do with it?

....

....

....

....

How can you create more time to focus on what is really important to you?

....

....

....

....

....

To be good at time management does not mean that you have to work longer hours; you simply have to work smarter. Most people spend a good portion of their time on things that aren't effective. You want to maximize your working hours. Use the time you spend working wisely, so that you have more time to enjoy life, relax, have fun, cook, exercise, and do whatever else you love.

TIPS FOR TIME MANAGEMENT

- Know how many hours you want to work each week.
- Identify the times of day when you do your best work.
- Note the times of day that are difficult for you to work.
- Build your schedule around your personal time cycles: when you work best, when it is best for you to exercise, to eat, to sleep, etc.
- Know your limit. How many hours a day and a week can you work before burning out?
- Acknowledge that there is a time in a day, after working a certain number of hours, when your efforts actually stop being useful.
- Clarify your goals and priorities, and make sure you spend most of your time working toward your biggest goals.
- Identify things you do that do not support your goals, and drop them.

WEEKLY TIMESHEET

If you plan to be a full-time Health Coach, plan to spend about 75 percent of your time scheduling and doing Health History consultations. The remaining 25 percent of

Notes:

your time will be spent following up with potential clients, keeping track of them, and preparing for your meetings. Once you start signing clients, you will probably spend about 50 percent of your time marketing your services and doing Health Histories, 30 percent of your time meeting with clients, and 20 percent of your time on follow-ups and preparation.

To help you master time management, we have created this weekly timesheet. Keep it, or one like it, in your office or in a journal. Before lunch each day, write in how many hours you spend on each category. Do the same again at the end of your workday. This is a good way to see where you are putting your energy and how long certain tasks take you. You may think that most of your time goes into marketing, but in actuality you may be spending hours upon hours on the Internet. At the end of each week, review this time sheet, making note of where most of your time went. Reflect on it, and decide if this was an effective use of your time. Make the appropriate adjustments in the following week.

BIG ROCKS

Named after a demonstration performed by a time-management expert, Stephen Covey, Big Rocks is a concept used throughout Integrative Nutrition. If you haven't yet watched

WEEKLY TIMESHEET

	Health Histories	Client Sessions	Writing/ Newsletter	Marketing & Networking	Paperwork/ Phone	Email/Phone	Other
Monday a.m.							
Monday p.m.							
Tuesday a.m.							
Tuesday p.m.							
Wednesday a.m.							
Wednesday p.m.							
Thursday a.m.							
Thursday p.m.							
Friday a.m.							
Friday p.m.							
Saturday							
Sunday							

Notes:

Joshua's Big Rocks Demonstration in the curriculum, we suggest you do! In the demonstration, the expert takes a jar and fills it with some big rocks. He asks his students if the jar is full. They say it is. He proceeds to dump gravel into the jar, and shake the jar around so the pieces of gravel fill up the spaces between the big rocks. He asks his students if the jar is full. They respond, "Probably not." Next, he pours sand into the jar, which fills in all the empty spaces between the gravel and the rocks. Again, he asks, "Is the jar full?" The students shout, "No!" Finally, he takes a pitcher of water and pours it into the jar until it is full to the brim. His point is not that you can always fit more into your jar, but that if you don't put in your big rocks first, you'll never get them in at all.

Each Monday morning, everyone on the Integrative Nutrition staff completes a Big Rocks list. This is an inventory of all the important tasks we are going to accomplish in the coming week, along with how many hours we plan to spend on each one. We list the tasks that take the most amount of time at the top. The reason we do this is to help us clarify our work for the week for ourselves and our supervisors. Some weeks we have too many hours, so we have to reevaluate our priorities, while other weeks we have extra time to work on upcoming or new projects.

Decide how many hours you would like to put toward health coaching this week and make a list of everything you would like to get done, both big and little. Make sure to add in time for phone calls, emails, and other miscellaneous tasks. Now identify the Big Rocks. What are the items on this list that you absolutely must accomplish this week? And, honestly, how long is it going to take you to make them happen? Be realistic in terms of your time when listing your Big Rocks. Notice if you have a tendency to underestimate or overestimate the amount of time it takes you to do things, and adjust your Big Rocks so that it is an accurate representation of the actual time spent on different projects.

Divide all the work you do into categories, such as "School Work," "Marketing," "Organization" and "Other." Then list the various projects within each category. For each category, note the number of hours you plan to spend on this work. You may want to chunk the time down, and list the amount of hours per project.

Doing your Big Rocks every Monday will keep you focused on the important things, and ideally prevent you from spending all your time on the little rocks, or things that don't really matter to you. If you do this each week, realistically representing your time, you will be saved from beating yourself up at the end of the week because you didn't get to the million other things on your list.

Keep your Big Rocks someplace visible and cross off your tasks as you accomplish them. The next week, list your top five accomplishments at the top of your new Big Rocks to remind yourself how well you are doing. The more you focus on your Big Rocks, and not the little pebbles, the more productive you will be. The first time you compile your Big Rocks it may take a little while, but after a few weeks, you'll breeze through it in about 20 minutes.

Notes:

ELISHA'S BIG ROCKS

MM/DD/YY-MM/DD/YY

TOTAL HOURS = 40 HOURS

3 Top Monthly Rocks: October
1) Develop marketing plan
2) Get Fit for Fall workshop
3) Coaching sessions

3 Top Weekly Rocks
1) Coaching sessions
2) Coaching admin—catch up
3) October newsletter

ACCOMPLISHMENTS		
		coaching admin: signed up 2 new clients newsletter: finished/sent out September newsletter workshops: researched possible spaces to hold Get Fit for Fall workshop
TOP ROCKS		
31 hours	20	coaching sessions –coach current 20 clients
	7	coaching admin –organize/file/paperwork for current clients (3) –prepare giveaways for current clients (1) –do 3 health histories (3)
	4	marketing –edit and send October Newsletter (1) –update IIN website text—focus on target market (2) –email new contacts (1)
OTHER ROCKS		
3 hours	3	Get Fit for Fall workshop –confirm venue and date (1) –begin to write content (2)
MISCELLANEOUS		
6 hours	2	self-care –yoga class (1) –massage (2)
	2	training –attend healing through nutrition seminar (1) –travel time (.5) –file notes (.5)
	2	email

URGENT VERSUS IMPORTANT

This exercise is another effective tool to explore where your time goes. There are four quadrants here: important and urgent, not important and urgent, not urgent and important, and not urgent and not important. Everything you do in your life fits into one of these quadrants. Please fill in each quadrant with your regular activities that fit each category.

In which quadrant does most of your time go? Quite frequently, people spend the majority of their time doing things that they categorize as being urgent but not important, and consequently things that are important get pushed aside. Use this exercise as motivation to cut out anything in your life that is not urgent and not important. Also, cut down the amount of time you spend on things that are urgent, but not important. Put the excess time and energy into things that are important to you but not urgent.

Notes:

URGENT VERSUS IMPORTANT

	IMPORTANT	NOT IMPORTANT
URGENT		
NOT URGENT		

Excerpted from *The 7 Habits of Highly Effective People: Powerful Lessons in Personal Change*, rev. ed., by Stephen R. Covey, New York: Free Press, 2004.

Surround yourself with people who respect and treat you well.

—Claudia Black

CHAPTER 5:

CREATING A SUPPORT SYSTEM

In this chapter we discuss three very important topics to put you on a path to success: support, self-care, and overcoming fears. Support refers to the key people in your life that will help hold you accountable and encourage you along your journey. Getting support systems in place now will set you up for success. Self-care is just as crucial! Being healthy will give you the energy you need to get out there and shape your career. Remember to walk your talk and take time for you. And finally, learning to acknowledge and overcome your fears will put you in a positive mindset for doing this work. Feel the fear and do it anyway!

SUPPORT PEOPLE

One step of the Golden Path is to get support! A happy and energized Health Coach is one who is getting support. The only way to get the support you need is to ask for it. You can't do everything alone, and by asking for help, your chances of success skyrocket. This goes for both your business and your personal life.

Health coaching is a giving profession, meaning you are constantly giving to your clients, prospective clients, and probably the majority of the people in your life. To ensure that there is a balance of give and take, you need to create a support system that works for you—a way to recharge your battery and discharge stress. Creating a support system early on in the program will help you lay the foundation for a successful year.

An ideal support system includes everyone in your life. You can never have too much encouragement. And know that it is possible to have everyone in your life be supportive of who you are and what you are doing. It is a sign of strength to allow others to support you, to be vulnerable at times, and to take others' ideas into account.

Notes:

List five supportive people in your life and how they support you.

1. ....

....

2. ....

....

3. ....

....

4. ....

....

5. ....

....

Find a way to appreciate these people for all they do. Tell them how grateful you are for having them in your life. Explain what they do that you find helpful, and encourage them to keep on doing it! Find ways to make these people more central in your life. Also, make sure it is a mutually supportive relationship in which both people benefit.

Now, ask yourself how you might be able to get this kind of support from others. Are there people in your life with whom you would like to be closer but find unsupportive right now? How can you ask them for the kind of support you need? Or could it be time to reduce their role in your life? If it is family members who are unsupportive, it is usually best to do whatever is in your power to be on good terms with them, without compromising yourself.

List five unsupportive people in your life and how they do not support you.

1. ....

....

2. ....

....

3. ....

....

4. ....

....

5. ....

....

Notes:

Without a doubt, you are going to come across some people who are unsupportive of your decisions. These people may truly care about you and only want the best for you. If that is the case, communicate with them openly about why you are making the choices you are making and why you really need their support right now. Hear them out and listen to their concerns, and then reply honestly.

It is possible that these unsupportive people may not be the best people for you to have in your life anymore. There are those in this world who are very jealous and may not want to see their friends doing well. There are also those who are scared of change and prefer everything to remain the same. If you are changing, such as beginning a new career, eating new foods, and making different lifestyle choices, you will be challenging their reality. Ask yourself if there are some people who you know in your heart you would be better off without. It is okay to let them go. You are not doing them, or yourself, any favors by continuing to be a part of a dysfunctional relationship. If breaking off contact seems too drastic, you can downgrade your relationship so that you see them less often and give them less of your energy.

YOUR COACHING

Coaching Circles are group-based coaching calls that provide you with guidance and support later in the program.

Coaching Circles are led by IIN Health Coaches who demonstrate coaching techniques, provide curriculum and business guidance, and support you with nutrition and primary food concerns. And because Coaching Circle sessions take place in a group atmosphere, you will also have the opportunity to connect and learn from your classmates.

YOUR ACCOUNTABILITY COACH

The people closest to you may not always be the best support people for your business. As much as they love you, their tolerance for hearing about another Sugar Blues talk or Health History might be low. Your Accountability Coach is a valuable support person for you because they know where you are coming from, and they are also just starting out as a Health Coach.

Having an Accountability Coach will help you to get the most out of the program, move forward with your goals, stay on track, and build a health coaching practice. You will select a fellow classmate and take turns holding 12 sessions over the course of the program. This is a great opportunity to practice the 6-month program so you know what it will be like with actual clients. On top of that, you will be able to get support with your own goals. The two of you should meet or speak twice a month for an hour. We strongly suggest you schedule calls or meet every two weeks on the same day and at the same time. By doing so, you are both more likely to participate and maintain consistency, which

Notes:

will lead to greater success. Your Accountability Coach's duty is to listen to you, celebrate with you, commiserate with you, be your brainstorming partner, and keep you focused on achieving your goals. This is also your duty to your Accountability Coach.

CREATING COMMUNITY

An important ingredient to the success of our school is community. As you may know, many of our students make some of the best friends of their lives while they are enrolled. This happens naturally because the school attracts people who are healthy, happy, and who want to do something that inspires them and helps others. We strongly encourage you to take advantage of the community you have through the school. Meet new people in your class by reaching out to those with similar interests. Having other Health Coaches in your life is priceless. They know how to listen and give good advice, and they can also support you in your career.

STUDY GROUPS

Integrative Nutrition has created study groups because we noticed that students truly enjoy supporting and getting to know one another. We highly encourage you to take advantage of this valuable resource. Attend study groups held by people in your area or over the phone. Even better, organize your own study group. Pick a topic related to business and invite however many people you would like. During the study group, share business tips, stories, challenges, and laughs. We provide outlines to give you ideas of what you can discuss when you meet. Feel free to use our outlines, or develop your own agenda items!

SELF-CARE

Remember the first step of the Golden Path is to be healthy! A common vice among Health Coaches is that we can put so much energy into taking care of others that we forget or don't have time to take care of ourselves. If you keep up this behavior, you will eventually burn out and have nothing left to give anyone. You will wonder where you went wrong, and you could even develop an illness.

Your body sends you messages through its ailments to take better care of it. As a Health Coach and a human being, you must learn how to discipline yourself to take care of your own mental, physical, emotional, and spiritual health.

Take note of the signs your body sends you when you are out of balance, burning the candle at both ends, or not taking good enough care of yourself.

Notes:

List the top five ways your body has signaled you to take better care of yourself.

1. ....

2. ....

3. ....

4. ....

5. ....

Be on alert for these messages. Lovingly listen to them and take the appropriate action to get back into balance.

We encourage you to practice extreme self-care. What do we mean by extreme self-care? At least once a day do something to energize or rejuvenate yourself. This will be different for everyone, and it will also look different depending on the day. It may mean getting a massage, spending time with nature, taking a bubble bath, cooking your favorite meal, going for a walk around the block at work, seeing a movie, or anything else that pleases you. It may be that you need to do two or even three things a day for yourself. Hopefully, self-care will become second nature to you over time, and you won't even consider putting everyone else's needs in front of your own.

STRESS

Stress has extremely negative effects on our overall health; it causes all sorts of illness, affects sleep and digestion, lowers the quality of life, and can lead to depression. Develop reliable and simple ways to reduce stress. Experiment with meditation, hot towel scrubs, drinking more water and herbal tea, running outside, or whatever else helps to quiet your mind so that you feel at peace. Eating well and doing regular physical activity are excellent ways to reduce stress and nurture yourself. Do whatever you need to make these things regular occurrences in your life.

What are the main sources of stress in your life at the moment?

1. ....

2. ....

3. ....

4. ....

5. ....

Notes:

What are two steps you can take to let go of these stressors or reduce or eliminate the stress they bring into your life?

First stressor ....

1. ....

2. ....

Second stressor ....

1. ....

2. ....

Third stressor ....

1. ....

2. ....

Fourth stressor ....

1. ....

2. ....

Fifth stressor ....

1. ....

2. ....

What are three things you know you can do to help yourself when you feel stressed?

1. ....

2. ....

3. ....

NEED MOTIVATION?

If you lack motivation, look inside yourself and be honest about what you are experiencing. Why have you not been prioritizing this program or starting your health coaching practice? Only you know the answer to that question. If you aren't sure, journal about what you are going through and ask for feedback from your Accountability Coach and other support people.

In our experience, lack of motivation is often caused by fear of success or failure. Deep down you want to be a Health Coach, but you lack confidence for one reason or another. You probably have thought patterns from a long time ago that still go on

Notes:

in your head and say that you aren't good enough or smart enough to do what your heart desires.

A helpful analogy here is the Hudson River. Everyone thinks it flows one way, downstream into the ocean. But the river is very deep and influenced by tides. Although it's hard to tell on the surface, the river's flow actually changes direction several times a day, often sending water back upstream. This is similar to what happens inside of you when you say you want something, but you are too afraid. Powerful feelings can pull you in the opposite direction from where you really want to go. Take a moment to think about any fears you have around being a Health Coach. Know that it is totally normal to have these fears.

COMMON FEARS STUDENTS FACE

- I'm not healthy enough, so who am I to be telling other people what to eat and how to exercise?
- If I actually succeed at this, I'll have to be perfect all the time.
- If I work for myself, I'll always be thinking about work.
- If I make money, I'll have to support everyone else in my family.
- If I outgrow my old lifestyle, I'll lose all my friends.
- It's not safe to depend on myself for a paycheck. I could go broke.
- If I do what I want instead of what my parents want, they won't love me anymore.
- What if my clients don't get well? They might blame me and be angry.
- If I own a business, I will lose free time and flexibility.
- I'm not smart enough to make good decisions, so my business could fail.
- If I spend all day listening to people talk about their problems, I'll feel depressed.
- If I get up in front of others and talk about nutrition, people will laugh at me.
- If I'm always helping other people, no one will help me.
- If I change careers, I will lose credibility with my business associates.
- If I do what I want to do, everyone will think I'm selfish.

Make a list of potential reasons why you might not want to be a Health Coach.

1. ....

2. ....

3. ....

4. ....

5. ....

Notes:

6. ....

7. ....

8. ....

9. ....

10. ....

It is worthwhile to spend some time acknowledging your fears. See if you can pinpoint where these fears originated. Remember that the past is over and anything is possible in the present. Use your journal and the support of the program to work through your fear, procrastination, and self-doubt.

On occasion, people simply are not motivated to be Health Coaches because it is not their calling in life. They may come to the program and start out as Health Coaches, but end up deciding that becoming a full-time parent is where their true happiness lies or that their lifelong dream is to move to another country. Perhaps you want to launch a product or program instead of doing health coaching. Or maybe you want to be a Health Coach, but you prefer to work in a doctor's office or a spa instead of owning your own practice. Entrepreneurship isn't right for everyone, and owning your own business takes a huge commitment of time and dedication. We'll cover career options throughout the program.

Whatever your dreams are, we want them to come true. Know that even if you don't have clients in a 6-month program, you can still be a source of inspiration and health to those who know you. Regardless of what you decide to do with what you learn at Integrative Nutrition, we are here to support you and help you accomplish your goals.

What does success look like to you?

....

....

....

....

....

Notes:

Notes:

Setting an example is not the main means of influencing others; it is the only means.

—Albert Einstein

CHAPTER 6:

HEALTH COACH DEFINED

In our current healthcare system, almost no time is spent discussing daily diet and lifestyle. The world needs well-trained professionals to teach people how to adopt a healthier lifestyle. At Integrative Nutrition, we educate our students to do just that.

A Health Coach offers guidance and inspiration to help clients shift their behavior to healthier habits by making step-by-step changes to their diet and lifestyle. The client learns about new, healthy foods and the concept of primary foods: relationships, physical activity, career, and spirituality. As a result of this partnership, clients develop a deeper understanding of the foods and lifestyle choices that work best for them, and implement lasting changes that improve their energy, balance, and health. Instead of prescribing one diet or one way of exercising, Health Coaches focus on teaching clients to become self-sufficient by observing their own unique responses to various modifications and choosing health-promoting behaviors that work for them.

HEALTH COACHING PROFESSION

As more and more awareness is given to preventative care, health coaching is seen as a vital aspect of creating healthy lifestyle changes. Health Coaches are becoming recognized as essential parts of people's health and well-being. Not only is there a shift to live healthier lives, people are finding that helping others become healthier makes their lives better too!

There is now a huge demand for Health Coaches. Not only are doctors hiring more Health Coaches than ever before, but patients are learning that working with a Health Coach is one of the most effective ways to improve their health. Health Coaches are needed to fill the gap between medical professionals and preventative healthcare. The goal is not to replace any existing healthcare professional; rather, health coaching serves

Notes:

to complement existing healthcare providers. As more and more medical professionals recognize the vital importance of Health Coaches, the demand will grow.

Given this unique role as coach rather than authority, it's important to leverage the title of Health Coach as an ally not only to the client but also to other health professionals. With millions of people suffering from preventable lifestyle-related diseases, the Health Coach is a complementary member of the healthcare team that can help bring about lasting behavior changes for more people, in less time and with a greater impact than the current model. In this role, Health Coaches support the mission to play a crucial role in improving health and happiness, and through that process, create a ripple effect that transforms the world.

WHAT DOES A HEALTH COACH DO?

A Health Coach is a guide and mentor who empowers clients to take responsibility for their own health and supports them to implement and sustain lifestyle and behavior changes that will contribute to the achievement of their personal wellness goals. Your work is about integrating changes into people's lives, giving them things to try, and building on what they've done before. You provide clients a bridge between foods and lifestyle, primary food and secondary food. Some common areas where a Health Coach may help a client to focus include weight management, food cravings, sleep, energy, stress management, and digestion—just to name a few.

WHAT DOES A HEALTH COACH NOT DO?

A Health Coach does not take the place of any medical practitioner; rather, he or she serves as the missing link—the patient guide—that helps develop strategies to enact real, lasting lifestyle changes that address not only the diagnostic label (e.g., pre-diabetic), but also serve to enhance the client's overall wellness.

There are many similarities with other professions, but health coaching is not better or worse, it's just different. A Health Coach does not diagnose, treat, or take responsibility for bringing about wellness changes in a client's life; rather, he or she guides and supports the development of and progress toward personal wellness goals. A Health Coach often works with generally healthy clients who may not necessarily be practicing many bad habits, but who are not practicing enough of the good habits.

Focus on ways to empower clients and avoid risk. Use the guide on the next page for safe success.

ART OF LISTENING

What makes a Health Coach unique is their ability to truly listen to their clients. The art of listening is one of the greatest skills in a coach's repertoire and the key to effectively working with clients.

SCOPE OF PRACTICE GUIDELINES

	GO FOR IT!	AVOID IT!
Conditions	Do work with people who are generally healthy with mild health concerns such as: • Headache • Fatigue • Sugar cravings	Don't say that you can cure disease or work with people with complex, advanced diseases such as: • Cancer • Kidney failure
Age	Do work with adults. Get written authorization from a legal guardian to work with children.	Don't work with minors without written authorization from their legal guardian.
Medical	Do suggest a client: • Ask their doctor about alternatives to medication • Get a second doctor's opinion if they're unsure	Don't suggest clients stop or change prescription medication or stop seeing their doctor.
Diet	Do suggest ways to "crowd out": • Caffeine, sugar, alcohol, tobacco, junk food, dairy	Don't exclude major food groups or recommend extreme detox programs.
Supplements	Do recommend: • Superfoods • Multivitamins • Mineral supplements	Don't recommend controversial supplements or very high doses.
Exercise	Do encourage clients to begin gentle, low-risk exercise changes such as walking.	Don't encourage clients to do vigorous exercise without consulting their physician.
Relationships	Do give people time to talk about their important relationships. Promote participation in social events to meet new people.	Don't promote divorce or conflict with friends and family.
Career	Do recommend that clients explore new hobbies and interests.	Don't recommend that your client quit their job.
Spirituality	Do advise clients to engage in self-reflection and experience nature.	Don't advise your client to change religious affiliation.
Liability	Do get liability insurance and contact IIN if any issues arise. Use the IIN agreement when working with clients.	Don't call yourself a Registered Dietitian or Nutritionist.

Many clients may not have a safe space to share their health concerns, personal goals, and aspirations, so being heard by someone else is very powerful. In the beginning stages of working with a client, and throughout the course of their program, a coach should listen and ask questions. This allows the client to think out loud and hear how they are expressing their own thoughts. Through this process they will bring awareness to the issue at hand, which can lead to action and forward motion. Clients start to become "unstuck" and the healing process begins.

The truth is, whether we know it or not, we all have the answers within ourselves. It's the job of a Health Coach to empower clients to find their own answers and then support them in their journey. Many of you might be nervous or fearful about finding just the right thing to say to your future clients, but the good news is that you don't have to know all the answers! This work requires good listening skills above all, so that you

Notes:

are fully present with your clients. This means listening with everything you have—ears, heart, mind, and gut. Get in touch with your intuition and begin to pick up on what's not being said. Words have different meanings for different people, so you will learn how your client thinks and speaks. For example, your idea of success may be very different from your client's. Ask him or her to describe what "success" looks like for them. How does it make them feel? This will give you a clear understanding of where they are, so you can meet them there. Reiterate and recap what they have said to help the client know they are heard and fully understood. As their coach, encourage and support your client's self-expression, allowing them to continually explore how they feel. Guide them to use these feelings to create clear goals and real change in their lives. This process can exponentially deepen sessions and provide a life-changing experience for clients.

Learning the art of listening is not complicated work, but it requires an open mind, dedication, and practice. As you begin to work with clients, we will support you in becoming an expert observer, noticing body language and eye contact, and allowing silence when appropriate. We will also arm you with key coaching tools including how to ask high mileage questions that will keep the conversation moving.

With all the skills that you will gain to help others become healthier and happier, imagine the impact of this work on your friends, family, community, and world!

HIGH MILEAGE QUESTIONS

Asking high mileage questions is an effective way to prompt your clients to get to the heart of the matter and surprise themselves with how much they already know. High mileage questions open the space for in-depth conversation around your clients' issues, values, and goals, and encourage them to connect the dots, draw their own connections, and make their own conclusions. Asking high mileage questions gets easier with practice, and you'll be inspired when your clients start to open up in a whole new way.

We will explore more high mileage questions in the curriculum. Here are a few examples of open-ended questions to help your clients communicate meaningfully during your sessions:

1. Are these feelings trying to tell you something?
2. Could this be a symptom rather than a source?
3. Did anything surprise you when . . . ?
4. How can you expand your life in that area?
5. How does it serve you?
6. What is out of balance?
7. What is the gift in this challenge?
8. What is your intuition telling you?
9. What are the moments of choice in this situation?
10. Why do you believe that to be true?

List a few ways in which you can begin active listening:

....

....

....

....

....

List a few of your own high mileage questions you can use when you practice Health History consultations:

....

....

....

....

....

Notes:

It is common sense to take a method and try it. If it fails, admit it frankly and try another. But above all, try something.

—Franklin D. Roosevelt

CHAPTER 7:

HEALTH HISTORY CONSULTATIONS

The way to get more clients is to schedule Health History consultations. A Health History is a free initial consultation that gives both you and your potential client a chance to get to know each other and determine whether or not you want to work together. The potential client gets to see what you're about—how you work and what the coaching process is like. You get to decide whether the other person is someone you want to work with. Because the session is complimentary, it increases the likelihood that someone will agree to meet with you. This also enables them to uncover their fundamental needs, so they see how working with you can change their life. By the end of the session, they will want to register for your health coaching program.

One step of the Golden Path is to do two Health Histories every week! If you do two a week, you WILL get clients. To start, we recommend practicing only with fellow classmates. Keep practicing, and we'll tell you when it's time to start reaching out to potential clients!

THE HEALTH HISTORY FORM

Become very familiar with the Health History forms. Take a moment now to look at all the questions. There are questions about the person's lifestyle and health—where they were born, what they do for a living, what their main health concern is, etc. There is also a section about food where the person can share what they ate as a child and what they are eating now. There are specific forms for men and women; please review both. Additionally, you can find forms in the Resources for working with children, teenagers, seniors, and Spanish speakers.

WOMEN'S HEALTH HISTORY

PLEASE WRITE OR PRINT CLEARLY. ALL OF YOUR INFORMATION WILL REMAIN CONFIDENTIAL BETWEEN YOU AND THE HEALTH COACH.

Personal Information

First Name: .... Last Name: ....

Email address: .... How often do you check email? ....

Telephone—Home: .... Work: .... Mobile: ....

Age: .... Height: .... Birth date: .... Place of Birth: ....

Current weight: .... Weight six months ago: .... One year ago: ....

Would you like your weight to be different? .... If so, what? ....

Social Information

Relationship status: ....

Where do you currently live? ....

Children: .... Pets: ....

Occupation: .... Hours of work per week: ....

Health Information

Please list your main health concerns: ....

....

Other concerns and/or goals? ....

....

At what point in your life did you feel your best? ....

Any serious illnesses/hospitalizations/injuries? ....

....

How is/was the health of your mother? ....

How is/was the health of your father? ....

What is your ancestry? .... What blood type are you? ....

How is your sleep? .... How many hours? .... Do you wake up at night? ....

Why? ....

Any pain, stiffness, or swelling? ....

Constipation/diarrhea/gas? ....

Allergies or sensitivities? Please explain: ....

Women's Health

Are your periods regular? .... How many days is your flow? .... How frequent? ....

Painful or symptomatic? .... Please explain: ....

Reached or approaching menopause? .... Please explain: ....

Birth control history: ....

....

Do you experience yeast infections or urinary tract infections? .... Please explain: ....

....

Medical Information

Do you take any supplements or medications? Please list: ....

....

Any healers, helpers, or therapies with which you are involved? Please list: ....

....

What role do sports and exercise play in your life? ....

....

Food Information

What foods did you eat often as a child?

Breakfast	Lunch	Dinner	Snacks	Liquids

What is your food like these days?

Breakfast	Lunch	Dinner	Snacks	Liquids

Will family and/or friends be supportive of your desire to make food and/or lifestyle changes? ....

Do you cook? .... What percentage of your food is home cooked? ....

Where do you get the rest from? ....

Do you crave sugar, coffee, cigarettes, or have any major addictions? ....

....

The most important thing I should do to improve my health is: ....

....

Anything else you want to share? ....

MEN'S HEALTH HISTORY

PLEASE WRITE OR PRINT CLEARLY. ALL OF YOUR INFORMATION WILL REMAIN CONFIDENTIAL BETWEEN YOU AND THE HEALTH COACH.

First Name: .... Last Name: ....

Email address: .... How often do you check email? ....

Telephone—Home: .... Work: .... Mobile: ....

Age: .... Height: .... Birth date: .... Place of Birth: ....

Current weight: .... Weight six months ago: .... One year ago: ....

Would you like your weight to be different? .... If so, what? ....

Social Information

Relationship status: ....

Where do you currently live? ....

Children: .... Pets: ....

Occupation: .... Hours of work per week: ....

Health Information

Please list your main health concerns: ....

....

....

Other concerns and/or goals? ....

....

At what point in your life did you feel your best? ....

Any serious illnesses/hospitalizations/injuries? ....

....

How is/was the health of your mother? ....

How is/was the health of your father? ....

What is your ancestry? .... What blood type are you? ....

How is your sleep? .... How many hours? .... Do you wake up at night? ....

Why? ....

Any pain, stiffness, or swelling? ....

Constipation/diarrhea/gas? .... Please explain: ....

Allergies or sensitivities? Please explain: ....

....

Medical Information

Do you take any supplements or medications? Please list: ....

....

Any healers, helpers, or therapies with which you are involved? Please list: ....

....

What role do sports and exercise play in your life? ....

....

Food Information

What foods did you eat often as a child?

Breakfast	Lunch	Dinner	Snacks	Liquids

What is your food like these days?

Breakfast	Lunch	Dinner	Snacks	Liquids

Will family and/or friends be supportive of your desire to make food and/or lifestyle changes? ....

Do you cook? .... What percentage of your food is home cooked? ....

Where do you get the rest from? ....

Do you crave sugar, coffee, cigarettes, or have any major addictions? ....

The most important thing I should change about my diet to improve my health is: ....

....

Anything else you would like to share? ....

....

Notes:

THE HEALTH HISTORY CONSULTATION

Later in this chapter, we will discuss how to find and invite people to come to your free initial Health History consultation. First, let's review what will happen before, during, and after the consultation. You can practice these steps with your fellow classmates and with your Accountability Coach. Remember—we'll tell you when to start reaching out to potential clients in the modules and in your assignments.

BEFORE THE HEALTH HISTORY CONSULTATION

- Decide where you are going to hold the consultation. In your home, in an office, on the phone, in a hotel lobby, or in a tea or coffee shop can all be agreeable options.
- Send a reminder email a day or two before your appointment. In this email, give instructions on where and when to meet you, and let the person know you look forward to seeing them.
- We recommend filling out the Health History forms during the session with the client. Prepare for your session by having a blank Health History, a pen, and a clipboard to write on. For phone sessions, you will verbally conduct the Health History and will be filling out the form according to the client's verbal answers.
- Bring blank copies of your Program Agreement form, Program Schedule form, Credit Card Authorization form, Welcome handout, and Goals handout. We'll cover all of this in the program; just note that when you conduct Health Histories with potential clients you'll want these forms on hand.
- Pick an outfit that is professional yet comfortable.
- Center yourself by quieting your mind right before the meeting.

BEGINNING THE HEALTH HISTORY CONSULTATION

- When you greet the person, give him or her a warm welcome. Show you are happy to see him or her. Acknowledge the potential client's presence and thank him or her for taking the time to talk with you.
- Connect by touch—shaking hands or hugging if appropriate. If you are on the phone, make sure the person knows you are happy to be talking with him or her.
- When you have the person fill out the Health History form while he or she is with you, give the person the blank form on a clipboard or something that makes it easy to write on. Filling out the form can be an emotional process, so one advantage of doing it in person is that you are there to provide support and address whatever comes up. Offer the person some water or tea, and get it while they are filling out the form.

Notes:

- If the session is by phone or video call, let the client know that you will be asking them a series of questions designed to prompt them to think about their health and that this information will help you determine if and how you can help them. You can also let them know that if they would like a copy of the form, you can send it to them for their records.
- Once you have the completed form in front of you, you can begin the conversation. Here are some sample questions you might ask to get the conversation started:
  "So, how was filling out this form for you?"
  "What's new and good in your life?"
  "How do you feel about coming to a Health History consultation?"

DURING THE HEALTH HISTORY CONSULTATION

- Use the form to guide you. You can go through the form in order, or let the conversation evolve based on what the person is saying. Ask questions based on what the person wrote on the sheet. Let them talk about their responses, especially their main health concern. The form is meant to stimulate conversation. You may find that your potential client wants to talk more about one part of the form and less about another. That's okay. Go where the client wants to go.
- Go over easy information first. Where they live, where they are from, how old they are, etc. You can ask questions such as: "How does it feel being 36?" "How was it growing up in Nebraska?" or "Do you like living in New York City?" This helps to make an initial connection.
- Listen, connect, and take notes. The more you listen, the more the person will open up. Connecting with the person will create trust. And if you take notes, the person will feel valued. However, avoid taking too many notes. You don't want to have your head in your paper the whole time.
- Breathe. Notice how much you like talking to and listening to this person. Empty your mind of everything that you have to do or any place you need to go. Stay present and trust yourself.
- When you get to the more complex subjects, such as weight, relationships, career and sleep, read between the lines and ask questions that draw the person out. For example, if the person wrote that they want their weight to be different, you can ask, "Do you want to look slimmer, feel lighter, or both?" A good question to ask if you see they spend many hours working is, "I see that you work about 45 hours each week. Does that feel like a lot to you, or does it feel like you have a good balance of work, rest, and play?" If they wrote that they don't sleep well and wake up a lot during the night, you can ask "Why do you think that is?"

Notes:

- People are not used to talking about their digestion in regular conversation, so you may find resistance around getting people to open up about constipation or diarrhea. It may be helpful to say something like, "Most people suffer from some kind of digestive problem. I see it all the time, and talking about digestion is one of the key elements to figuring out what foods are best for you." Or share something about yourself such as, "I used to have terrible constipation, but since I changed my diet, it's cleared up, which I'm thrilled about."
- If possible, make the person laugh. If you can get someone to laugh in your office, that is a huge step forward. Most people take health care too seriously. Having fun with the person will make them feel comfortable and lighten the mood.
- **Do not give advice during the Health History.** We cannot stress this point enough. Let the person do the majority of the talking. Ask questions to take them deeper into what they are talking about. In the Health History, you are simply uncovering a client's need and talking about your program. Once someone becomes your client, then you can introduce recommendations.
- Share how you relate to the person's issues. When someone knows that you are human too, and you have worked through your own health issues, they will feel closer to you. However, be careful not to talk about yourself too much. Mention some health conditions or health concerns that you have cleared up either once or twice throughout the Health History.
- Remember and write down key points to bring up later in the conversation. If the person shared earlier that they take allergy medication, you can say, "In my 6-month program, I can work with you to help you understand what is going on with your allergies." Remember, for now you are just practicing with classmates, so it's okay to say this!
- Notice if there are any areas of the form left blank. It could be that the person did not list something because they are avoiding it. Use your judgment. You may want to say, "I notice that you did not write anything down for this question. Why is that?"
- Restate and paraphrase what the person shares with you. This shows you understand what is being communicated to you and gives the person the opportunity to clarify anything that is unclear. When the person says something, you can say, "So what you are saying is . . ." or "What I'm hearing you say is . . ."
- Briefly explain the concept of primary and secondary foods. It will be helpful for the person if you talk about the importance of both what we eat and our lifestyle, how if we are not happy or fulfilled in one aspect of our life, such as relationship or career, we will not be healthy no matter what we eat. Remember to avoid giving any advice. Simply introduce the concept.
- Ask the person "What are the biggest challenges standing between you and your goals?" This is a strong question that allows you to see where the person's

Notes:

mindset is and how your service could bridge that gap. From a coaching perspective, you are having the person look at their situation from a new perspective, which most often allows for an "aha" moment.

- Do not avoid silence. Let the person speak and when they are done speaking, you don't have to start speaking right away. Sometimes if you allow silence, the person will take this as permission to go even further with their thoughts. Real healing can occur here. Even if the silence feels awkward to you, it's okay to experiment with allowing it.
- When going over the person's main health goals, ask him or her to prioritize these concerns in order of concern. Then ask them "How are they impacting your life? What other areas do they affect?" You are reframing the impact of these health concerns and opening an awareness the person probably hasn't considered before. As a coach, your job is to show a client what is possible, and this is the first opportunity for that.
- At the end of the Health History, after you've gone over what the person is eating, ask, "What's the most important thing you should change about your diet to improve your health? On a scale of 1-10, how important is it to address this? If in 6-12 months nothing changes, what would your life look like?" Write all this down. You will come back to this as you talk about your program as a solution.

ENDING THE HEALTH HISTORY CONSULTATION

- Tell the person that you've really enjoyed getting to know them better, and mention one specific thing that you liked about the session.
- Ask them, "How was that for you?" and "What was something you found valuable in our session?"
- Restate the person's main health concerns, the level of importance, and the one thing they know they should already be doing. Then repeat back to them how these concerns affect other parts of their life and what the future looks like if they don't change. For example, you can say, "Today, we've established that your main concerns at this time are losing weight and having more energy. On a scale of 1-10, you put these concerns at an 8, which is pretty high. You already know you should be eating better by eating lunch rather than drinking a coffee. And if this doesn't change, a year from now, you foresee major conflicts with having the energy to travel to see your son in college, which means missing out on his first year of playing college football. Should we work together, we would work together to make very small changes over a period of time to ensure you reach your goal of having the energy and the health to be available for your son's amazing life events."

Notes:

- Ask them, "Would you be interested in hearing about my 6-month program?"
- We'll talk more in Chapter 11 about how to close the deal and end the Health History consultation—that is, turn a potential client into a paying client! You will practice this with your classmates as well. When it's time to start looking for potential clients, you'll know how to close the deal and sign them up right away!

AFTER THE HEALTH HISTORY CONSULTATION

- Follow up with the potential client via email or phone. Express your appreciation for your new client if they have signed up for your program, or reiterate that you would love to stay in touch and continue offering support for their goals. Mention something personal to make them feel special. Keep a log of all your Health Histories in one place. You may want to create a spreadsheet or use a piece of paper from your Health History folder. A suggested template is at the end of this chapter.
- Reflect on your session. What worked? What didn't work? Take notes for yourself and keep them in the binder, folder, or notebook where you keep your Health History information. Your coaching skills will improve as you practice, refine your style, and gain experience.

LISTENING

You should do very little talking during the Health History. People love to talk about themselves, especially with someone who is a good listener. Most health professionals today have very limited time to speak with their clients or answer questions. When people come to you, it will be a much needed breath of fresh air. They will be thrilled to have the space to speak about what is going on with their health and their life. By simply speaking and being listened to, the people who come to you for Health Histories will make connections around their health that they would not make if it were not for your presence.

What are five things that you already do that make you a good listener?

1. ....

2. ....

3. ....

4. ....

5. ....

Notes:

LISTENING TIPS

Most people live in their heads, thinking about what they have to do tomorrow, what happened yesterday or an hour ago, pretty much anything except the present moment. Because we are all living in our own heads, we are rarely listening to what other people are saying. Likewise, it is rare that someone actually listens to us without interruption or judgment. When done well, listening delivers tremendous benefits.

As a Health Coach, you are offering anyone who comes to you for a Health History the priceless opportunity of being listened to. The more you develop your listening skills, the better Health Coach you will be.

In order to listen well, put all the thoughts about yourself out of your head. Focus on the person you are listening to. This will greatly improve the quality of your communication. Listening is an art that fosters understanding, affirmation, relatedness, and appreciation.

Tips for listening well, both on the phone and in person:

- Remain curious and ask pertinent questions that bring the person deeper into what he or she is talking about.
- Summarize what is said to determine if you accurately understand the speaker.
- In person, keep strong eye contact. On the phone, it's good to make comments to let them know you are listening and comprehending what they are saying.
- Try to sit in one place. Avoid moving around.
- Learn to be comfortable with silence and being quiet. Don't talk in awkward silences; sometimes this is when the client reveals the most important information.
- Listen with your whole body: ears to hear the message, eyes to read body language (in person), the mind to visualize the person speaking (phone), intuition to determine what the speaker is actually saying.
- Meet in an environment conducive to listening. Avoid coffee or tea shops with loud music, tables that are very close together, or outside parks with a lot of children.

When listening, avoid:

- Looking at your watch or around the room instead of focusing on the speaker's face.
- Multitasking: Avoid writing a lot, cleaning, looking around for something, and cooking if you are conducting the session over the phone. When you are meeting a client in person, avoid reading email, texting, and playing with your hair or a pencil.
- Constantly interrupting or finishing the other person's sentences.

Notes:

INVITING PEOPLE TO A HEALTH HISTORY CONSULTATION

Remember to honor your worth when extending invitations to Health History consultations. What you are offering is free, but it is incredibly valuable. Even if the person doesn't express interest in signing up for your program, simply talking about his or her health with you for 50 minutes will be extremely beneficial.

Even though you are not ready to see clients, start doing Health History consultations now with classmates to get familiar with the process. We recommend at least two a week. The first 10 you do will be the most difficult, so get them out of the way as soon as possible. Practicing Health Histories will build your confidence, and you will find your own unique style and become more comfortable with the process.

As you begin your work as a Health Coach, we recommend that you practice Health Histories with fellow students, instead of with family, friends, or people who may become clients. This will help you build your skills and your confidence and prepare you for even greater success when you do the consultation with potential clients. You can ask your fellow students to practice with you, either by phone or in person. We recommend you post on Facebook and ask who would be interested in practicing with you, and also that you respond to other students' posts.

An exciting part of being a Health Coach is talking to strangers about what you do. Potential clients are everywhere: at the health food store, the gym, yoga class, the bookstore, the bank, church, temple, on the bus, on the Internet, everywhere!

List five places where you could find someone who would want to do a Health History consultation with you when the time is right. Remember that you can include any online communities with which you are involved. You can start going to these places now to say hello and build your contact list.

1. ....
2. ....
3. ....
4. ....
5. ....

If you're not very comfortable talking to strangers, that's okay. You will learn. Start off slowly and build up your muscle for starting conversations with people.

COMMUNICATING WITH POTENTIAL CLIENTS

It's important now to become familiar with the Health History forms and put together a list of people you will contact when you are ready to start inviting people for a free consultation. Once we instruct you to do so, you will start to contact other people besides

Notes:

fellow classmates. Please take a moment now to make a list of five people, other than classmates, to invite to a Health History session. Have this list ready to go for future use.

1. ....

2. ....

3. ....

4. ....

5. ....

For now, start building relationships. Let people know what you are up to. Keep in touch with them periodically by email or phone.

We'll let you know in the modules and your assignments when it's time to start reaching out to people other than your classmates. At that time, you can send out a professional, warm email to all of your contacts, inviting them to a Health History consultation. We have provided a template for you to use for this purpose, which you can find in the Health History Resources. You can also send a casual email to your close friends to see if they are interested, or if they know someone who might be interested in doing a Health History consultation with you.

If someone asks you for more detail about what a Health History consultation is, you can say, "We will spend about an hour going through your Health History form and discuss what you eat, your lifestyle, and your goals for your health. We will also get a sense of how it would be to work together. How does that sound?"

Share how excited you are and how much your life has improved since changing your diet and lifestyle. You can give them an example of a health concern that you have cleared up or something that is going really well with you as a result of getting involved with the school and health coaching. This will inspire them to want to have more of what you have!

Here are some examples of what to say when inviting people to a Health History consultation:

- "I am studying to become a Health Coach and I am able to start seeing clients. Would you be interested in sitting down with me for about an hour to discuss your health?"
- "Do you have an hour this week to sit down with me and talk about your health? We can look at what you are eating and how that is affecting your health."
- "Have you ever thought about all the different areas of your life that affect your health? I'd be happy to talk with you about it further in a free consultation."
- "As a Health Coach I work with people to help them improve their diet and lifestyle. Would you like to sit down with me and discuss what is happening in your life and with your health?"

Notes:

- "I am a student at the Institute for Integrative Nutrition, studying to be a Health Coach. I am learning about how food, diet, and lifestyle have a tremendous impact on our overall health, happiness, and well-being. Not only am I learning how to improve my life, I am also learning how to help clients look better, feel better, and reach their health goals."
- Ask the person, "I'm curious, what is one area of your health you would like to improve?" or "What is your main health concern?" After he or she responds, you can say something like, "I'd be happy to sit down with you and have a conversation about your health goals. Would you be interested in doing a Health History consultation with me?"
- If inviting a person to do a Health History is scary, you can practice telling people that you are studying to be a Health Coach. From there, they may ask what a Health Coach is or what you are studying in school. You can tell them, "I help people discover how their diet and lifestyle choices affect their health." Listen to how they respond and if it is positive, you can say, "Would you be interested in doing a free consultation with me?"
- Another approach is to talk to people about something you learned in class. For example, if you are in a social setting you can say: "The other day I was listening to an audio lecture from the head of nutrition at Harvard and he said . . ." From there, they may ask more about what you are studying. If they sound interested, you can invite them for a Health History consultation.

Be yourself. Say whatever is true for you. With time and practice, you will find your personal style and language.

SCHEDULING HEALTH HISTORY CONSULTATIONS

Read the next sentence very carefully. If someone expresses interest in doing a Health History with you, schedule it on the spot! Set the exact time and place where the Health History will be. You can say, "Great! I am free on Tuesday and Thursday nights and Sunday afternoons. Would any of those times work for you?" Or you might say something like, "I would love to set up a free consultation with you. My schedule can get full very quickly, so is it okay if we schedule it now? What days and times work best for you next week?"

This means you should start carrying a planner with you at all times, because you never know when you are going to meet potential clients. You also want to make sure you get the person's phone number and email address. Let them know you will email them the details of when and where to meet you. Within 24 hours, email them the address, your phone number, and the date and time of your appointment. You will also send them a reminder about your appointment 24 hours beforehand.

If you skip this crucial step of immediately scheduling appointments, you will lose out on potential clients. People are not going to knock down your door to schedule a

Notes:

Health History with you. It's not because they don't want to work with you; it's because they are busy and they do not prioritize their health. They put their jobs, relationships, and a million other things ahead of their own well-being. They need you to be the advocate for the importance of their health. You can do this for them by being assertive in scheduling the initial consultation. You are not doing anyone any favors by playing small or being shy.

If you don't have your schedule, or if it's not an appropriate situation in which to schedule the Health History, get the person's contact information and be in touch within 24 hours to set up the appointment. Do not delay!

FREQUENTLY ASKED QUESTIONS AND SUGGESTED ANSWERS

Sometimes, when scheduling a Health History or during the consultation itself, people will ask you questions you may not have answers to. In these situations, it is best to answer the questions honestly. If you don't know the answer, you can say, "That's a great question; I will look into it and get back to you," or, "That question is outside of my area of expertise. I recommend that you consult . . ."

Also, you can practice ahead of time by anticipating potential questions and deciding on the best responses. You can also write down questions people ask you during the Health History and keep a list of them for future reference.

What is a Health History?

"During a typical consultation, we will spend about an hour going through your Health History, your goals for your health, and what you've always imagined for your life. We will also get a sense of how it would be to work together. How does that sound?"

What is a Health Coach?

"A Health Coach guides you to reach your health and life goals by making step-by-step changes to your food and lifestyle, at a pace that's comfortable for you." If people who are not clients ask you for advice, try not to give them recommendations. Instead, say, "That is a great question, and those concerns you mentioned are the types of things we would cover together if you were to become my client."

What about confidentiality?

"Like any other health professional, I keep everything clients share with me strictly confidential."

How does the program work?

"I work with clients in 6-month health coaching programs to reach their goals for their health and life. During the six months, I meet with my clients to create a plan, step-by-step, so they feel and look great. Together, we look at their current diet and lifestyle and customize a way to upgrade their food and other aspects of their life. I also

Notes:

offer my clients bonus materials, like books and handouts on health-related topics and other fun ideas to help improve their health. Would you be interested in a free Health History consultation?"

Why is it six months?

"Studies show that if you do something for six months, it is much more likely to become a long-term habit. My goal is that after six months of working together with a client, they will have a deeper understanding of the foods and lifestyle that work best for them. I want them to take what they learn through working with me and use it for the rest of their life."

KEEPING TRACK OF CLIENTS

As you begin inviting people to Health History consultations and lining up potential clients, you will need a way to keep track of it all. At a minimum, we recommend that you keep track of the person's name, their email and phone numbers, the date of their Health History consultation, and any relevant notes that you will want to remember. We have included a sample Health History Tracking Form at the end of this chapter. You will also receive an electronic copy in the Health History Resources. You can edit it in any way that makes sense to you. The important thing is that you keep track.

HEALTH HISTORY EXCITMENT

We understand that the idea of doing a Health History with someone may be a new concept for you. You probably have myriad thoughts and emotions about this, from fear to excitement and nervousness.

List three things that you are nervous about:

1. ....

2. ....

3. ....

You can use your fellow students and Accountability Coach to help you work through anything that you are nervous about. Remember to feel the fear and do it anyway! We ask that instead of focusing on what is scary, you focus your attention on your excitement. In fact, nervousness usually comes out of excitement. Allow yourself to be happily energized about this new adventure you are beginning.

List three things that you find exciting about doing Health Histories:

1. ....

2. ....

3. ....

HEALTH HISTORY TRACKING FORM

Name	Phone	Email	Date of HH	Potential Client?	Follow-up Notes

Don't ask what the world needs. Ask what makes you come alive, and go do it. Because what the world needs is people who have come alive.

—Howard Thurman

CHAPTER 8:

ATTRACTING THE RIGHT CLIENTS

Many of our graduates work as full-time Health Coaches. In order for you to get to this point, you have to put in a lot of work and practice doing Health Histories, workshops, marketing, and networking. Even if you think you are not good at it or don't like marketing yourself, this chapter—and the curriculum taught in the program—will support you in finding ways of marketing yourself that best suit you. Once you figure out how to attract the clients you want, you will be able to focus on building your practice.

TARGET MARKET

In the early stages of health coaching, we recommend you do Health Histories with fellow classmates. As you do Health Histories with all different types of people, you will naturally start to identify those who are attracted to you and who you most enjoy working with. You should also think about who you already know and imagine yourself working with. For example, maybe you want to work with new moms. Once you start doing Health Histories with people who may become clients—that is, non-students—you can narrow your marketing efforts to focus on setting up Health Histories with new moms. You can ask yourself, where can I go to meet this group? What are their concerns? How can I create an email or flyer that will address those issues? New moms then become your target market. Other target markets might be busy executives, college students, marathon runners, yoga instructors, or people with a specific health concern (such as celiac disease, Candida, migraines, sleep problems, stress, or weight loss). For now, focus on understanding why it's important to have a clearly defined target market and start brainstorming on who you may like to work with.

Notes:

BENEFITS TO HAVING A CLEAR TARGET MARKET

- It is easier to market your services when you know who you are trying to reach.
- You can become an expert in a few particular health concerns, rather than learning about new health concerns with each new client.
- People seek health practitioners who are experts in their health concern.
- You will enjoy health coaching more if you are working with people who are interesting to you.
- People in this target market most likely know a lot of other people like them who will also be ideal clients for you.

Answer these questions to help you identify your target market:

1. What health or life issues are you currently working on or have you worked through? Your own experience and expertise may make you a perfect Health Coach for people who are dealing with a challenge you've already faced.

....

....

....

....

....

....

2. What type of person would you enjoy working with? Perhaps you've noticed in your Health History sessions that you connect well with a particular type of person. List a few different types of people here. Get as specific as you can (e.g., women with eating disorders, single dads, twenty-somethings who live in New York City, women going through menopause, people with diabetes, children ages six to ten, corporate professionals, traveling professionals, athletes looking to improve physical performance).

....

....

....

....

....

....

Notes:

3. What hobbies or passions do you enjoy? What is your current profession? Your spiritual community? Think about what you already do, and know that will help you discover who you would like to work with.

4. Out of these groups, who can afford your 6-month program fee?

5. Now that you have identified your target market, where can you find them? For example, working mothers may spend time at day care, or be involved with working mom groups or school functions. You can go to the places where your target client hangs out, and share with people what you do as a Health Coach. List those places here.

6. What are the characteristics and qualities of people in your target market?

Age range:

Male or female:

Education level:

Notes:

Career:..

Income:..

What are their needs, concerns, and goals?..

Who else serves these people?..

7. Who do you know who can introduce you to your ideal client?

....

....

....

Once you have identified the type of people you are trying to reach, you can narrow your networking and marketing efforts. This allows you to more effectively design and write your materials, as well as improve how you communicate what you do.

DYNAMIC INTRODUCTION

What do you say when people ask you what you do? You should be able to summarize everything that you do in one or two sentences. This is what we call your "elevator speech." As you probably already know, one of the basic steps to getting clients is to clearly communicate what you do.

> Example 1 (not recommended):
>
> **What do you do?**
> I'm a Health Coach.

What does *that* mean? Taking this approach can be a dead end because it doesn't convey what you actually do. Remember that health coaching is a relatively new field. A lot of people still don't know what it is or what health coaching means.

> Example 2 (not recommended):
>
> **What do you do?**
> I'm a Health Coach, so I am super holistic. I help all sorts of people implement self-care techniques to manage stress and improve relationships and cook more at home with whole foods and get really healthy. I get people to love healthy food! I used to eat lots of pastries and drink coffee and now I'm a vegan and I LOVE it! I feel so fresh and light! I gave up gluten, too, and I feel so clear! I just want my clients to feel the same way about life that I do.

It's too much. Get the picture? You just can't stop yourself and you want to say every little thing about your life and your diet and the school. While your enthusiasm is appreciated, this might be overwhelming for most people. Less is more.

> Example 3 (recommended):
>
> **What do you do?**
> I work with women who want to improve their appearance naturally. My clients want to lose weight and improve their skin quality, so I teach them how to make better decisions that fit into their busy lifestyle. My clients love that they can make simple changes that create big results.

Begin with the RESULTS that your target market wants. Results impact action for consumers. People want to know what's in it for them. It is your job to tell them.

Here's another, very simple example to show variety since we're all different:

> Example 4 (recommended):
>
> I work with men who are addicted to sugar and want to reduce their cravings and have more energy.

Practice organizing your sentences like this:
I work with [target market] who [problem] and want to [solution].

Try out a few for yourself:

1. I work with ....

who ....

and want to ....

2. I work with ....

who ....

and want to ....

3. I work with ....

who ....

and want to ....

Notes:

Notes:

Here are a few more examples:

1. I work with young professionals who want help reducing their stress and having more energy.
2. I work with busy moms who are struggling with preparing quick, healthy, enjoyable meals for their families, while also making sure they are taking care of themselves and their own health.
3. I work with men who are overworked, overstressed, and want to have more energy and incorporate delicious, healthy foods into their diets.

This elevator speech should be your first step in introducing yourself to someone. During any conversation, you should be sure to listen and have the communication flow. Don't talk too much or try to say everything that you do in less than one minute. Share, ask questions, and be genuinely interested in other people. Think about how you can explain your work in a way that is easy for them to understand, and so they recognize the benefits of what you do. And always remember to get the person's contact information so you can add them to your mailing list.

COMPANY MISSION STATEMENT

Throughout this program, we discuss knowing your intentions and having a clear vision for doing this work. It's one step of the Golden Path. That's because building a business is hard work—and given all the demands on your time, it's important to stay on track. Many students find that writing a mission statement for their business helps keep them focused and energized. Note that a mission statement for your business is similar to a vision or intention for yourself. The main difference is that it's used to help guide the direction of your business versus guiding your personal path.

After you've identified your target market, you can develop a mission statement for your business. A mission statement is a sentence, bullet point list, or paragraph illustrating the goals and purpose of your business. It's the vision of your company put into words. Though this is not immediately necessary, it will help you clarify what inspires you to do this work.

Example:

Jane Smith Health supports busy moms in maintaining a healthy family and a high level of self-care. As a Health Coach, my mission is to improve the health and happiness of my clients.

Use this space to write a first draft of your company mission statement. This is just a first draft; it doesn't need to be perfect. You will refine it as your business grows.

....

....

Notes:

MISSION STATEMENTS

Disney: To make people happy.

FedEx: FedEx will produce superior financial returns for shareowners by providing high-value-added supply chain, transportation, business, and related information services through focused operating companies. Customer requirements will be met in the highest quality manner appropriate to each market segment served. FedEx will strive to develop mutually rewarding relationships with its employees, partners, and suppliers. Safety will be the first consideration in all operations. Corporate activities will be conducted to the highest ethical and professional standards.

Google: Google's mission is to organize the world's information and make it universally accessible and useful.

Institute for Integrative Nutrition: Our mission is to play a crucial role in improving health and happiness, and through that process, create a ripple effect that transforms the world.

As you can see, mission statements range from very simple to fairly complex. Some companies include their target market and/or their ethical position.

Use this mission to guide you. This can be a powerful motivational tool for you, keeping you clear about the bigger picture of why you are doing this work and what is driving you to accomplish your goals. When you are unsure what steps to take with your business, think back to this mission statement and ask yourself, will taking this action support the mission of my company? Also use your mission to help you reach your target market. By speaking clearly and confidently about why you are doing this work, people will become interested in you and want to learn more.

INTENTIONS CHECK-IN

In Chapter 1 we asked you to state your intentions and develop your vision for doing this work.

Do you use your vision to guide you in the program and in setting up your business?

Notes:

If not, why?

....

....

....

How do you feel?

....

....

....

Has your vision changed? If so, how?

....

....

....

What can you do differently in the future to stay true to your vision?

....

....

....

Notes:

Notes:

What the mind can conceive,
it can achieve.

—Napoleon Hill

CHAPTER 9:

THE BUILDING BLOCKS FOR A BUSINESS

Now that you are learning to become a Health Coach and thinking about building your own practice or related business, it's time to make sure you are organized from the beginning. Although this may seem overwhelming at first, if you take it one step at a time, you will move forward with ease.

Having a legitimate business will help you look and feel more professional. Please keep in mind that you can start your marketing efforts before you set up your business officially. For many of you, having your own practice may be a lifelong dream. We will review some basic steps for getting your practice up and running, including getting organized, creating your office, determining your business name and your title, picking a legal structure, registering your business, and creating a website.

If you ever feel overwhelmed, remember to refer back to the Golden Path for guidance!

Use the following section to see if you have your necessities covered. If you answer "no" to any of these questions, take action to change your answer to "yes" as soon as possible.

BASIC OFFICE SUPPLIES

1. Do you have a phone? **(Yes/No)**

   If you have more than one phone number, have you chosen which one you will use for your business? **(Yes/No)**

   What is the number for your business? ....

   Have you changed your voicemail or answering machine greeting so that it is professional? (e.g., "This is Jane Smith, Health Coach. I cannot take your call right now, so please leave a message and I'll get back to you as soon as possible. Have a great day!") **(Yes/No)**

Notes:

2. Do you have a professional email address? (e.g., jsmith@yahoo.com) **(Yes/No)**

   If you have more than one email address, have you chosen which one you will use for your business? **(Yes/No)**

   What is the email address for your business? ....

   Note: You can get free email at yahoo.com, hotmail.com, or gmail.com. We suggest that you use your name if possible (e.g., janedoe@yahoo.com or janedoehealthcoach@yahoo.com) rather than something less professional, such as jane623@yahoo.com).

3. Do you have the following office supplies?

   Computer or pocket calendar/scheduling system **(Yes/No)**

   File folders **(Yes/No)**

   Pens **(Yes/No)**

   Pads of paper **(Yes/No)**

   File holder **(Yes/No)**

   Paper clips/staples **(Yes/No)**

4. Do you have a printer or access to a local copy shop, FedEx office, or a library? **(Yes/No)**

ORGANIZATIONAL SYSTEMS

As a Health Coach, you will have appointments, follow-ups, lectures, cooking classes, and events. You do not want to lose any information. There are various types of systems available to help you stay organized.

FILE FOLDERS

Paper filing systems can be very helpful. If you do not have a filing system already, you can buy small, portable filing cabinets or boxes that fit file folders. You can get these supplies at any office supply store.

Here are some suggested labels for your files:

- **Health History Forms:** for blank forms.
- **Completed Health History Forms:** for people who have filled these out but did not become clients. People who become paying clients will get individual folders for their forms.
- **Health History Notes:** for storing your ideas about what worked and what you want to improve.
- **Handouts:** for hard copies of all of your health coaching handouts.

Notes:

EMBRACE TECHNOLOGY

Some people are afraid of technology. Are you avoiding technology? Do you know how to use your computer, email, smartphone or tablet? As a Health Coach, your time is invaluable and using technology can certainly save you time. By learning how to work with technology, you can benefit from the fast level of service that it provides. Also, 90 percent of your clients will most likely have good technological skills and will expect you to communicate with them in this way. This is part of providing good customer service.

Here are a few fundamental things you should know how to do on your computer:

- ☐ Print
- ☐ Read email
- ☐ Send email
- ☐ Cut and paste
- ☐ Save email into folders
- ☐ Send attachments over email
- ☐ Create Microsoft Word documents

If you do not know how to do something from the list above, identify someone in your life who could show you. Perhaps you have a friend or family member who is good with computers.

- **Clients:** for information on individual clients. Within this file, each client should have his or her own hanging file to keep that client's documents.
- **Financial Information:** for copies of payment checks, receipts, and any other pertinent financial information.

COMPUTER ORGANIZATION

Along with your file folders and paper work, you will also want to create computer folders to save important information relevant to your business. We will provide you with many resources including forms, handouts, outlines, and other documents to get your business started. Once you get these, we recommend that you save them onto the hard drive of your computer. You may also want to email them to yourself so you have a backup.

Here are some suggested folders to create on your computer desktop to help you stay organized with your health coaching documents:

Notes:

- **Health Coaching:** within this folder you will create additional folders for Health History Forms and Client Handouts.
- **Classes:** within this folder, you can create a new folder for each talk you give (e.g., Sugar Blues, Eating for Energy).
- **Newsletters:** for your newsletters.
- **Marketing:** for tracking business marketing ideas, plans, and action steps.

COMPUTER FILES OR FILE FOLDERS

Even if you are extremely computer savvy, please know that you cannot keep everything on your computer when it comes to health coaching. Your clients may be filling out Health History forms in person and you will have other documents that you will want to save. You should have an actual file folder for each client that contains his or her paperwork, as detailed earlier.

SCHEDULE ORGANIZATION

Some people prefer to do all their scheduling electronically, either on their computer, Blackberry, iPhone, or other smartphone. Other people prefer to use an old-fashioned pocket, desk, or wall calendar. Use what works best for you. Being organized means putting everything into your schedule. You should schedule when you plan to exercise, when you are having dinner with your family, and other details of your life. Even if it is something that you are sure you won't forget, if you don't put it into your schedule, your chances of forgetting about it or double booking yourself are much higher. Your scheduling system should be foolproof. The benefit of having a pocket calendar or handheld device is that you can always have it with you. Electronic calendars can be set with reminders, which is great if you are a forgetful person or like to have that extra reminder.

CONTACT ORGANIZATION

As you begin your health coaching practice, you will meet many people. Some of these people will be potential clients, others will be contacts who may be able to refer clients to you or help your business in some other way. You will want to keep track of important people you meet so that you can be sure to follow up with them when needed. Some people like to keep track of all their contacts on their computer, while others prefer a notepad or Rolodex. Any way that works for you is great. Just make sure that you have a consistent process to stay organized. It will also allow you to track the conversations and interactions you have with potential clients, business partners, or other organizations with whom you may do business. This will help with your marketing efforts and all of the tasks required to keep building these relationships.

Notes:

If you choose to keep track of your potential clients on your computer, you have a couple of options. The best option is to organize your contacts in an Excel spreadsheet or the address book/contact system that comes with your email service.

The point is to have your contacts organized and ready to go, so that you are all set to work with clients when the time comes. If you do not wish to purchase a contact management software package or create an Excel spreadsheet, you can do the same kind of tracking in a low-tech kind of way. Some people prefer to keep track of their acquaintances using a simple address book, or you can use the Client Contact form to record information about people you meet, which is located in the Marketing Materials Resources. You can store these forms either in a hanging file or an online folder you create for "Contacts."

FORMS

All the forms you will need to run your health coaching practice are provided in the 6-Month Program Resources. You should save each to your computer and spend time reviewing the content. You can also customize the forms as you see fit, adding your logo, name, or contact information. However, please retain Integrative Nutrition's copyright notice on all forms.

We recommend that you print out some forms to have on hand, such as the Health History forms, Program Agreement, and any other forms that you use on a regular basis. We cover the forms in detail in Chapter 12. One suggestion is to have client folders ready to go, each containing a blank copy of all the forms you use to sign on a client. This way when you have a Health History you can just grab one of the folders, rather than printing out and organizing all the paperwork each time.

You may want to staple the Client Progress form to the left side of the folder and the Giveaway Checklist to the right side. After each session, you can easily mark down how the session went and what you gave to your client. Find a way that works for you to organize all your forms and paperwork; it will save you a lot of time and stress in the future. It will take some trial and error to determine the systems that work best for you.

OFFICE SET-UP

When you first begin health coaching, it's completely okay for you to not have an office. You can meet your clients in a coffee shop, library, bookstore, their home, your home, or a hotel lobby. Any place has advantages and disadvantages. You will want to meet your clients in a comfortable setting where you can speak about personal topics. Experiment with different venues to see what feels appropriate.

Eventually you may want to get office space. An office space will allow you to stay in one place to see your clients and guarantee that you have the exact environment you want. You may rent an office or create one in your home.

CLIENT CONTACT FORM

CLIENT CONTACT INFORMATION

Name:	**How you know this client:**
Cell Phone: **Work Phone:**	**Email:**
Address:	**City, State, Zip:**

Special Information: (work, name of pet, spouse or partner, important details to remember that will make them feel special)

CLIENT CORRESPONDENCE

Date	what you talked about, what you need to follow up with and when
2/20/XX	initial call to set up Health History scheduled for 3/22 at 7 p.m. in the lobby of the Marriott email her on 3/21 with reminder notice
(other dates here)	

Notes:

If you choose to rent an office, consider renting in a massage therapy practice, a wellness center, or a therapist's office with other health professionals who might refer clients to you. You can also rent space from community centers, YMCAs, and churches at reasonable rates. Also look into co-working spaces that supply private meeting rooms at hourly prices specifically for entrepreneurs.

If you use your home as your office, it's helpful to pick an area where you will see clients. It may be at your kitchen table or on your couch. Perhaps you have a room that you can turn into your office. If you don't have an area that works, think about purchasing Japanese screens and sectioning off a small area of your home where you can fit two chairs and a small table. You'll need at least two comfortable chairs in your office. You'll also need a clock, strategically placed so that you can easily view it during your sessions and keep track of time. You may also want to have attractive decorations, a hot pot for making tea, the option to play relaxing music, and a bookshelf to display your health and wellness books. You will also need office space to do all of your paperwork and correspondence. This may or may not be the same place where you see your clients.

CREATING A BUSINESS NAME

There is no one-size-fits-all formula for picking a fantastic business name. But you can consider a few things, such as the kind of business you do, your target market, and your unique style or personality. Your business name should be distinctive, memorable, suggest the services you offer, and be easy to spell and pronounce.

The options for your business name are endless. You can use your first or last name as part of it, which is recommended, such as Jane Smith Health or Health with Jane. Or, you can pick a powerful name that conveys what your business is about without including your name. Words such as "health," "nurturing," and "wellness" are popular among our students and graduates.

Write six possible business names here:

1. ....

2. ....

3. ....

4. ....

5. ....

6. ....

Which of these names best represents what you do? What sounds the strongest to you? If you are not sure, you can ask your friends, family, fellow students, and Accountability Coach what they think.

Notes:

We suggest giving yourself a few weeks before finalizing your decision and registering your business name. Make sure that someone else does not already have the rights to use the name you have chosen. Remember though, the most important part of your business is YOU. Your energy and enthusiasm will speak louder than your business name.

Here are steps you can take to conduct a name search:

1. A quick and easy place to start is with an online search engine, such as Google. When you Google the name you like, what else comes up? Is there already another business with this name?
2. Go to www.godaddy.com or www.register.com and do a search for the domain name that you'd like to use. If another company has reserved a domain name that contains the business name you want, you probably won't be able to use it because the domain name qualifies as a trademark if the website is used commercially.
3. Get in touch with your county clerk's office. There you can check a list of all the assumed business names. In some states, you can also check with the state corporation commission to view a database of all business names.
4. If someone else is using the business name you want to use, you shouldn't use it. Before you decide upon a name, you might also want to check that your business name can be used as a website address, also called a domain name or URL. These days, most successful businesses have websites. Having your website match your business name allows potential clients to find you quickly and easily. For example, if your business name is "Health with Jane," you might want to use www.healthwithjane.com as your domain name. It can be difficult to find a domain name that is not already taken, so you may have to be flexible with your choices.

YOUR TITLE

Upon successfully graduating from Integrative Nutrition, you will receive a certificate as a Health Coach. The title that you can add to your business cards and other marketing materials is Health Coach.

Be careful about picking titles that require certain qualifications that you do not have. For example, you cannot call yourself a registered dietician in any state unless you are registered with your country's dietetic association (e.g., Academy of Nutrition and Dietetics for the US, Dietitians Association of Australia, or the British Dietetic Association). Your diploma will give you the designation of Health Coach, so graduates who choose to use a designation other than Health Coach must be aware that they are solely responsible for understanding and fulfilling any licensure or certification requirements

Notes:

of that title. Many titles (such as Nutritionist, Dietician, and Counselor) are protected by regulations that vary from state to state. You may contact your local government or visit your State Board of Dietetics and Nutrition to keep abreast of current regulations and legislation around those titles.

We are part of a dynamic, evolving field. It's exciting to be part of a growing movement of wellness practitioners. However, this also means that the laws are evolving and will continue to change.

DETERMINING YOUR BUSINESS STRUCTURE AND REGISTERING YOUR BUSINESS

Once you choose your business name and title, you can register your business so that you are in adherence with state and local regulations in your area. The process of registering your company with your state and local governments will vary depending on the business entity type. This section describes the most common forms of business entities.

All this business information may seem overwhelming. Breathe. Read each section slowly and carefully. We will cover it more in the program, and we are available to provide additional support. We've included the information here to give you a clear picture of your options.

SOLE PROPRIETORSHIPS

Most new businesses, and most students at Integrative Nutrition, start as sole proprietorships because it is the easiest, cheapest, and quickest way to create a business. In fact, about 70 percent of small businesses are sole proprietorships. This type of business is an option if you are going to be the only person who owns the business. If you have co-owners or partners, sole proprietorships are not allowed, unless your partner is your spouse.

A sole proprietorship is a business that is owned by one individual and is unincorporated. This is the simplest form of business organization to start and maintain. In a sole proprietorship, the business and its owner are one and the same. The business has no existence apart from you, the owner. Therefore, you are solely responsible for your business and all liabilities are your personal liabilities. The record keeping is very simple because your business doesn't have to file income tax returns or pay income taxes. All the money that is made is considered your income. If you are a sole proprietor in the US, you don't need a federal identification number for your business, so you may use your social security number. This may vary per country.

Sole proprietorships are so easy to set up and maintain that you may already own one without knowing it. If you are a freelance writer, a massage therapist who is not on an employer's payroll, or a salesperson who receives only commissions, you are already

Notes:

a sole proprietor. Even though a sole proprietorship is easy to start and maintain, you may have to comply with local registration or permit laws, and obtain a business license to make your business legitimate.

You can begin to work right away as a sole proprietor. Keep it simple at first, and let your business evolve as you do. It's unnecessary to start out by creating a complicated business structure.

LIMITED LIABILITY COMPANIES (LLCs)

In order to create an LLC, most US states require two owners, who can be spouses. An LLC is set up like a sole proprietorship in that all the profits go directly to the owners, but there is a distinction between the owners and the business, protecting the owners from any personal liability. The paperwork for creating an LLC is less complex than for a corporation, but more complex than for a sole proprietorship. In the US, an LLC requires a federal identification number. It's like a social security number for your business. SBA.gov provides more information on this process. Please research your country's registration process. Most countries have online resources to guide small businesses in their registrations and paperwork process.

CORPORATIONS

Corporations provide a business entity that is separate from the owner as an individual. It can be expensive to start a corporation, but the owner avoids liability. Minimum requirements for maintaining a corporation include conducting annual meetings, filing minutes in your corporate books, and filing the required documentation with the state on an annual basis. While double taxation is sometimes mentioned as a drawback to incorporation, the S corporation (or Subchapter corporation, a popular variation of the regular C corporation) avoids this situation by allowing income or losses to be passed through on individual tax returns, similar to a partnership. The main reason for incorporating is to limit your personal liability. You would pay yourself a salary. In the US, a corporation needs a federal identification number, like an LLC.

SETTING UP A SOLE PROPRIETORSHIP

Unless you have a strong business background and are up for the task of creating a corporation or LLC, we recommend starting your business as a sole proprietorship. You can always transition to another kind of business structure in the future, but for your first year as a Health Coach, a sole proprietorship will likely provide you with everything you need.

For the US, after you have made certain the business and domain names you want are available, you may fill out a simple "Doing Business As" (DBA) form with your

Notes:

local government. A DBA is a business filing that allows business owners to operate a company under a name other than their own name at a minimal cost. In most states, if your business is your first and last name, such as Jane Smith Health or Healing with Jane Smith, a DBA is not required. However, if you want your business to be called Holistic Healing, you will need a DBA since that business name is not your legal name (Jane Smith).

Having a DBA allows you to use a name without filing a legal entity, such as a corporation, partnership, or LLC. It also protects the business name from being used by anyone else. Most states and counties require that you file a DBA to legally run a business by a name other than your own, even a small home-run business. Also, most banks won't let you open a business account unless you have registered your business name.

Filing a DBA is simple and takes little time. First, call your county clerk's office to learn about the local fees and procedures in your area. They can tell you where to get the DBA form, also called an Assumed Business Name Form, and where to submit it. Follow the instructions provided by the county clerk and submit the proper form and filing fee. Once your DBA filing is approved, you will get your Business Certificate and your business is officially registered. You can now start using the name as your official business name. Some states, such as California, also require that you publish an announcement in a local newspaper with your business name. Please check in with your local county clerk's office, either in person or on the web, to read more about the regulations in your state.

SATISFYING ALL REGIONAL AND LOCAL REQUIREMENTS

Once you have registered your business and, if necessary, gotten a federal identification number, you will need to make sure that you are complying with all regional and local requirements for running a business. For example, you may need to purchase a business license from your county. Your county's website will most likely have the information you need to make sure you are complying with county requirements, and you can use your state website to find out how to satisfy state requirements.

If you are practicing outside of the United States, please look into your local requirements. Be sure that you are complying with all the necessary rules and regulations.

TAKE ACTION

Throughout the program, you will learn a great deal of information about health and nutrition. However, it is the process of starting to work with clients during the program that will enable you to get the most out of this education.

People are often used to buying a product and then owning it. We encourage you to break this trend when it comes to your education at Integrative Nutrition. Instead of

Notes:

RESOURCE GUIDE

Your state's website will have information on how to select a business structure as well as the specific regulations for each option in your area. Visit the website (e.g.,www.state.ny.us, www.ct.gov, www.newjersey.gov) and search in the "Business" section.

You can also contact the U.S. Small Business Association website at www.sba.gov for more information on the advantages and disadvantages of each business entity mentioned earlier, and to find a Small Business Association in your area.

Other local assistance options include Small Business Development Centers, Service Corps of Retired Executives (SCORE), Veterans Business Outreach Centers, and Women's Business Centers. You can also contact your local Chamber of Commerce, which has many options to support business owners. Look in your local phone book for any of these organizations.

You may also want to consult with an accountant, lawyer, or anyone else you know who is knowledgeable about your state's laws and your personal situation.

Many national governments have established resources to connect small business owners with the appropriate guidance and resources for complying with all registrations, licenses, and reporting. Please reference your country's small business association to ensure the proper setup for your business.

merely absorbing the information we teach and keeping it inside your brain, we want you to go out and teach others what you are learning here. Make your education an active experience.

It is through your work with clients that our curriculum will genuinely start to make sense to you. You will see how desperately most people need someone to talk to about their health. By taking on clients, you will learn to become a leader and a partner in the change that is happening around wellness in this country. As you help others develop healthy habits and find balance in their lives, you will notice that you too will experience growth, improved health, increased happiness, and more fulfillment.

For now you should be practicing Health Histories with fellow classmates. We will tell you when you are ready to start having Health History consultations with potential clients and seeing clients in a 6-month program. Some of you will get one client; some of you will get 20. Your clients will pay you, or maybe you will barter services as a student. Either way, it is extremely important that you start seeing clients as a student because you will have the staff and a community of students to support you and answer any questions that may come up.

Throughout the years, we have seen many students who learn all about nutrition, improve their own health, and plan to do health coaching after they graduate. But this plan rarely works. These people end up putting off getting clients and never get around to it. You do not want to be one of these people. We encourage you to use the school to help you improve your own health and then go out to help others.

Notes:

We make a living by what we get,
but we make a life by what we give.

—Winston Churchill

CHAPTER 10:

FINANCIAL BASICS

We find it helpful to have a separation between business and personal finances. Some small business owners pay their expenses out of personal accounts and deposit business income and income from other sources into family checking accounts that are shared with a spouse. While this may be okay in the beginning, as you grow your business, you can avoid complications by having one bank account for business and one for personal or family expenses.

For example, if you do business under a name other than your own, your bank may not allow you to deposit checks that are made out to your company name. Additionally if you have your business money in a joint account with someone else, what happens if you have to write a check for your business the same day your husband, wife, or partner drew on that same money for something else? If you keep your business money separate from your personal account, when it comes time to do taxes, it will be much easier to figure out your deductions, fees, expenses, and so on.

As mentioned earlier, if you have a sole proprietorship, your money and the business's money are one and the same. It is not necessary for you to keep a separate business account, but it can be helpful. If you keep your business finances separate from your personal finances, you can put all the money you make from health coaching into a different account and pay all your business expenses from the same account. Having a separate business account will ensure that you keep track of how much money you are putting into and getting out of your business.

Once you register your business, you will receive a Business Certificate or your country's equivalent of that. Most banks require official paperwork from your registration to open a business bank account. Please inquire with your bank regarding what paperwork you need to open a business account.

Notes:

Many banks offer free checking for small business owners. You can also usually get a no-fee debit or credit card. Figure out how many deposits and how many payments you expect to make a week. Chances are it will only be a few per week, in which case you will be able to get a low-cost or free bank account. A basic plan usually has unlimited checking each month.

Find a reputable bank that you have used in the past. It's probably easiest to use the same bank you use for your personal account if it has a business branch. You can call them, schedule a visit, or drop in to find out what your options are when it comes to small business bank accounts.

ACCEPTING PAYMENTS

Many of our graduates are very skilled coaches; they are great listeners who are intuitive and genuinely enjoy talking to people. Coaching is the easy part for them. The hardest part is asking their clients for money.

To help you overcome any fear about asking people to pay you, we are going to be very clear about the different options you have when it comes to getting paid. Do you want your clients to pay in full up front or in monthly installments? Do you want them to pay by cash, check, or credit card?

GETTING PAID UP FRONT VERSUS IN MONTHLY INSTALLMENTS

Of course, it is always exciting to get paid in full at the beginning of your program. When you first start out as a Health Coach, you may keep your fees a little lower as you get your feet wet. So paying in full may be quite doable for your clients.

As you get more experience and raise your rates, your clients may want to pay in monthly installments. To get started we generally recommend charging around $75–95 per month as a student, and $195 per month once you graduate. You might consider encouraging your clients to pay in full by offering them a discount for doing so. For example, "save 10 percent if you pay in full" or "get $100 off the full price if you pay in full."

Some graduates actually prefer to have their clients pay in monthly installments. This can be accomplished with both checks and credit cards. If you choose to make monthly payments an option to clients, set it up so that you are not chasing down money each month. In this chapter, we provide suggestions for setting up hassle-free monthly payments.

As you get new clients, simply add them to the list, and then enter each payment into the appropriate cell. Using this system, you will know how much you have earned each month, and at the end of the year you can easily tally the total income you have earned.

Notes:

CASH, CHECK, OR CREDIT CARD

Cash: Everyone likes to get paid in cash. However, if you are not skilled at money management, this may not be the best way for you to get paid. Cash is easy to spend because it goes into your wallet and you forget that it was your paycheck from your client. Also, if your rates go up, it may not be feasible or convenient for your clients to pay you in cash. If your client wants to pay with cash, they should pay up front. If they say they will pay you in cash each month, you will have to remember to ask them for the money at your sessions. You don't want to be discussing money during the program. You want them to pay you in full up front, give you post-dated checks, or give you a credit card that you will charge each month.

Check: Checks are a great way to get paid. Unlike credit cards, you will not have to pay a fee for accepting a check as payment. We highly suggest that you ask your clients who want to pay you by check to give you six post-dated checks—one for each month you will be working together. That way, you will not have to ask your client for payment each month, freeing you up to focus on what's really important in your work with them. Have your client date the checks for the same date of every month. The 1st and the 15th are usually easiest for convenience. Once you receive the checks, be sure to keep them in a safe place. Keeping checks from all clients for a certain date in one convenient spot will make your bank runs easier. It is good customer service to deposit checks within three days of their date.

Credit Cards: Credit cards are very convenient for your clients, and will allow you to easily process payments, but there is a fee. This is also great when working with phone clients. The easiest way to accept credit cards is to use PayPal. This lets you accept credit cards, bank transfers, debit cards, and more—at some of the lowest costs in the industry. Plus, your customers can pay you instantly, even if they don't have a PayPal account, via American Express, MasterCard, Visa, Discover, and debit cards.

Another way to accept credit cards is to set up a merchant account through your bank. If you already have a business account, your bank may be able to help you accept credit cards as well.

Finally, many of our graduates who have many clients use DirectPay (www.directpayinc.com) to set up an online account that accepts credit cards. With DirectPay (DP), you simply collect the credit card information from your client, log in to the DP website, and enter in the information to charge the client. The money is then transferred from the client's credit card directly into your business bank account. If you choose this route, take a look at the Credit Card Authorization form in the 6-Month Program Resources.

Notes:

MANAGING FINANCES

A critical part of running a business successfully is having a system and structure in place for managing your finances. This step is important for tax purposes, making financial decisions, collecting payments, and projecting financial goals long-term. Poor financial planning will decrease your income and will jeopardize the success of your business. Accounting is simply a process of tracking what you spend and what you make.

STEPS FOR FINANCIAL PLANNING

Step 1: Set Up a System to Track Your Finances

As mentioned, opening a separate bank account allows you to easily keep track of your finances. You can use a spreadsheet or database program on your personal computer, keep a ledger and record manually, or purchase a software system like Quicken or QuickBooks.

Keep on top of this work. You should plan to spend time each week updating your records. It is also important that you keep all of your receipts and tax forms from year to year, since you could be asked by your country's tax-collecting agency to show proof of your earnings and expenses.

Step 2: Track Your Expenses

A great thing about health coaching is that you won't have many large expenses. No inventory, no employees. The biggest expense you will have is rent, if you are renting an office space, and your client giveaways. We suggest that you spend approximately 10 percent of your client revenue on giveaways. So if your client is paying you $200 per month, you have $20 each month to spend on gifts.

Per tax regulations, you are eligible to deduct expenses for your business from your income. These expenses must be "incurred in connection with your business, ordinary (similar to others in your field), and necessary." Basically, any money you spend to run your business can be deducted, either in whole or by percentage. Your accountant will know the specifics.

You should track all items, whether you paid cash, check, or credit card. Keep every receipt, and organize them by category in a large manila or accordion envelope. If you don't have a receipt, record the amount, item, and date with whatever system you have in place.

These are the types of expenses you may want to include:

- All goods you purchase for clients including: books, CDs, DVDs, food samples, self-care items.
- Office equipment including: computer, fax, copy machine, phone, chairs, table, frames, plants, lighting.

Notes:

- Business use of home or rental office. You are entitled to deduct the percentage you actually use for seeing clients and running your business.
- Business supplies: paper, CD-ROMs, pens, files.
- Email, Internet, and computer costs.
- Phone bill. You may deduct a percentage, based on how much you use your phone for business.
- Marketing and promotion—ads, flyers, brochures, networking event fees, business cards, website creation, designer fees, hiring people.
- Renters' and liability insurance.
- Legal and professional services.
- Continuing education, including: workshops, seminars, events related to your field, learning a complementary modality. Find out from your accountant what is legal.
- If you take your clients to an event, you can deduct a certain percentage of that expense.
- Event expenses for clients, including: the cost to rent a room for a workshop or food purchased for a cooking class.
- Transportation and lodging, including: speaking engagements, out-of-state conferences, or business meetings.
- Association fees.
- Bank fees.
- If you rent a car or use your own car, you can deduct a certain percentage for gas and mileage based on how much you use your car for business.
- If you rent an apartment and your office is in your home, a percentage of your rent may be deductible.

In terms of what you spend on Integrative Nutrition tuition, US tax law states that education expenses incurred to change careers are not deductible. Education expenses that are extending your knowledge of your current profession are deductible, based on IRS guidelines. Again, your accountant will know what and how much you can claim as expenses.

Step 3: Track Your Revenue

You should record all income you earn related to your business—cash, check, and credit card payments.

Types of revenue from health coaching:

- Client fees from your program
- Speaking engagements
- Group program revenue
- Corporate workshops
- Income from writing

Notes:

- Consulting income
- Any products you sell
- Referral fees given to you by other practitioners

Track this revenue in your ledger or with your software or Excel, organizing it by month and by client. By using a software program, it makes it much easier to add, analyze the figures, and to have a detailed and organized record to give to your accountant. If you have other income from your day job, you should also keep accurate records for this and provide all of the income to your accountant, who will be able to properly prepare your tax forms.

Step 4: File Your Taxes

We recommend that you set aside 30 percent of your income for taxes. For example, if you collect $200 from a client, set aside $60 for taxes. It is important to note that the tax laws are very complicated. And while this book is meant to provide an overview of financial planning, it is not meant to take the place of a qualified accountant. By spending money on an accountant, you actually save money, since he or she will know exactly how to provide the greatest savings for you and your business. Being self-employed means that you have the chance to keep a large percentage of what you make, since you are allowed to deduct expenses for your business. And tax laws are designed to support businesses. If you really don't want to hire an accountant, you can purchase tax preparation software, such as TurboTax for the US.

MONEY PERSONALITIES

Usually when people go into business for themselves, issues about money come up. After all, this may be the first time in your life when you are directly asking people to pay you for your time. Please know that what you are offering your clients is incredibly valuable, and you deserve to get paid well for it. It's important to be clear on your ideas about money so that you do not create blocks for yourself when it comes time to get paid. When people pay for something they tend to value it more. Additionally, if you are earning a good income, you have the flexibility to do more charitable work, as you are meeting your financial needs through paying clients.

MONEY BELIEF SYSTEM

What are your earliest memories of money?

....

....

....

What were/are your parents' views of money?

Notes:

What do you enjoy about money?

What difficulty do you have around money?

For further reading about issues with money, we recommend *Creating True Prosperity,* by Shakti Gawain, Novato, CA: New World Library, 1997, and *Secrets of the Millionaire Mind,* by T. Harv Eker, New York, NY: Harper Business, 2005.

BUDGETING

We may not like the word "budgeting" because of restrictive associations, so what about reframing it to "healthy spending"? The key to being financially healthy is making sure that you are spending (and saving!) your income wisely.

Use the suggestions below to see if you're on track:

- 50% of your take-home income (after taxes) goes toward needs like housing, transportation, food, childcare, insurance, and mandatory debt pay-down.
- 30% goes toward wants, the fun things that bring you joy.
- 20% is set aside for savings.

Don't worry if you are nowhere near this ratio! Simply use it as a guideline to work toward. Starting to save even 1% or 2% is a step in the right direction. (Adapted from Manisha Thakor, http://manishathakor.com)

Notes:

What is your reaction to the suggested percentages?

Where do you think you are right now?

Needs:

Wants:

Savings:

Which one is your priority? Does your budget reflect that?

What would you need to change to match your budget with your priority?

What could this change open up for you? How would it impact you in the next six months? The next year?

Notes:

TYPICAL MONEY PERSONALITIES

Throughout the years, we have identified that our students fall into different categories in terms of their relationships with money. Take a moment to see which one you identify with. Get support around letting go of any troubled past with money and recognizing that you can have a future full of abundance and wealth.

The Under-Earner: These people charge nothing, or very little for services. They believe this should be free to everyone. They usually ask for about $25 per month for their 6-month program. These students have a hard time raising their rates and asking clients for money.

The Over-Giver: These people doubt their abilities as Health Coaches and make up for their insecurities by over-giving. They often spend a lot of money on giveaways and food, and their sessions usually go longer than the allotted 50 minutes. They spend a lot of what they earn on their clients and end up with little profit.

The Over-Spender: These people wish to portray themselves as successful. They spend lots of money on upscale offices and expensive clothes to help themselves feel professional and cover insecurities about doing this work.

In all of these cases, remember that your financial health and your belief in your own self-worth are tremendously important. The truth is, how you approach money in your career is how you look at it in all areas of your life. If you take this opportunity now to form a healthy, balanced relationship with money, it will change your life. By keeping yourself financially healthy, stress is usually reduced, which contributes to your overall health and happiness.

Describe how you would feel once you reach this budget goal:

What action will you take to make this vision a reality?

Notes:

PROFESSIONAL LIABILITY INSURANCE

Be sure to have all your clients sign the Program Agreement that we provide you because it also contains a legal waiver. After you graduate, you may want to purchase professional liability insurance if you can afford to do so. Prices may range from $250 to $500 per year.

Whether or not you purchase it is up to you. Additionally, many home insurance and renters' insurance companies will have a work-home policy. They offer addendums and riders, which cover things like personal injury, as well as protecting business equipment in case of damage. You can check with your insurance company to see what they offer and learn more about other options.

CHECK-IN

We've just given you a lot of new information about how to start a business. Right now you may be feeling excited, nervous, overwhelmed, or confident. Wherever you are is totally fine. Remember to stay focused, follow our instructions, and ask for support when you need it.

Take a minute to check in with yourself. How are you feeling about your business? What have you accomplished so far? What has been the most challenging part? What are you most looking forward to?

Notes:

Notes:

The surest way not to fail is
to determine to succeed.

—Richard Brinsley Sheridan

CHAPTER 11:

SUCCESSFULLY SIGNING ON CLIENTS

Generally, people attracted to health coaching are intelligent, unique, intuitive, and generous. Sometimes, however, new Health Coaches have challenges around asking for money. If you want to be successful as a Health Coach, you will have to overcome blocks around money and fully understand the value of your work. We will support you in this process, but the best way for you to learn is to practice closing the deal. Closing the deal is the part at the end of a Health History where you ask your potential client if they want to work with you. Closing the deal is about having a conversation that allows your potential client to understand the value of your work. When they can clearly see the benefits that they'll receive in your program, closing the deal is much easier. It's up to you to help them see what's possible. Even if you do not intend to be a Health Coach, as a holistic health practitioner it is important to feel comfortable talking about money and own your worth when it comes to setting your rates or prices.

Practicing the closing the deal conversation allows you to fully understand how to sign on a new client. For some people it comes easily, but for others it is the most difficult part of the Health History. In this chapter, we will walk you through the different aspects of closing the deal and provide you with the tools to do this successfully.

CLOSING THE DEAL AND ENDING THE HEALTH HISTORY SESSION

After you go through the Health History form, leave about 10 to 15 minutes to close the deal. Here are some steps to take:

Notes:

- Mention one thing you enjoyed about your potential client and the session.
- Ask them, "How was this for you?"
- Ask them, "What was one thing you found valuable in our session?"
- Restate the person's main health concerns, the level of importance, and the one thing they know they should already be doing. Then repeat back to them how these concerns affect other parts of their life and what the future looks like if they don't change. This is your transition to presenting your program as a solution to the challenges they face implementing what they already know they should be doing.
- Explain in detail what they get from your 6-month program. Talk about how you set goals together so you both know what you are working toward and that as a coach, you give them accountability and self-awareness. You will help them evaluate their goals and how to implement them within each session and you will explore, together, more ways to improve the person's health. Then you can present the features of your program. (You may want to get out your Program Agreement, which clearly lists everything that is included in your program. Sometimes having a visual of all this information is helpful.)

    o Two 50-minute appointments each month for six months, which will include discussion of the client's progress, recommendations, and a full set of notes.

    o A variety of handouts, recipes, books, CDs, foods, and other materials.

    o Monthly special events like a health food store tour and group discussions related to health and wellness. (The health food store tour is optional for you to include, and you may want to just give or loan them a copy of the DVD from the school.)

    o An invitation to bring guests to the special events.

    o Email support in between sessions.

- Let them know that all of this is included in your fee.
- Ask them, "How does all of this sound to you?" or, "How do you see this program being a benefit to help you to reach your goals?"
- Ask, "Do you have any questions?" They will probably ask how you accept payments. Explain that they can either pay in full or monthly installments. Explain that they can pay via cash, check, or credit card (if you take cards).

Example of Specific Language for Explaining Program Cost

"The program is $95 per month, and that includes everything: our meetings, recommendations, handouts, helpful books, and email support in between sessions." Note we recommend $95 per month while you're still a student. We discuss suggested rates later and also in the curriculum. Charge what feels right for you.

Notes:

Power Statements

The following statements are useful tools for you to close the deal successfully, wrapping up Health Histories in a way that will make potential clients more likely to sign up. Use these as you like and feel free to adapt them to your style:

- During the six months that we'll be working together, I am committed to teaching you a set of skills you will be able to use for the rest of your life.
- I will offer you recommendations that are enjoyable, easily integrated, and step-by-step, to work toward your goals.
- When we begin to work together, I think a perfect place to start would be (mention three things identified in the Health History).
- We would work together for the next six months, which gives us time to get to know each other and to make slow but lasting changes.
- I could give you a list of 25 things to do and you would probably do them for a week—and then the list would go under the bed with the dust bunnies.
- We would check in with what is going on with you and see how the recommendations went from our last session.
- You would always leave with a few recommendations to put into action in the two weeks between our sessions.
- Much of the program is driven by you, and no two programs are the same. Each one is completely individualized, based on your goals, your needs, and the pace at which you want to go.
- In addition to our 12 sessions, I support you with books, materials, recipes, food samples, and handouts that enhance the changes you are making.

Power Questions

These questions are very helpful in closing the deal and having the potential client focused on how to make the program work:

- What are your top three goals?
- How will you feel once you've reached these goals?
- How would you like my support to reach these goals?
- When do you think we could start working together?

PROGRAM AGREEMENT

The Program Agreement is a document that you will give people once they say they want to sign up for your program. It is important to have every client sign this form. It contains your program offerings, price, disclaimer, and a legal waiver. Be sure to update your current information on fees and services before giving the form to your client. International students will need to customize the agreement to their region's legalities.

Notes:

PROGRAM AGREEMENT

Welcome. During the coming six months, you will learn ways to help yourself achieve a healthier diet and lifestyle. Please read the following. If anything is unclear, please ask.

This Agreement is made today between the Coach of the Program and the person named at the end of this document [the Client]. The Program in which you are about to enroll will include all of the following:

A. Two 50-minute appointments each month for 6 months, which will include discussion of your progress, recommendations, and a full set of notes

B. Monthly special events like teleclasses, group seminars, and/or workshops related to health and wellness

C. A variety of handouts, recipes, books, CDs, food samples, and other materials

D. An invitation for guests to attend special events

SCHEDULING

As your Coach, I understand that my clients have busy schedules and I take pride in not keeping them waiting or keeping them longer than planned. Each session will end 50 minutes after it was scheduled to begin. Please be on time. If the Client needs to cancel or reschedule the appointment, the Client must do so 24 hours in advance; otherwise, the Client will forfeit that appointment and will not have an opportunity to reschedule it.

Program begins.............................and ends..("End Date")

This program expires if all 12 sessions have not been completed within two months after the End Date specified above.

PAYMENTS AND REFUNDS

The Client understands that the regular cost of the Program is $195 per month for six months. However, registration today reduces that cost to $150 per month. Payments of $150 are due on the first meeting of each month, and may be made by credit card or check. If the Client selects to pay the full cost of the program today, the cost shall be reduced by another $100 (for a total cost of $800).

In the event of the Client's absence or withdrawal, for any reason whatsoever, the Client will remain responsible for the pro rata share of the program that has been delivered, plus a cancelation fee of $50.

The Coach reserves the right to cancel the program if at any point she or he feels it is not advantageous for the coaching program to continue. If this happens, the Client is only responsible for the pro rata share of coaching services received.

DISCLAIMER OF HEALTHCARE-RELATED SERVICES

The Client understands that the role of the Health Coach is not to prescribe or assess micro- and macronutrient levels; provide health care, medical, or nutrition therapy services; or to diagnose, treat, or cure any disease, condition, or other physical or mental ailment of the human body. Rather, the Coach is a mentor and guide who has been trained in holistic health coaching to help clients reach their own health goals by helping clients devise and implement positive, sustainable lifestyle changes. The Client understands that the Coach is not acting in the capacity of a doctor, licensed dietician-nutritionist, psychologist, or other licensed or registered professional, and that any advice given by the Coach is not meant to take the place of advice by these professionals. If

Notes:

the Client is under the care of a health care professional or currently uses prescription medications, the Client should discuss any dietary changes or potential dietary supplement use with his or her doctor, and should not discontinue any prescription medications without first consulting his or her doctor.

The Client has chosen to work with the Coach and understands that the information received should not be seen as medical or nursing advice and is not meant to take the place of seeing licensed health professionals.

PERSONAL RESPONSIBILITY AND RELEASE OF HEALTHCARE-RELATED CLAIMS

The Client acknowledges that the Client takes full responsibility for the Client's life and well-being, as well as the lives and well-being of the Client's family and children (where applicable), and all decisions made during and after this program.

The Client expressly assumes the risks of the Program, including the risks of trying new foods or supplements, and the risks inherent in making lifestyle changes. The Client releases the Coach from any and all liability, damages, causes of action, allegations, suits, sums of money, claims, and demands whatsoever, in law or equity, which the Client ever had, now has, or will have in the future against the Coach, arising from the Client's past or future participation in, or otherwise with respect to, the Program, unless arising from the gross negligence of the Coach.

CONFIDENTIALITY

The Coach will keep the Client's information private and will not share the Client's information with any third party unless compelled to by law.

ARBITRATION, CHOICE OF LAW, AND LIMITED REMEDIES

In the event that there ever arises a dispute between Coach and Client with respect to the services provided pursuant to this agreement or otherwise pertaining to the relationship between the parties, the parties agree to submit to binding arbitration before the American Arbitration Association (Commercial Arbitration and Mediation Center for the Americas Mediation and Arbitration Rules). Any judgment on the award rendered by the arbitrator(s) may be entered in any court having jurisdiction thereof. Such arbitration shall be conducted by a single arbitrator. The sole remedy that can be awarded to the Client in the event that an award is granted in arbitration is refund of the Program Fee. Without limiting the generality of the foregoing, no award of consequential or other damages, unless specifically set forth herein, may be granted to the Client.

This agreement shall be construed according to the laws of the State of [your state]. In the event that any provision of this Agreement is deemed unenforceable, the remaining portions of the Agreement shall be severed and remain in full force.

If the terms of this Agreement are acceptable, please sign the acceptance below. By doing so, the Client acknowledges that: (1) he/she has received a copy of this letter agreement; (2) he/she has had an opportunity to discuss the contents with the Coach and, if desired, to have it reviewed by an attorney; and (3) the client understands, accepts, and agrees to abide by the terms hereof.

Client name .... Signature ....

Date ....

Notes:

As soon as people agree to sign up for your program, hand them this form and give them a moment to read it. We recommend that you state out loud your cancellation and refund policies, as well as the disclaimer that you are not a doctor. You want to be certain that your client understands these important details.

You must have all your clients sign the Program Agreement. Without it, there is no contract between you and your client, meaning your client could back out of the program at any time. Being clear about the Program Agreement is in the best interest of both parties involved. Some clients will want a copy for their records, so bring two copies to each Health History.

SCHEDULING CLIENTS

As soon as your client signs up for your 6-month program and you both sign the Program Agreement, pick the days and times that you will have your sessions. Scheduling all your future sessions at the end of the first Health History will reduce the amount of back and forth you have with the client throughout their program. If they are not able to choose every date, at least schedule the first two months. Use the Program Schedule provided to help you organize these dates. Fill out the Program Schedule with your clients after they sign the Program Agreement, and give them a copy or tell them you will give them a copy. Be sure to reiterate what it says on the bottom of the Program Schedule, which is that the sessions last 50 minutes from the scheduled start time. If clients show up late, their sessions still end on time. Also stress the importance of your 24-hour cancellation policy. Once they sign up, send them a reminder email with the start date, time, and location of their first session. In this email also thank them for agreeing to participate in your program, and remind them of the benefits they can expect. It's important to add scheduled dates you set on the Program Schedule to your calendar right away.

PRICING YOUR PROGRAM

When pricing your program, start out with a cost that feels comfortable to you but also compensates you fairly for your time and expertise. The process of pricing your program may bring up issues you have around money. Please reach out for support around this issue.

Our students all come from different backgrounds. Some of them are young and just out of school, and the idea of making $50 per hour is very exciting. Other students come from professional backgrounds where they are used to making over $100,000 a year. It's important for you to acknowledge where you are on this spectrum and be gentle with yourself along the way.

We recommend students start around $95 per month. Some of you may already be used to charging this much. Maybe you are a massage therapist, nutritionist, physician,

Notes:

PROGRAM SCHEDULE

Client name: ______________________________

Appointment day: ______________________________

Appointment time: ______________________________

	Individual sessions		Group events
Month 1	________	________	________
Month 2	________	________	________
Month 3	________	________	________
Month 4	________	________	________
Month 5	________	________	________
Month 6	________	________	________

Additional notes:

____

____

____

____

____

____

I understand that you have a busy schedule and I pride myself on not keeping you waiting and not keeping you longer than planned. Your session will end 50 minutes after it was scheduled to begin.

Please arrive on time. If you have a need to cancel your session, please do so at least 24 hours in advance.

or private yoga instructor. If this is the case, you can charge $150 or more for your first few clients. If charging $150 a month is scary for you, then you have two options: feel the fear and do it anyway or lower the fee. Perhaps you want to charge your first client $50 per month. If you do this, we encourage you to charge your second client $100 per month and so on.

You can raise your rates to $150, $195, or even $250 after graduation or after you have gained more clients. Many graduates then raise their rates to $300 or $350 after another six months or a year of health coaching. Some go on to charge $450 or even $500 per month. People can afford these prices. It's up to you to ask for what you are worth. When setting your fees, consider how many clients you actually want to work

Notes:

with and how much money you want to make from health coaching this year. Also consider your target market and research similar professionals such as massage therapists, estheticians, chiropractors, and nutritionists to gauge pricing for your area.

LOWER-INCOME CLIENTS

It's important to first work with paying clients so you can meet your own financial goals and build your confidence around asking for money. If, at some point, you want to offer your services to people who tend to not have as much flexibility with how they spend their money—such as young people, senior citizens, or single parents—you have a few options.

Offer a Sliding Scale

When potential clients ask how much your program costs, you can say something along the lines of, "I have a sliding scale from $75 to $150 per month. What works for you?" You can use these parameters or create others. Be sure that you're still getting paid fairly for your services.

Group Programs

Another possibility is to offer group programs. You can then charge less per person while still making the same amount of money for your time. We will discuss group programs in Chapter 18.

Grant Funding

Applying for grants may work for you, especially if you want to work in schools or within certain communities.

DISCOUNTS

People love to save money. So if you want to charge $95 per month for your program, an effective strategy may be to tell potential clients that your program costs $150 per month, but if they sign up today (the day of the Health History), you will give them a discount so that the program is $95 per month. However, we discourage you from offering arbitrary discounts just to close the deal. If you live in an area where rates are lower or if your target market is one that cannot afford high rates, like students, then you will take this into consideration when determining your rates—not in the middle of closing the deal. Cutting your rates is a slippery slope, and remember that the rates you charge are more than fair given the value you provide. Be comfortable with what you charge!

ASKING FOR MONEY

If this chapter about money makes you anxious, know that you will survive. You can still become a successful business owner, even if right now you are nervous about asking for money. Here are some strategies to help you overcome your concerns and confidently ask for the money you deserve:

1. Start your practice by taking on a client with whom you barter services, so that you become confident in the value and effectiveness of your work. Then when you start asking for money, you will be very clear about what your clients are paying for.
2. Work on clearing up your money issues in your personal life. If you have difficulty asking for money in a business setting, this issue is probably coming up in all areas of your life. Are there a lot of people who owe you money? Do you owe money? Do you have difficulty asking for what you want? Are you afraid of money? Do you feel that you don't deserve money? Practice asking people for money they owe you. Nurture and value the money you have. Get in the habit of happily receiving compliments, favors, gifts, and money from others.
3. When closing the deal, focus on the other person, not on yourself. Learn that receiving money from your client benefits them by making it much more likely that they will reach their health goals. When you ask a potential client for money, the conversation is not about how much they value you, but about how much they value themselves. Asking your client for money is asking them to make a commitment to their own health. Paying you is an important action, symbolizing their investment in their well-being. Remember, when people pay for something, they value it more.
4. When you ask for money, all kinds of feelings may come up. Relax, stay focused, and keep listening to the person. Your role is to show them everything they will get for their money and point out all the great benefits, and then support them to invest in themselves. You can point out that it is unfortunate that people spend so much money on clothes, cars, houses, and going out to eat, but not on their bodies, which will be with them forever. You can support them to turn that around in their own lives.
5. Learn that payment for your work helps you have a positive relationship with your client. Money is energy. In order for you and your client to build a healthy, working relationship, the energy flow between you should be equal. You will be giving this person a great deal of your time and energy, not only in sessions, but also when you photocopy handouts, buy gifts, teach a cooking class, and plan for your sessions together. You can view money as the way that they send energy back to you, a way to create a give-and-take relationship so you both feel energized.
6. An exchange of money for your services helps clarify boundaries between you and your clients. As a Health Coach you will be warm, friendly, and loving, but you are also a paid professional. It's important to keep this boundary clear, especially when it comes to the occasional client who misuses your time, bounces checks, or treats you like a parent or best friend. Having clear written agree-

Notes:

Notes:

ments, and the appropriate exchange of money helps you set limits, keeping the coaching experience positive.

TIPS ON ASKING FOR MONEY

- Feel your fear, and do it anyway. Don't give into your fear about asking for money, because it will make your business stagnant.
- Practice your closing the deal statements with your Accountability Coach. Asking for money is simply a muscle that needs flexing.
- Write down all the things that could happen when you ask for money: the person could say no, they could give you the money but resent you, and so on.
- Write down all of your fears to get them out of your mind.
- Always be honest. Don't answer questions that you don't know the answer to and don't promise anything that you can't deliver.
- Make sure potential clients know what they are getting for their money. Go over the Program Agreement and/or show them your rate sheet so they are clear.
- Tell a success story to illustrate what is possible if they work with you.

CASE STUDY

Here's an example of one student who was not appreciating her true value.

Christina was charging $25 per month for her 6-month program. She wanted to charge more, but was uncomfortable doing so. She consulted with another student coach to help her raise her rates. The coach asked Christina how working with her clients was going. Christina said it was great. She loved working with her clients and they were seeing many results. However, Christina was a dancer and really enjoyed working with other dancers. She didn't think it was fair to charge a lot for her program because she said dancers don't have a lot of money.

The coach asked Christina about her favorite client and the benefits her favorite client received from the program so far. Christina began to list them: the client had lost 10 pounds, she moved out of her parents' house and got her own apartment, she began cooking for the first time ever, she quit a job she hated and got a new, better paying job, she entered a new, loving relationship, and she cleared up her digestive concerns. The client was also beginning to develop a spiritual practice and getting closer with her friends. And this was only the beginning of month four! "So," the coach repeated to Christina, "your client has cleared up health concerns, lost weight, is cooking, moved into a new apartment, got a new job, and has fulfilling relationships."

"Yes," Christina replied. The coach asked, "Christina, how much would you pay someone to help you with all of that?" Christina replied, "Thousands." The coach asked, "So, why are you charging your clients only $150 for your program?" In reality, Christina was not keeping her prices low because dancers couldn't afford more than $25 a month. She was keeping her prices low because she couldn't see how much her services were worth.

Notes:

SUCCESSFUL BARTERING

The most important thing when bartering is to make sure it is an equal trade, and that you are receiving something you want. Perhaps you'd like to trade with a massage therapist, a private yoga instructor, or a web designer. A good protocol to follow is an hour of your time for an hour of theirs.

It's also smart to pick someone to barter with who may turn into a referral source for you. For example, pick a yoga instructor who has a large clientele. He or she may share the results of your work with his/her clients, who may then want to come see you. Other people to barter with may include hair stylists, personal trainers, chefs, life coaches, Reiki practitioners, music teachers, language teachers, or writing coaches.

Even though bartering may seem casual, it is crucial that you sign an agreement with your barter clients. This will make you look more professional and prevent your bartering clients from rescheduling, canceling, or not fulfilling their part of the agreement.

POSITIVE FEEDBACK

One way to help you realize your value as a Health Coach is to consistently ask for feedback.

At the end of each Health History, coaching session, or cooking class, ask the client or participants what they enjoyed. Really listen to what they say and allow it to sink in. Also, at the end of each 6-month program, ask your clients to fill out the Completion Form and the Last Session Evaluation Form. These documents are available in the online resources. Having your clients write down all the benefits they received from their work with you will help you (and them!) comprehend exactly how valuable you are.

We share this story with you because you may have something similar going on. We know that what you have to offer is priceless. Your clients will change dramatically as you introduce them to healthier foods, primary foods, and new cooking techniques. The high-quality listening you offer will change their lives.

It is interesting to note that many graduates who are charging $100 a month have difficulty signing clients. However, once they raise their rates to $200 or $250 a month, people sign up without batting an eye. This change happens because the coaches did not recognize their own value, so neither did the potential clients who came to see them. If you own what you are worth, others will follow.

Notes:

WHAT ARE YOU WORTH?

1. List everything that your clients get as part of your 6-month program:

2. What benefits have your clients and/or friends and family received as a result of knowing and working with you?

3. What makes you an excellent Health Coach?

DEALING WITH REJECTION

As you begin your practice, about half the people who come to you for a Health History will sign up for your program. Some graduates have a higher closing rate than others. Regardless of where you fall on this spectrum, recognize that in this business you will always have to deal with rejection. It's a good idea to have a plan to help you cope with any feelings that come up and to learn and grow from your experiences.

Do not be too hard on yourself when someone does not sign up. Maybe that person would have been a difficult client who would have caused a lot of strife. Maybe that person was too stuck or distracted to make a commitment to change at this time. Maybe it's not as clear as this, and you are left wondering if you could have done more. There is no "rejection;" there is only an opportunity to learn, grow, and do better the following time.

Whatever the situation, when someone doesn't sign up after a Health History, ask yourself what you might have done differently. Were you focused on the person and listening as deeply as possible? Could you have used more power statements? Do you need more confidence when asking for money? Write down what you learned and what you want to do better next time. Then take a deep breath and move on.

It is very normal to have emotions come up when someone turns you down. You might feel sad, angry, guilty, or frustrated. But remember to put things in perscpective. The only thing that has happened is that someone has chosen not to work with you at this time. Acknowledge and then let go of your feelings. Keep a journal, make some art, or go for a run—whatever works best for you. As time goes on, you will come to understand that a certain level of rejection is normal, and you will not be bothered by it. The most important thing is to not let it paralyze you. Instead, let it motivate you to take the next step forward. Learn from it and move forward in new ways.

Notes:

Kindness is the language which
the deaf can hear and the blind can see.

—Mark Twain

CHAPTER 12:

YOUR PROGRAM OFFERINGS

Throughout our more than 20 years of experience running the school and teaching people how to be Health Coaches, we have found that the 6-month program meets the needs of most clients. In this chapter, we outline the components of the 6-month program.

We provide a structured session outline to guide you through the 6-month program sessions. Sometimes when students start out, they tend to spend an exorbitant amount of time getting ready for sessions, researching what to give clients, creating more forms, and reading up on health concerns. While it is important to do great work, the program we provide works very well, so you don't have to use your time changing the content. Simply be there to listen, love them up, and help them make step-by-step changes.

BASIC PROGRAM

THE BREAKDOWN OF THE 6-MONTH PROGRAM

- Two 50-minute appointments each month for six months, which will include discussion of the client's progress, recommendations, and a full set of notes
- A variety of handouts, recipes, books, foods, and other materials
- Email support between sessions
- Monthly special events like a health food store tour and group discussions related to health and wellness
- An invitation to bring guests to the special events

Notes:

WHY SIX MONTHS?

Studies show that six months is the amount of time needed to create long-term habits. Supporting your clients for six months around making better food, exercise, and lifestyle choices increases the probability that they will continue with these activities after the completion of your program. The monthly events or seminars that are part of your 6-month program are a great way for your clients to meet one another and create a community, as well as an opportunity for you to meet their guests and practice your public speaking.

Giveaways

Your 6-month program includes the gifts that you give each client at the end of every session. These gifts do not need to be fancy or expensive. Useful choices include cooking utensils, tongue cleaners, books, and food samples. We provide you with a giveaway checklist in the 6-Month Program Resources and recommend that you keep a copy in each client folder to keep track of what you have given them. You can keep a bag or a bin in your office space containing extra client giveaways. That way, each time you have a client, you can look in your treasure chest and pick something out. When you come across a good giveaway, buy a bunch and throw them into your stash.

Popular Giveaway Items

- Beans
- Grains
- Recipes
- Strainer
- Thermos
- Chopsticks
- Water bottle
- Tongue cleaner
- Wooden spoons
- Organic toothpaste
- Organic tea and a tea ball
- Louise Hay affirmation cards
- Fresh greens (bok choy, kale, collards, etc.)
- *Integrative Nutrition: Feed Your Hunger for Health and Happiness*
- *The Self-Healing Cookbook* by Kristina Turner
- Blank journals for writing or using as a food journal
- Dry-erase markers (to write loving notes on the mirror)
- Condiments (umeboshi, hot pepper sesame oil, gomasio, etc.)

For giveaways such as books and journals, it may be helpful to buy wholesale on Amazon.com. Their prices are already discounted and you can have them shipped

Notes:

directly to phone clients, if you like. If you are a member of Amazon Prime, then most shipping is free. Visit Amazon.com to learn more about Amazon Prime. Integrative Nutrition has a storefront on Amazon, including the *Integrative Nutrition Journal*, the *Healthy Shopping* DVD, and more!

Most clients appreciate getting a binder in which to keep all the handouts that you give to them. You can purchase binders at an office supply store for less than $1 each. You may want to tape your business card to the front or insert it inside. You can give this to your clients when they sign up or at the beginning of their first session. It is also helpful to give them dividers for their binder so they can create sections in whatever way makes sense to them. Or you can do it for them: one section for session notes, one for recipes, and one for handouts. This giveaway helps your clients stay organized around their self-care.

PROGRAM FORMS

We have included everything you need to conduct a coaching session in the 6-Month Program Resources.

Forms to use during a Health History consultation:

- Health History
- Program Agreement—serves as a disclaimer and a legal waiver
- Program Schedule—gives your client the dates you are going to meet
- Credit Card Authorization form—gives you permission to charge your client's credit card
- Welcome form—welcomes your client to your program
- Goals form—asks your client to think about his or her goals for working together

Fast forward to the end of the Health History. Let's say the Health History went well and the potential client has agreed to work with you as a client—you successfully closed the deal!

As discussed in the previous chapter, when you sign on clients, you'll give them the Program Agreement and the Program Schedule. You'll discuss payment and give them the Credit Card Authorization form if they are paying by credit card. And you'll give them the Welcome form and the Goals form to look over before their first session.

Forms to use before coaching sessions:

- Handout Checklist—helps you keep track of what handouts you give your clients
- Giveaway Checklist—helps you keep track of what giveaways you give your clients

Notes:

As mentioned earlier, you'll be providing clients with giveaways in your sessions. As you prepare for your session and select your giveaway, use the Giveaway Checklist to keep track of what you bring each client. Use our suggestions or come up with your own giveaways—whatever works for you.

You'll also give your client a few handouts in each session. In the 6-Month Program Resources, there is a Client Handout Library. Select handouts you think your client will enjoy or handouts that you want to discuss with your client in the session. You can even use handouts from the curriculum. Fill out the Handout Checklist when you select the handouts to help you keep track.

Also before each session, read over the Session Notes and Client Progress form from the previous session to refresh your memory about what you discussed in the last session. (See below for more information on these forms.)

Forms to use during coaching sessions:

- Revisit Form—allows you to see what progress your client has made and what is on their mind coming into the session
- Session Notes—use to take notes during the session. You can also use a notepad.
- Handouts—you'll discuss whatever handouts you select and bring from the Client Handout Library
- Circle of Life—use this with clients at Sessions 1, 6, and 12 to see what primary foods are imbalanced and track your client's progress throughout your program

Now, it's time for the session. If you are coaching over the phone or video calling, you will want to send the Revisit Form to your client ahead of time and look it over before the session starts. If you are coaching in person, you can give your client the Revisit Form at the start of the session. You can also send it to your client ahead of time. Experiment and see what works best for you.

All sessions should look the same, that's why there is a session structure in your 6-Month Program Resources titled Session Outline. The structure of the session has been built specifically to yield results that support long term change. Each section of the session was intentionally built in based off of experience and research of human development psychology and successful coaching. This structure actually leads to more freedom for the client to discuss what's vital for them to say in that moment which leads to that oh so treasured "aha" moment, which is clinically known as a generative moment. The content of the sessions will vary from client to client, as it is always based on their goals. But each session should look the same in terms of the general flow.

Our structure follows the acronym:

C - create connection with what's new and good
O - open conversation with the Revisit Form
A - allow your client to lead the session
C - convey your recommendations
H - handouts and giveaways to close the session

Notes:

We as humans have a tendency to want to hash out what isn't working, but as a coach, you will retrain the client's brain to focus on what is going well. The study of positive psychology tells us that focusing on positive thoughts rewires our brains to think in terms of accomplishment, opportunity, and possibility. This is the 'C' of your session structure.

Start by asking, "What's new and good?"

The next part of your session is the 'O,' opening conversation with the Revisit Form. Throughout the program, you will tailor sessions to your client's needs with the Revisit Form. Or you can encourage them to email you questions or specific topics they would like to discuss before the next session. In fact, clients who share with their coaches before a session what they'd like to talk about move more quickly into those generative, or aha, moments. Take your time in this part of the session because reviewing what may or may not have worked is a fantastic place to learn about clients and the thought process, where they trip up, and how they deal with themselves. This is where your client can really lead the session and where high mileage questions can assist in uncovering resistance to change.

After opening the conversation, you will let the client lead the conversation which is the 'A' of the session structure. The 'A' section is less of a separate section and more of a theme that spans the two sections of reviewing previous recommendations and introducing new information. The new content portion of your sessions will be driven by client goals set at the beginning of the program and further refined by the Revisit Form. Even with new content, keep clients engaged by asking high mileage questions and relating it to their situation. Remember—your client will heal him- or herself, with you serving as a guide on the side.

Each session you will want to provide your client with a few recommendations to try out. Make sure they are realistic and that you take it step-by-step. If your client feels overwhelmed it is unlikely he or she will try out what you recommend. Ideally, the client eventually learns how to set their own recommendations and the coach simply holds the client accountable to the commitment. This is the 'C' portion of the session, convey recommendations. You will give your client the handouts you selected for each session which is the 'H' section of the structure. For example, if you bring the Glorious Greens handout you will want to speak with your client about the benefits of greens and to incorporate more greens into his or her diet. You may want to share recipes or give a gift that relates to greens such as a vegetable steamer. At the end of each session, you will want to ask your client to recap his or her goals and what they intend to work on before your next session. You can also solidify the client's experience by asking him or her, "What was most valuable about today's session?" Asking a closing question like this keeps communication open for the client to give you feedback and it makes the client clarify the experience for themselves.

At sessions 1, 6, and 12 we recommend you give your client the Circle of Life form. This will help clients assess where they are with their primary foods goals. At the end of your sessions you can show your client their three completed Circle of Life forms to note how much change they have made in their lives.

Notes:

In addition to giving your client the Circle of Life at session 6, some coaches also give their clients the Halfway Revisit Form. This is to be used instead of the normal Revisit Form, and it allows your client to reflect on the first half of the program. It is a useful tool for you to see how your client is progressing and if you need to change anything about how you work together. Experiment with the Halfway Revisit Form and see if it is a form you want to use in your practice.

Form to use after coaching sessions:

- Client Progress form—use to record the main topics covered in the session, any recommendations you have made, positive changes noticed, and any items that require follow-up

After each session you will fill out the Client Progress form. This form will contain the same information as the Session Notes, but in a summarized format. You will use the same Client Progress form for all 12 sessions. You will also want to review this form prior to your next session to review where you left off.

Forms to use in your last session:

- Program Summary form—a summary you create to highlight your client's progress throughout the program, which helps to celebrate your client and can be used to discuss working together beyond the 6-month program
- Client Accomplishments form—a summary of all your client's accomplishments, written by you the coach, which is used to help create the Program Summary
- Completion of Your Program form—a summary of all your client's accomplishments, written by the client

Throughout your client's program, we recommend keeping detailed notes of their progress. Include even the small things. Write them down word for word. This can be recorded in your Session Notes, in the Client Progress form, or in another format that works for you.

We recommend wrapping up a client's program with a Program Summary, which is introduced by IIN graduate and successful Health Coach Nancy Weiser in the audio lecture "Beyond the 6-Month Program" that is later in your curriculum. This is a document you will create using the Program Summary form based on your client's improvements. The Program Summary form outlines each section and what to include and is broken up into three sections:

1. Summarize the Health History
2. Restate the client's goals
3. List client accomplishments

Notes:

We include a Client Accomplishments form for you. You will revisit your notes and compile all the accomplishments you noted throughout the program. You will bring this with you as part of the Program Summary to the final session.

In the final session, you will give the client the form titled Completion of Your Program. You will instruct your client to write down everything he or she feels they accomplished throughout the program. Then you will read your list of client accomplishments from your own notes and have your client write it all down, too. Writing it down reinforces the accomplishments for them. This leaves your client with a long list of accomplishments on which to reflect.

The Program Summary is for your clients to keep as a reminder of how far they came. Clients often don't remember how much they have changed over six months. The Program Summary effectively reminds them of every little improvement and each step toward achieving their goals.

In addition to the Program Summary, you will want to ask your client to write a testimonial for you. The Testimonial Request form is located in the Marketing Materials Resources.

All of these forms were designed so that you can start seeing clients without needing to recreate the wheel. As you gain more coaching experience, you may design your own forms. Use what works for you. There is nothing "wrong" with choosing to eliminate or replace some of the forms. What works for some may not work for others. The important thing to keep in mind is that you get out there and start changing lives!

When you can't change the direction
of the wind—adjust your sails.

—H. Jackson Brown Jr.

CHAPTER 13:

INTRODUCTION TO MARKETING

Marketing is any method of attracting and retaining customers through communication and building trust. It is important to focus your energy on marketing. In order to be successful, you should choose marketing activities that you enjoy and will bring you the most reward. It is not just your website, flyers, and elevator speech. All of your business activity becomes part of your marketing effort, including the way you set up your office, how you greet strangers, the words you use in your newsletter, and the clothes you put on each morning. You are your best marketing strategy, a walking billboard so to speak. When someone chooses to work with you, they are choosing you, your enthusiasm, your energy, and the benefits you offer.

The key to successful marketing is discovering what works for your personality and the personality of your business. Some graduates get 90 percent of their clients from workshops, while others never lead workshops and get their clients from referral systems with other health professionals. Some graduates make a constant effort to get into the press and advertise in holistic magazines. There is no one-size-fits-all rule when it comes to marketing. Explore the different resources available and choose what feels right to you and what produces the most results. Identify your ideal clients, figure out where to find them, and learn how to contact them. You can then add them to your contact list and begin reaching out to build trust and share the programs and courses you have to offer.

MARKETING OVERVIEW

Some of the core methods of getting clients are listed here:

- Website
- Brochures

Notes:

- Newsletter
- Workshops
- Health fairs
- Target market
- Networking
- Business cards
- Social media

All of these methods will be covered in the curriculum. You will experiment with which ones work best for you.

DEVELOPING A MARKETING PLAN

Developing a basic marketing plan helps motivate you to stay on top of your marketing. This will help you choose the methods that will best support your business goals, while staying within your budget. A professional marketing plan usually includes an analysis of your target market, how you would like to be positioned in the market, an analysis of your competition, past attempts at marketing and their success rates, and your current strategy and expenses. Approach your marketing plan as a work in progress that requires adaptation and innovation. One month your newsletter could bring in a few initial consultations. The next month you might want to design and send out a holiday postcard to everyone in your pipeline, letting them know about special discounts. This may yield positive results as well. Then you can compare which strategy worked best and do more of that type of marketing.

How many clients do you have now? ....

How many clients do you want to have by graduation? ....

Who is your target market?

....

....

How would you like to be positioned in the market?

....

....

....

Notes:

Who are your competitors?

Make a list of marketing techniques you would like to try, such as getting on the radio, publishing an article, increasing word of mouth and referrals, or boosting your online presence.

How and when do you plan to implement these techniques?

Who can support you or how can you get support to make this happen?

What day of the week is designated as your marketing day?

How many hours on this day are spent on your marketing materials and events?

DO WHAT COMES NATURALLY

When deciding which strategies are most effective for your practice, strongly consider what you enjoy doing and what comes naturally to you. Some marketing techniques will be second nature, while others will feel like pulling teeth. Perhaps you don't enjoy

Notes:

writing but are an excellent cook and love teaching cooking classes. You can reach out to a classmate for help with your writing in exchange for you helping them learn how to teach a great cooking class. If you absolutely hate leading workshops, the people who attend are going to sense it, so it will not be an effective marketing tool for you. Discover what kind of marketing you enjoy and do it often. The more natural and creative your marketing techniques are, the more success you will encounter.

Please keep in mind that you are your best advertisement. You are a walking billboard for your business. Your health and happiness are instrumental in generating business, so don't waste precious time doing things that make you unhappy. The more you are focused on doing what you love and the more you are out and about looking like your radiant self, the more people will want to know who you are and learn how they can get some of what you've got.

BUSINESS REVENUE PLAN

Next, let's take a moment to be more specific about your income goals. When you are clear on how much income you would like to generate, you can have a better idea if your goals are realistic. Then, plan accordingly to reach those goals. For example, if you know you would like to have four new clients next month from a workshop, it's important to start the marketing and planning process now instead of waiting until the last minute. You can also decide from which sources of income you would like to earn revenue (workshops, group coaching, individual coaching, corporate wellness, and so on.)

Your business income plan can be simple or complex. We recommend keeping it simple in the beginning. Here is a formula for a simple business plan:

- First, decide how much money you want to make from health coaching over the next year. Write that here: ________________
- What would that work out to, on average, per month? ________________
- Next, figure out what you want to charge for your services. Most of our students start out at $95 per month while they are still in the program. After they graduate, they typically increase their rates to $195 per month. From there, rates can go to $250 per month, $295 per month, and higher.
- How much do you want to charge your clients each month? ______________
- Now, divide how much you want to make each month by how much you want to charge your clients each month. This is the number of clients that you will need to reach your income goal.
- Write that here: ________________

Example: You want to earn $24,000 from health coaching this year. You would need to earn $2,000 per month. If each client you work with is paying you $195 per

Notes:

month, you will need to have 11 clients. Note this is a simplified example, not including the money you spend on clients for items like giveaways, but the example serves to get you thinking about how many clients you will need to do this work part- or full-time.

From here, you can plan how many Health History consultations you will need to do each month. On average, 50 percent of your Health History consultations may become clients. This percentage will improve as you gain more experience, but this is a good reference point to use when you're starting out. So if you want to get four new clients, you will need to do eight free consultations. If you do eight free consultations each month for three months, you should have about 12 clients.

The next step is to determine how you will get eight people to come in for free Health History consultations. Eventually, you will create a more detailed marketing plan.

BENEFITS MARKETING

A very important part of successful marketing is being able to effectively communicate the benefits of your work. Virtually all of your potential clients will be concerned with what we call WIIFM, which stands for "What's in it for me?" If you can answer this basic question for them, they will be interested in becoming your client. Through understanding a person's motivation, you can better speak to their needs.

In promoting our work, we are often tempted to talk about the "features" (6-month program, health care items, group sessions, etc.). Ultimately, a person will become your client if they find value in your services. You need to show them how your program can meet their needs. The types of goals a person wants to accomplish by working with you include feeling better, looking better, and having more joy and passion in their life. They are looking for a return on their investment in your program, whether it's losing weight, sleeping better, reducing stress, or reaching other health goals. You have to offer people what they want in order to motivate them to sign up for your programs or classes. All of these benefits should be included in your marketing efforts, whether in person, at a workshop, during a Health History, or in your written materials.

What are some of the benefits your clients receive from your work?

....

....

....

....

BUSINESS REVENUE TRACKING

	JAN	FEB	MAR	APR	MAY	JUNE	JULY	AUG	SEPT	OCT	NOV	DEC	TOTAL
PROJECTED INCOME													
INCOME SOURCE 1													
INCOME SOURCE 2													
INCOME SOURCE 3													
INCOME TOTALS													
ACTUAL INCOME													
INCOME SOURCE 1													
CLIENT 1													
CLIENT 2													
CLIENT 3													
CLIENT 4													
CLIENT 5													
CLIENT 6													
CLIENT 7													
CLIENT 8													
CLIENT 9													
CLIENT 10													
CLIENT 11													
CLIENT 12													
CLIENT 13													
CLIENT 14													
CLIENT 15													
CLIENT 16													
CLIENT 17													
CLIENT 18													
CLIENT 19													
CLIENT 20													
CLIENT 21													
CLIENT 22													
CLIENT 23													
CLIENT 24													
CLIENT 25													
CLIENT 26													

BUSINESS REVENUE TRACKING PAGE 2

	JAN	FEB	MAR	APR	MAY	JUNE	JULY	AUG	SEPT	OCT	NOV	DEC	TOTAL
INCOME SOURCE 1 TOTAL													
INCOME SOURCE 2													
SOURCE 1													
SOURCE 2													
SOURCE 3													
SOURCE 4													
SOURCE 5													
SOURCE 6													
SOURCE 7													
SOURCE 8													
SOURCE 9													
SOURCE 10													
SOURCE 11													
SOURCE 12													
INCOME SOURCE 2 TOTAL													
INCOME SOURCE 3													
SOURCE 1													
SOURCE 2													
SOURCE 3													
SOURCE 4													
SOURCE 5													
SOURCE 6													
SOURCE 7													
SOURCE 8													
SOURCE 9													
SOURCE 10													
SOURCE 11													
SOURCE 12													
INCOME SOURCE 3 TOTAL													
TOTAL ACTUAL INCOME													
INCOME COMPARED TO GOAL													

Notes:

What are some of the problems that your clients want to solve by working with you?

....

....

....

....

In what ways can you include these benefits and speak to these problems in your marketing communications?

....

....

....

....

YOUR CORE MESSAGE

Remember back in Chapter 8 when we had you develop your elevator speech? Now we are going to take that tool to the next level. Practice this formula for an elevator speech:

My name is .... I work with (target market)..
who (what you help your target market with) ....

This is a dynamic way to introduce yourself, but only at the first level. After this introduction, people will usually want to know more about how you work with your clients. Please keep in mind that it's important to tailor your conversation to the person with whom you are speaking. Be careful not to talk too much, and remember to discuss the benefits of your work as it relates to that individual.

As you listen and stay present, you will increase the likelihood that they will attend a Health History consultation and eventually become a client. Ask questions that will make them think about how they could benefit from your services (e.g., "How do you see this work being beneficial to you and your life?") Explain your work in a way that allows the person to understand it. Be clear; try not to use too much health jargon. At some point, you may want to explain that you work with clients in a 6-month program designed for their individual needs in which you introduce them to new foods, teach them healthy cooking and shopping techniques, and support them in maintaining a healthy, active lifestyle.

To help potential clients understand the benefits of your program, you can ask, "What is your main health concern at the moment?" When they respond, you can share with them how you have worked with other clients who had similar concerns by look-

Notes:

ing at how their diet affects their health. If you haven't yet worked with any clients, you can say that by working together you will address their concerns. You can then offer this person a free 50-minute consultation to discuss their concerns further and see firsthand how you work with your clients.

Do not overlook the importance of explaining how clients benefit from your program. For example, a Health Coach who works with busy professional women who want to eat well and have more energy might mistakenly say, "I offer a 6-month program that includes detailed recommendations, a health food store tour, cooking classes, books, and handouts." This statement does not tell anyone about how these services actually help the busy professional women. A more effective way to present this information would be to say, "I work with busy professional women to incorporate healthier options and more home-cooked foods into their lives. My clients experience reduced stress and increased energy."

You will find that you adapt your message slightly, depending on with whom you are speaking. For example, if the person asking you about your business is overweight, you might add that your clients also lose weight.

A significant disadvantage is dealing with the general public's lack of knowledge about the importance of health. Many people don't realize how much better they will feel if they start eating healthier foods and adopting more health-promoting lifestyle

BARRIERS TO SUCCESS

- You can't decide where to begin. Marketing your business seems like an overwhelming project with too many considerations and choices. You want to make sure you do it all perfectly, so you worry about how to best spend your time. Struck by "analysis paralysis," you start and stop, sit and stew, or just do nothing.
- You aren't sure how to put the pieces together. You know you should be leading workshops, writing a newsletter, and doing Health Histories, but you think that you should first finish your brochure, design your logo, or read one more nutrition book. You don't have a system, a program, or a plan.
- You can't stay motivated. With no boss holding you accountable; it's easy to procrastinate around marketing. If you don't see immediate results, you can get discouraged and lose motivation. It's difficult to not take it personally when someone doesn't sign up for your program.

If you have ever had any of these thoughts or if you are having them now, you are not alone. People who market service businesses rarely fail due to lack of information about effective sales and marketing techniques. They fail because they don't use the information at their fingertips. Use the techniques that we suggest to overcome these barriers.

Adapted from *Get Clients Now: A 28-Day Marketing Program for Professionals Consultants and Coaches,* 2nd ed., by C.J. Hayden, New York, NY: AMACOM, 2007.

Notes:

choices. Your marketing efforts should involve educating people around the importance of what you do. Don't assume that anyone already knows what you do as a Health Coach. Explain to people how you work with clients and how those clients can benefit from your services for the rest of their lives. You can do this in your articles and brochure, on your website, at your workshops, and at networking events.

CLIENT FUNNEL

Marketing is about building relationships. In order to successfully build these relationships you need to develop a plan to help generate leads. A lead is also referred to as a prospective client or potential client. These people are intrigued by what you have to offer but are not ready to register in your program. Even though you're not officially seeing clients yet, take some time to brainstorm ideas of how you will find leads. The Client Funnel is a marketing tool we use to keep track of your leads and turn them into paying clients. At the beginning, the focus is on getting more contacts and reaching as many people in your niche market as possible. As you foster new relationships, people learn more about you. This helps to build trust and the desire to work with you. Eventually this will lead to enrollment into your 6-month program.

Lead generation occurs as you network through live events, social media platforms, referrals, and advertising. As you make new contacts and generate leads into your business you're building trust and inviting them to things such as your teleseminars, workshops, or giving them a book you wrote. This can lead to an initial Health History, which promotes enrollment into your 6-month program.

Please take a minute to write down the top three lead-generating activities you will start with:

1. ....

2. ....

3. ....

Running your own business requires determination, planning, and the ability to stick with it. The marketing plan you develop and the steps you take now will affect the success of your practice in both the short and long term. Often times, business owners who do not consistently market themselves may end up in a position where they are struggling to find clients down the road. Follow the steps we've outlined to create a plan and understand that developing a business requires that you build visibility and trust with your target market.

As you build awareness of your services, stay in touch and allow people to see the value of your work as it relates to the benefits they can achieve (WIIFM), and you will be more likely to succeed. Some leads will become paying clients right away and others will stay in your funnel for longer. For example, a potential client signs up for your

Notes:

THE CLIENT FUNNEL

The key to having a thriving health coaching practice is to attract clients consistently. To get clear on how this happens, top Health Coaches use a tool called the Client Funnel. The Client Funnel illustrates the usual four steps a lead takes to become your client:

1. Become a LEAD
2. SCHEDULE a Health History
3. COMPLETE a Health History
4. SIGN UP for your program

Learn how to successfully move people through your funnel and pinpoint strengths and weaknesses in your marketing. Focus on doing more of what works, and strengthen any weak areas.

We will go into more detail on this process throughout the curriculum. For now, please familiarize yourself with each step of the Client Funnel. To be continued!

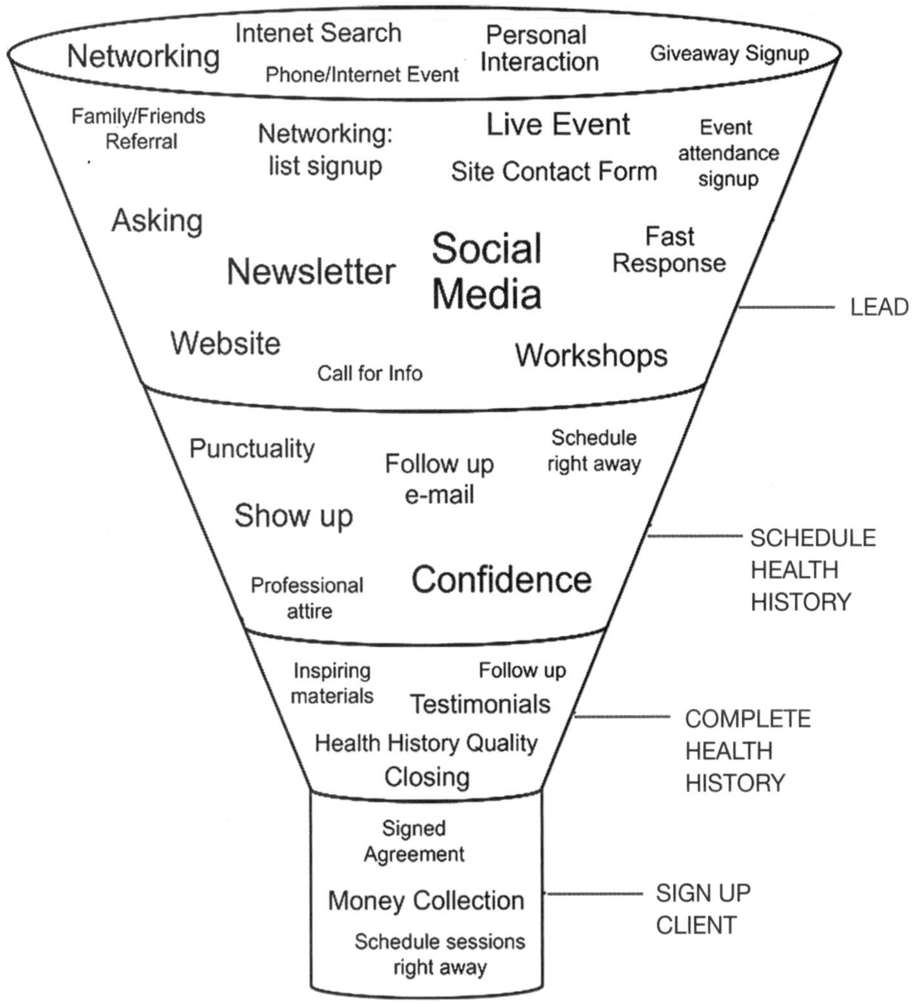

Notes:

newsletter and four months later they decide to attend your workshop; they attend the workshop and then contact you a week later for a Health History; and two weeks later they begin your program.

The following strategies will help you build awareness with leads and ensure long-term success:

- Build your contact list continually by always asking each person you meet to join your newsletter or email list.
- Offer frequent invitations to visit your workshops, group events, or teleclasses in order to provide people with numerous opportunities to understand how you can help them.
- Provide low- or no-cost ways for leads to learn more about you, such as free Health History consultations, free articles, newsletters, or a free chapter of your e-book. Find ways to build community by bringing people together in groups through volunteer activities, social outings, or local events.
- Follow up with every new person you meet, and stay in touch with them.
- Be consistent, stick with your plan, and trust the process.

What strategies will you use to build relationships and create a successful Client Funnel over time?

What steps will you take to start implementing these strategies now?

Notes:

FILLING THE PIPELINE

"Filling the pipeline" means getting more leads into your funnel or finding ways to meet and connect with new people. The concept of filling the pipeline comes from *Get Clients Now!* by C.J. Hayden. In her book, Hayden outlines her marketing and sales system for getting clients. The first step is to fill the pipeline.

According to Hayden's principles, you should focus on this stage of marketing if you are brand new in business, do not have enough people to call, have called all of your prospects in the past 30 days, or your prospects don't need or can't afford you. At this point, you need to increase your visibility and outreach. Some ways to do this are by leading a workshop, attending an event, or writing an article for a local paper or online publication. If you want to have a booming business as a Health Coach, your goal should be to have a constant stream of initial Health Histories. To produce this desired outcome, you will need to consistently add people to your pipeline.

Marketing is a numbers game. You often have to meet, contact, and connect with many people in order to generate a client. For example, when booking a workshop at a spa, you might need to meet the receptionist, the manager, and then the events coordinator. At the workshop, you will meet all the attendees. One of the attendees may refer a friend to you who becomes a client. Your new client is the fifth person in your chain of interactions around that workshop; notice that you had to interact with four other people to sign this one client. Other times, you may run into a stranger at a health food store who becomes a client right away. Keep in mind that anyone you meet could become a client, refer a great client to you, or know of a location or business where you could lead a workshop. The truth is that you never know where your next client may come from, but the more people who know you are a Health Coach, the more quickly your client base will grow.

GUIDELINES FOR FILLING YOUR PIPELINE

- Always follow up with leads.
- Research places near you where potential clients hang out: gyms, spas, schools, religious centers, bookstores, etc.
- Lead workshops at least once a month in various places so you are always in front of a new audience: schools, your church or temple, community centers, corporations, etc. Think big!
- Find subtle ways to incorporate your work as a Health Coach into conversations with friends and acquaintances.
- Make new contacts and continue gathering phone numbers to call.
- Conduct a master outreach via newsletters, phone calls, and emails to potential clients and/or referral partners.
- Increase visibility: get published, lead more workshops, and add people to your newsletter recipient list.

Notes:

- Create an association with a company, school, doctor's office, hospital, or organization that will give you consistent access to all the new people who walk through their doors.

Once you have mastered filling your pipeline, follow through with all the people in your pipeline. Add them to your newsletter recipient list, send them emails to check in, invite them to workshops or cooking classes, and keep them updated on your programs and referral systems. It can take many newsletters or multiple meetings before people are ready to work with you or send you referrals. Keep in touch with all of your contacts and stay visible. Eventually, you want everyone in your pipeline to be so impressed by the work you do that they share it with people they know and, consequently, clients seek you out. Remember—you will always have to put effort into filling your pipeline.

Notes:

Notes:

Pleasure in the job puts perfection in the work.

—Aristotle

CHAPTER 14:

FINDING AND KEEPING CLIENTS

Building your business is about building relationships. The more people you meet, the more likely you are to find prospective clients and create the possibility of having clients referred to you. Understanding and practicing networking will help you spread the word about who you are and what you do. As your network of contacts grows, your chance of success grows along with it. People like working with people they know. As you become increasingly recognizable as a holistic health practitioner, you create what we call VFT:

- **Visibility**—being seen.
- **Familiarity**—the more often you are in contact with people, the more they remember you and your services.
- **Trust**—being reliable, responsive, and knowledgeable fosters this relationship.

Networking is a way to expand the circle of people you know in order to increase the buzz about your business. If 100 people know that you are a Health Coach and they each tell one person who tells one person about you, your chances of getting a phone call are dramatically higher than if only 20 people know you are a Health Coach. And if 1,000 people know about you, your phone will ring even more!

One effective way to network is to attend key events where you can interact with your ideal clients. You can also attend events frequented by potential referral partners (chiropractors, physicians, fitness instructors, yoga teachers, etc.). This way, you can build relationships and increase the likelihood of connecting with their clients/patients. There are many benefits to networking, such as:

- Becoming known in your community as an expert in health and nutrition.
- Getting new ideas from others on how to provide your services and how to build your business.

Notes:

- Creating the opportunity to schedule more Health Histories.
- Building referral systems with other professionals.
- Adding people to your contact list.
- Having fun by meeting other people and learning who they are and what they do.

WHERE TO NETWORK

You can network anywhere: on the train, at the gym, on the Internet, at a restaurant, or at a more formal networking event. Here are some descriptions of places to start networking:

- **Networking groups:** There are specific groups that exist for the sole purpose of bringing people together to make contacts and help one another build their businesses. Some of these groups include Business Network International (BNI) (www.bni.com) and National Women Business Owners (www.nwboc.org).
- **Associations or organizations in your field:** Many groups already exist for people who are interested in health and nutrition. Do a bit of research to locate these organizations in your area. You can do a search online, ask around at gyms, yoga studios, and schools, and read the newspaper to see if there are any groups already in place. This is a great way to connect with other coaches, especially those with different target markets.
- **Trade and professional groups that your target market attends:** Many professions have associations and groups to which they belong. For example, if you are interested in working with women business professionals, you could attend various networking events for those women in your area.
- **Trade and professional groups that your referral partners are likely to attend:** Referral partners are critical to growing your business, whether they are doctors, chiropractors, yoga teachers, hair stylists, or personal trainers. They each belong to groups and attend events based on their professions. You can attend those events, get to know them, and let them get to know you.
- **Lectures, workshops, and conferences:** There are conferences on a variety of topics including health and healing, sports, entertainment, the arts, exercise, and finances. Find out when these events happen and attend them. You may even want to lead a workshop of your own.
- **Online options:** Social networking websites, blogs, and Twitter are popular avenues for sharing your work. Consider trying one avenue and see how it works for you. Remember, however, that the key is to get out and meet people!
- **Social, cultural, or sporting events, including mixers and parties:** You never know when you are going to meet a potential client or referral partner. When

Notes:

you start health coaching or your business, it is helpful for you to socialize and connect with people whom you haven't seen in a while. You could get clients at your high school reunion, by meeting up with an old friend, or by meeting new people when you are out.

- **Charity events and fundraisers:** You may want to donate a Health History, a cooking class, or even a condensed version of your 6-month program to a charity to help increase your visibility. When you attend the event, you can tell people that you donated your services, and that will start a conversation about what you do as a Health Coach.

Where do you think you could most successfully network your services?

....

....

....

....

....

....

HOW TO NETWORK SUCCESSFULLY

- Do the research and find out what is happening in your area with your target market and with your referral partners. Make a list of all the events and groups you can find.
- Contact the groups and associations you have researched. Get a copy of their calendar and ask questions about their events and members.
- Pick a couple of networking groups related to your niche market, hobbies, and interests. Start to attend events.
- Networking is like dating; you may not click with every group you attend, but you are gaining valuable experience in the process. Try different groups and see which one feels right.
- Start your own group. A great way to network is to contact people who also have their own business. You can meet once a month or so to get to know one another and share ideas on business building. Begin to refer your clients to people in your group and ask them to refer their clients to you. Effective people to invite may include doctors, lawyers, businesspeople, acupuncturists, massage therapists, hair stylists, and accountants. We cover mastermind groups in Chapter 26.

Notes:

NETWORKING TIPS FOR INTROVERTED PEOPLE

- Take a small step outside your comfort zone. Even researching events is a great beginning.
- Be patient.
- Get support.
- Invite an extroverted friend with you to the event. They can introduce you to people and help you feel more at ease.
- Introduce yourself on the phone to the event leader, and go to tea with them as a first step before diving into the group.
- Volunteer. This is a perfect opportunity to help others and meet people.
- Use our tips for good conversation skills and icebreakers for small talk.
- Speak to the people you feel most drawn to.
- Avoid large groups that are intimidating; instead speak to one or two people at a time.
- Start by asking others questions about what they do. Get them talking. Then, either they will ask what you do, or you can tell them.

WHEN ATTENDING A NETWORKING EVENT

- Start talking to people, especially those you are drawn to, or ask the event organizer to introduce you to a few people. The more people you meet and add to your contact list, the more likely your business will grow. Be passionate about what you do. Use your elevator speech.
- Use a firm handshake, look people in the eye, and make a good connection.
- Listen, be friendly, and show interest in others. Practice starting conversations and communicating effectively.
- At events, select a few "key" people with whom to align yourself. Organizers and promoters usually know most of the people, and they can be a great resource for you. You could even volunteer at an event and introduce yourself to all the attendees.
- Always give people your business card and be sure to get everyone else's cards as well. Have an organized way to keep track of the business cards you collect. Make notes on the back of the business cards so you can remember what you talked about and how to follow up with them.
- Be gracious. Ask people to put you on their mailing list. Show them you are interested in what they do.
- If you find yourself stuck in a conversation with someone, you can politely excuse yourself to get water or use the restroom. Always be considerate, but don't waste your valuable time with people who drain you.

Notes:

Remember that your goal is to connect with people and build your contacts. In addition to sharing what you do, it is important to listen, create a connection, and get people's contact information. You may even offer to send them something useful (an article you wrote or the name of a great book) as it relates to the conversation you shared. This is a productive way to stay in touch.

When you get home that night or the next day, record the contact information of the people you met. Keep track of them—remember that you want to create VFT: Visibility, Familiarity, and Trust. Subscribe them to your newsletter if they have given you permission.

You have to be proactive and take the initiative to contact others since they probably won't contact you, so send them a follow-up email. Try to attend at least two networking events per month. Networking and building a business take time, and it's okay to make mistakes. Just remember to keep moving forward!

NETWORKING MISTAKES

- Talking too much.
- Lack of eye contact.
- Asking for business, being pushy.
- Showing up in casual, sloppy clothes.
- Only hanging out with people you already know.
- Forgetting to offer or invite people to do anything.
- Going to the event hungry and eating the whole time.
- Focusing on getting clients rather than building relationships.

MAKING SMALL TALK

When you are out there approaching people, it's helpful to have some icebreakers to start the conversation. These phrases are subtle and non-intrusive ways to help you connect with a new person and not feel any pressure. They will get you and the other person talking and might lead to a Health History or a workshop connection. If not, at least you are building your communication confidence:

- Ask open-ended questions that require more than a simple yes or no answer. For example, at a health food store you can ask, "So what do you know about whole grains?"
- Make a simple comment to stimulate conversation. For example, "Those apples look very fresh. Do you buy them at the farmers' market often?"
- Make an occasion statement that refers to something that is going on around you. For example, "I've never been to this networking event before. Have you ever attended?"

Notes:

- Give a compliment. For example, "I like your bag. Where did you find that?"
- Ask for someone's opinion. For example, "I've never been to this health food store. What do you recommend?"
- Make a general comment. For example: "This workshop is one of the best I've been to."

HEALTH FAIRS

Some Health Coaches use health fairs as a way to increase their visibility in the community. Some health fairs are open to the public while others are private, intended for a particular business or organization. You can find out about health fairs by searching online and by talking to other health practitioners. It may be useful to sign up with a health fair organizer, so that you can be informed when they host events. Most of these organizers are local, so ask around to find one in your area.

The main objective of a health fair is to build your contact list. Health fairs take a lot of time to set up and attend, so only use your time in this way if you are confident you will get something valuable, such as new contacts in your target market or more Health History consultations.

Health fairs are not the first place to spend your marketing hours, as they may yield slower results. Make sure you first focus on direct outreach, public speaking, referral partners, and Internet marketing. At the fair, you will most likely have a table or booth to display your business. Here are some things you might want to bring with you to the fair:

- Brochures
- Business cards
- Sign-up sheet for your newsletter
- Tablecloth (unless one is provided for you)
- Large sign with your business name on it
- Sign-up sheet for free Health History consultations
- A free giveaway: food samples, tea, organic chocolate
- Bouquet of pretty flowers in a vase to draw attention to your table
- A raffle opportunity: people fill out a small questionnaire with their name and contact information and get entered into a drawing for a free month of health coaching, a book, or a basket of healthy goodies

DRESS TO IMPRESS

The importance of maintaining a professional image cannot be emphasized enough. How you present yourself to the world sends a message about how you view yourself.

Notes:

Dressing professionally does not mean that you need to wear a business suit every day. It means that you should dress in a way that makes you feel good about yourself and reflects your work as a Health Coach. If your target market is yoga teachers, wearing a business suit to a workshop is inappropriate. Likewise, if your target market is corporate professionals, wearing flip-flops and jeans will not make the best first impression. You want to dress in a way that your target market can relate to. You also want to be comfortable and confident in your clothing.

Keep in mind that you never know where your next client might be. You could meet him in the grocery store, at Starbucks, at a restaurant, or on the train. For this reason, consider dressing to impress every time you leave the house.

MARKETING MATERIALS

Your marketing materials should convey who you are and what you do. We provide you with newsletter templates, business cards, brochures, and a website to get you started. While you are a student, we want you to focus on marketing yourself, building business relationships, and practicing Health Histories, not spending your precious time and money at your computer designing marketing materials.

As your business grows, you may eventually create your own logo, color scheme, and style for your marketing materials. The look and feel of these materials should be consistent with how you want people to experience your services. For example, if you work primarily with women, you might want your marketing materials to feature colors and images that appeal to that group. If you work with male athletes, you may want your materials to have a different look.

NEWSLETTER

Your newsletter is a fundamental part of your health coaching practice. Each time you meet someone, you should ask them if they would like to join your newsletter list. This way, as you add more and more people to your list over time, you are increasing your prospects. Again, the more you reach out to people, the more likely they are to remember you and want to work with you.

Newsletters are a relatively simple way for you to get information out to a lot of people at one time. It can be part of a Free Stuff section of your website, a giveaway that you offer during networking, or part of your 6-month program. Also, writing your newsletter is an educational and creative outlet for you. Let your personality come out and write it in a way that expresses who you are. To help you with this, we provide you with several newsletters to get you started. You can use these newsletters just as they are, tweak them to make them more "yours," or write your own, using them as idea generators.

Notes:

You want to make sure to always include a warm introduction, a personal message from you that welcomes your reader to the newsletter. People like to see that you're human. You can include pictures of you to show you are walking your talk.

Speak to one specific person in your newsletter. Think of a person that you know would get great results from working with you, and that you would enjoy working with. This helps you create a genuine connection with the reader. When you write to one person, you're more likely to connect with a greater number of people that are like that person, and as a result, they are more likely to hire you.

Write about something that is interesting and valuable to the reader, and enable them to see you as someone they can turn to. We recommend you focus on one message per newsletter, keep it short and sweet, and write frequently. Start with two emails per month.

Here are some additional items you can include:

1. **Special offer or invitation**—Here you offer the reader something, which could be an invitation to your upcoming event or seminar, a consultation promotion, a new product you have developed, or an upcoming program you would like them to join. Even if you have no classes planned, you can still invite them to a consultation. Be certain to write about the benefits of the promotion you are offering, and provide clear action steps on how they can sign up and/or take advantage of your offer.
2. **Client testimonial**—Share the successes of one of your star clients, once you have them. Talk about how their life improved by working with you and how you helped them. Keep it short and to the point, and include their name and picture if you would like.
3. **About you**—This section is where you talk about who you are and what you offer. Don't assume that every reader knows you well.

Here are some tips for writing newsletters:

- Make sure you include the results of your program. People are not interested in wellness but rather the impact of wellness.
- Don't try to connect with everyone. Refine your target market so you can focus on them in your newsletters and speak to them.
- Write conversationally, as if you were talking to a friend.
- Use an attention grabber in the first line or two.
- Be personal. Share what is going on in your life as it relates to your work.
- Tell stories. You want your readers looking forward to what you have to share.
- Write short and frequent newsletters.
- Focus on one main message for each. Make sure whatever parts you include all tie together.
- Use an exciting and captivating subject line.

Notes:

- Make sure you write about big issues pertaining to the top things your clients struggle with. Give little challenges or tips to use in their daily life.
- Showcase your results by providing client testimonials and your own success.
- Write often.

DIFFERENT WAYS TO SEND OUT YOUR NEWSLETTER

- **Online newsletter service:** This is the most professional option. There are several online newsletter services that you can use to send out your newsletter. Constant Contact (www.constantcontact.com), Mail Chimp (www.mailchimp .com), AWeber (www.aweber.com), and Mad Mimi (www.madmimi.com) are just a few examples. They have pre-designed templates, or you can design your own. You simply copy or type your newsletter into their website and schedule it to be sent at a certain time. Once it goes out, you can track who read your newsletter, when they read it, and what links they clicked on (if any). Having an email newsletter sign-up box on your website is essential.
- **Email:** You can simply copy your newsletter into the body of an email and create an email distribution list. This option is useful when you're first getting started, but it's much better to transition to a reliable service as your business grows.
- **Snail mail:** While this is an option, we do not recommend it because it is time consuming and expensive.

LOGOS

Logos can help brand your business. Rest assured, many successful graduates have full practices well before they consider developing a logo. It takes time to figure out how you want to represent yourself as a Health Coach, and it's useful to get clearer on this before you commit to a logo.

A good graphic designer will work with you to understand what you want the image of your business to represent. Through this process, the designer will show you some options for logos. He or she may also help you pick colors and fonts for your business and design your business card. Before hiring a designer and agreeing to the fee, you should be very clear on what exactly you are paying for. How many drafts of your logo do you want? Usually, this kind of work demands three drafts: the first draft illustrates brainstorming about the look, feel, and colors; the second draft shows the direction you have chosen; and the final draft is tweaked to get it exactly as you like it. It can cost $300 to $1,500 for the design of a logo, and you can hire someone from a service like

Notes:

MARKETING MATERIALS

- **Business cards: IIN provides you with a business card.** The front of your card should include your name, title (e.g., Health Coach), company name, telephone number, email address, website address, and logo (if you choose one). You have until the end of the program to order your cards, so you have the time to decide on your business name and title before ordering. That said, we encourage you to order them sooner rather than later so you can start handing them out.
- **Brochures:** Brochures are great to take with you to networking meetings and to give out at talks. Your brochure can include parts of your mission statement: who you work with, the concerns they have, the benefits they get from working with you, and what makes your services unique. You should include your name, title, company name, address, phone number, email address, and website address. You may also want to include a short bio. **We provide you with a brochure template to get you started**, located in the Marketing Materials Resources. Later, a company such as VistaPrint can help you create an original brochure, or you can create your own using software such as Microsoft Word or PowerPoint.
- **Your bio:** Your biography is a few sentences of background information on who you are and what you do. You may have a couple of versions of your bio that you can use in different circumstances. It should include pieces of your mission, such as who you work with and how you help them. You can also include your educational background and any special training or certifications. We will give you a biography example in Chapter 16.
- **Website: IIN provides you with a customizable website.** Your website should expand on your core mission even more than your brochure does. The look and feel should match your other marketing materials. Experiment with your Health Coach Website Editor. You have the option of adding or hiding some of the pages on your website. Consider using the Recipes Page or adding a Free Stuff Page. This page can offer your favorite recipes, articles you have written, or back issues of your newsletter. This page is a great marketing tool—a way to get people to linger on your site a little longer than they might have otherwise. Please be sure to share your website with everyone you know, and have this be a place for potential clients to learn more about you and your work. This helps them understand how your services will benefit them.

99designs.com. If you know a skilled graphic designer you could barter with, that may be a good option.

Alternatively, you can use an online service, such as Vistaprint.com, that has a selection of logos. You can pick one that works for you and create your own business cards, brochures, notepads, postcards, and more. You can also upload your own original logo onto these materials and print them out. Please keep in mind that this is not required when you start out. What's most important is developing a consistent marketing plan.

Notes:

A man is but the product of his thoughts—
what he thinks, he becomes.

—Mahatma Gandhi

CHAPTER 15:

INTERNET MARKETING

YOUR WEBSITE AND DOMAIN NAME

As an Integrative Nutrition student, you will automatically receive your own beautiful website with information about your program offerings. This saves you the time and expense of designing a website. You will have the ability to customize your site to fit your practice and needs, and to reflect your unique work as a Health Coach. You will be able to change the theme, colors, fonts, text, and add resources that appeal to your target market. In order to attract the most prospects we suggest you follow these simple steps:

- Know what your niche market likes in order to attract the right people. For example, you want to use soothing colors on your website if your target market needs help with stress relief.
- Make it easy for people to find information. If they can't find how to contact you, they won't. The less clutter and easier it is to find relevant information the better.
- Give clear instructions on what you want them to do next. Tell them what you have to offer, why they would want it, and what the next step is.
- Follow up with interested prospects to build a relationship.

If you want to have a different web address than the one we provide, you will have to purchase a domain name from a provider, and have it routed to your Integrative Nutrition provided website. If you decide to purchase your own URL, we suggest that you go to www.register.com or www.godaddy.com, or any of the more reliable web

Notes:

domain and hosting companies and follow the instructions there. They have services that will allow you to direct your Integrative Nutrition website to the name you choose. We encourage you to make your website name match your business name so it's easier for people to remember.

If buying a domain name at this time feels like too much work, you do not have to do it. Your efforts are better spent working toward doing Health History consultations and building your name in your community and with your target market. Do not waste time figuring out how to build a complex website before you have your first five clients.

In Chapter 9 we asked you to think about your business and domain name. Did you buy a domain name? If not, when will you do this?

....

Have you activated your Health Coach Website? If not, when will you do this?

....

How do you plan to promote your website?

....

INTERNET PROMOTION

Almost every business, from corner bakeries to major corporations, is harnessing the power of the Internet for marketing. As a Health Coach, it is important to stay current with your marketing strategies and find simple yet effective ways to use the Internet to your advantage.

Begin by using the website we provide for you. Make sure you include your website address (the URL) on your business card and list it in every letter and email you send. You can also send your URL to all of your contacts and referral partners, letting them know you have a site with valuable information about your services. Your website can educate potential clients, provide them with additional information after an in-person meeting, and motivate them to take action to learn more about you. Remember, not all clients will be ready to sign up for your 6-month program right away. Some will remain leads in your Client Funnel for some time as they get to know you. Your website and blog are great ways for leads to learn more.

Talk about your website when you give workshops to show that you are credible and organized. Also mention it in your newsletter. You can promote your services and have readers visit your site for more detailed information and to learn how to schedule their complimentary Health History session. In addition, you can ask your colleagues and referral partners to mention your work and your website in their newsletters and on their websites.

At some point, you may choose to develop a website on your own. If you do this, use a qualified and trained web designer to ensure that your site is professional and

Notes:

persuasive. However, we caution you to not spend all your time and money designing a fancy website. Internet marketing is important, but getting out there, doing your work, and meeting people is the most important and effective marketing strategy.

SEARCH ENGINE OPTIMIZATION

Try this experiment: Google yourself and see what comes up. If nothing comes up, or if the first few hits are not related to health coaching, you may want to increase your visibility on the web. If you meet a prospective client and tell them all about your business but they can't find any information about you online, they may question your credibility.

There are various steps you can take to increase your visibility online. For instance, you can write an article for a website and be sure to include your full name, website, and contact information. You can also hire a newsletter company to send out your newsletter each month and archive your past newsletters on the web for you. Constant Contact, Mail Chimp, or other services can assist you with this.

Another tactic is SEO, which stands for search engine optimization. Why does this pertain to you as a Health Coach? You want your website to be easily and frequently found in search engines to get you more business. When people search for certain topics related to your specialty on the Internet (i.e., Google) you want your name and business to appear frequently. You can achieve this by using the best keywords in the right places on your website and have other sites link to your site.

Follow these simple tips to customize the SEO:

1. **Choose the best keywords for your practice.** In order to be found more easily in search engines like Google or Yahoo you need relevant keywords that people are using to search.
2. **Strategically place keywords on your website.** Use those top keywords in a few main places on your website: title, the URL, in webpage content, hyperlinks on your page, etc.
3. **Create buzz and backlinks.** Buzz refers to how much attention any one site is getting. You want yours to be at the top of that list. The more other sites link to yours the more buzz you create. Those are referred to as backlinks. In order to create your own buzz you have to make sure there are other sites talking about you. The more visible you are in business directories, blogs, sites, and the media the better!

SOCIAL MEDIA

Another way to promote yourself online is to join networks such as Facebook, Twitter, LinkedIn, or other networking and social media sites. Remember bio-individuality: no

Notes:

one site will work for everyone. Play around to see which one works best for you and your business. These sites are a great way to establish your business and connect with old and new friends.

Using social media in an effective way can seem overwhelming at first since there are many outlets and options to choose from. Establishing an online presence that represents you and your business helps you to network with both peers and potential clients. Clients will often take the time to research online before committing to a program, so it is important that your social media presence is engaging, trustworthy, and reputable. Make sure to act as your authentic self when engaging in social media. The intention is not to promote yourself, but rather to have conversations and exchange quality content. The information here provides a few examples of ways to promote yourself and your practice on the Internet.

FACEBOOK

Facebook provides a clean, user-friendly platform for you to reach out to friends and acquaintances about your business. To set up an account, all you need is an email address. You can either use your personal account or set up a separate page for your business. Be aware that your profile is the backbone for your business page. You will categorize your business depending on your services. Similar to how you invite people to be your friend through your profile, you can invite your friends or other people to "like" your business. Then, you can upload your picture or business logo, list your website, and include other relevant business information.

Michael Ellsberg, a social media expert, suggests using your personal page for your business. He believes clients hire you for your personality and lifestyle, not because of your business profile. He suggests adding in a touch of your personal life to your business, and you should therefore use your personal page to promote your business. Facebook allows certain posts to be visible to certain groups of friends which you control, so you can still keep some information personal while also promoting your business. This works well for those of you who want your business to be very personal and who share your business frequently with your personal networks. It's also much easier to maintain one page on Facebook and easier for people to find you.

Other social media experts suggest creating a separate fan page (or business page) in addition to your personal page, to keep your personal life and business promotion separate. This helps your business maintain a professional image, for those of you who want to keep your personal posts away from business completely. You can use a business page like a personal page. Friends or fans can comment on your wall, share photos, and communicate through messages. Creating a business page means you have a second page to keep updated as frequently as you update your personal page, so this option may be more cumbersome for those that are less familiar with social media in general.

Facebook has many applications that can help you sell your brand and your services. For example, if you are giving a Sugar Blues talk you can create an "event" where

Notes:

you include the location, time, and description to inform your fans. If the event was recorded, you can upload the video using the "video" application. Photos and videos have the best ability to reach others on Facebook, so be sure to upload and share as much visual content as possible. It is essential to log on to your page and send updates regularly so that your business will show up in their profile's "News Feed" section. Visit www.facebook.com to get started.

TWITTER

Twitter is another easy way to increase your online visibility. To start an account, all you need is an email address. Once you create an account, you can use Twitter to post messages of up to 140 characters. These messages ("Tweets") can include thoughts, quotes, photos, links, and other useful information your target market may find beneficial. There are no invitations or friend requests, and it's more important to share valuable content than to have a large number of followers. Think of Twitter as microblogging. Instead of writing posts on a blog, you can choose to write short, key messages to keep your clients and potential clients informed. It's also a great place to find news, so you can stay updated on the latest reports and trends in health. Visit www.twitter.com to get started.

LINKEDIN

LinkedIn is primarily for business contacts. You can think of LinkedIn as an online rolodex. In order to set up a profile, you must include a business name and category. When you set up your profile, summarize your professional accomplishments so that former colleagues, clients, and partners can easily find you. Your network consists of your connections (clients, partners, and former colleagues) and their connections, linking you to thousands of qualified professionals. You can also join groups, to stay connected with like-minded communities. You might want to consider setting up a LinkedIn profile so that you will have a place to publicize your events to a professional community. Go to www.linkedin.com to get started.

BLOGS

Consider creating a blog, which is short for "web log." A blog is a kind of online journal where you write about yourself and topics of interest to you. If you are going to use this as a marketing tool, update your blog regularly to provide current health-related information. That way, if someone is searching for that information on the web, they will come across your blog and learn about what you do. This is probably the fastest way to increase your visibility online.

It allows prospective clients to learn more about you as it provides a no-risk way for others to experience your ideas. By blogging regularly you enhance your connection to readers and potential clients.

Notes:

You can go to www.blogger.com, www.wordpress.com, or www.tumblr.com to create a blog. You simply need a photo, your biography, and the ability to regularly update your blog.

Social media is constantly evolving, and there are other smaller networks that are growing in popularity that you may want to pay attention to. Pinterest is a "virtual pinboard" that allows users to share photos and links. It's a great resource for sharing recipes. Go to www.pinterest.com to get started.

To learn more about social media and to stay up to date on new trends and changes, some valuable resources include:

- www.personalbrandingblog.com
- www.mashable.com

What are some ways that you want to enhance your online business presence?

What social media platforms do you use now for your personal use?

Which platforms will you use for your business?

Notes:

Take a deep breath, this is just an introduction to Internet marketing! Just choose one platform to experiment with now and see how it works for you. We cover these topics more in depth in the curriculum.

FOCUS YOUR MARKETING EFFORTS

Feeling overwhelmed by all the marketing options at your fingertips? Don't be. One of the key ingredients to successful marketing and getting clients is to choose a set of simple but effective things to do and then consistently following through with this plan. Instead of wasting time doing a little bit of various marketing techniques, it helps to choose one and consistently do it. Simplicity is key.

Here are a few steps from C.J. Hayden, business coach and author:

- Choose a few marketing strategies to use at one time. The more active and personal they are the more people will want to know about you and what you have to offer.
- Over the next month, develop three marketing ingredients to focus on. Map out when and where these will occur and be intentional on doing them. Be sure they fit your business and personality well.
- Then, employ these activities consistently for one month.

List your three strategies:

1. ....

2. ....

3. ....

Spend time mapping out what that month will look like. Make a to-do list with particular tasks and accomplish them. Each day look at your list and decide which ones you will do that day. Keep in mind that it should be simple yet consistent. And always, have fun with it! People will be drawn to your joy and passion.

In order to succeed, your desire for success should be greater than your fear of failure.

—Bill Cosby

CHAPTER 16:

PR, PRESS KITS, AND ADVERTISING

MARKETING REVIEW

In Chapter 13 we introduced you to marketing methods. Some are listed here:

- Website
- Brochures
- Newsletter
- Workshops
- Health fairs
- Networking
- Business cards
- Social media

Check in with your marketing efforts.

Which of these techniques have you already tried?

....

....

....

....

....

Notes:

What has been most effective for you so far?

What marketing materials do you use regularly?

Do your materials reflect your target market? Are they in alignment with your mission statement?

What methods would you like to add to your marketing repertoire?

INTRODUCTION TO PUBLIC RELATIONS

While social media allows you to promote yourself, learning traditional media methods of exposure can further your mission of helping others and establishing a healthy business. Two avenues for more exposure are public relations and advertising. Pursuing public relations exposure is not right for everyone; however, having a general understanding of the process is helpful for every business owner at any stage.

Notes:

First, what's the difference between public relations and advertising? Generally, a business does not pay for public relations placement. You pay for advertising space. The most common form of public relations is an unpaid interview via television or radio or in print via newspaper or magazine (online or hard copy). The most common form of advertising will be purchasing an ad or sponsoring an event. Second, being featured in media stories or interviews adds credibility to your business. It positions you to the public as someone who knows what you are talking about.

Position yourself as a resource to your target market, as a teacher rather than a salesperson. In all your material, keep messages sharp and focused. Speak in real terms to real people, not generically to everybody. Knowing your target market and even a niche within your target market will support successful media placement.

HOW TO GET IN THE MEDIA

The media frequently relies on "subject matter experts" when they are compiling stories. A journalist can't possibly know it all. This is where you come in handy! You can submit a press kit to journalists and reporters at publications that serve your target market and offer yourself as an expert contributor. Offer yourself as a news-making partner, an expert who can be contacted to help any journalist working on a story.

Getting PR may take a little bit of research. Do some investigation into your local press. What television shows feature stories about health? Is there a popular magazine that lists the events going on in your town for the week or the month? What are all the different print publications that your target market might read? What is a hot topic in the news right now, and how can you relate it to your business? Health and wellness are huge issues in the press—everything from obesity to prescription drugs, from Medicare to the latest nutritional supplement is explored.

Contact the media to let them know you are an expert in the field of health and nutrition, and that you would like to share your knowledge. If possible, find a contact person within the organization and ask them for the protocol to submit a story or get interviewed. Some people will prefer to speak with you first, while others won't speak with you until they have seen your press kit or other information. Snail mail, telephone, email, fax, and personal delivery are all functional resources when approaching the media. Give them a heads up before you send the press release or press kit, so they know to look out for it. After getting any kind of PR, send a thank-you letter and maybe a small gift to your contact person at the organization. Let them know that you truly appreciate them and that you would love to work together again in the future.

You can also submit pre-written articles as an outside contributor. This is also called syndicating articles. If you enjoy writing and have a knack for it, this is a strong option for you. Syndicate articles by writing pieces that are completely educational, do not push a product or service, and help people solve a problem. An ideal article length for online syndication runs 600 to 750 words. When syndicating an article, give permission to use the article as long as there is a brief biography and a link back to your website is

Notes:

included. In your brief biography, describe your services and target market with a link to go to your website.

For example:

Jane Austen helps women who have tried every fad diet out there to create a custom eating lifestyle, eliminate food frustration, and find freedom in food. For her most effective quick slimming strategies, go to her website at www.yourwebsite.com/slimmingstrategies.

After you send the release, follow up. Call your contacts, confirm that they received the release, and answer any questions they may have. Tell them you are interested in

WRITING PRESS RELEASES

A press release is a one-page announcement prepared for distribution to the media about you, your services and, if applicable, a particular event. You want to give journalists information that is useful, clear, timely, and interesting.

Here are steps you can follow to write a press release for a workshop:

- On your computer, design a one-page listing. At the top of the page, use the heading "For Immediate Release" or "Press Release." Below this, place your name and your contact number.
- Design a catchy title such as "Eating Sugar the Right Way" or "Increasing Your Energy Forever." The more unique your title, the more interest people will show. Place this in bold and center it on the page. You can use all caps as a way to make it stand out more.
- Write the date of the release and the city of origin (e.g., January 16, 2014—New York, NY).
- In the first paragraph describe briefly what the press release is about.
- The second paragraph describes what makes your workshop unique and interesting. Don't "sell," just make it stand out by educating readers about the event with stimulating text and intriguing details.
- Provide the actual event details in the second paragraph as well, such as the date, location, and time.
- The third paragraph should be a one- or two-sentence summary about you, the workshop presenter.
- Include your contact information at the end.
- The content of the press release, beginning with the date and city of origin, should be typed in a clear, basic font and be double-spaced.
- Make it fun, timely, and accurate. Throw in a fact or two to add credibility. In addition to announcing workshops, you can also design press releases about you, your work in your community, or your health coaching practice.

having this release considered for publication or announcement, and ask what the steps are to make that happen. Be courteous and professional. They may or may not publicize you or your event, but at least you are developing relationships with key individuals in the media. Relationship building is essential in promoting your business, so keep these people on your contact list, and continue to send them information.

Notes:

PRESS KITS

A press kit highlights your professional accomplishments and promotes your practice. A traditional press kit is a printed informational packet or a CD of the same documents. An online press kit is a page on your website with links and uploaded files.

YOUR PRESS KIT SHOULD CONTAIN

1. Cover letter detailing why you are providing the press kit
2. Contact info, including email address, phone number, website, and social media links
3. Biography highlighting your professional and educational experience
4. Professional headshot and a few action photos of events you have conducted
5. Media exposure, including articles and videos you have created or have been featured in
6. Testimonials from clients and business partners
7. Information on current products and upcoming launches

YOUR ONLINE PRESS KIT SHOULD CONTAIN

1. Contact info: email address, phone number, social media profile links
2. Links to download two versions of your biography: short (100 words) or long (300–500 words)
3. Professional headshots: small and large file sizes (one for web, one for print)
4. Media exposure, including articles and videos you have created or have been featured in
5. List of future and past live appearances, beginning with your most recent
6. Testimonials from clients and business partners
7. Information on current products and upcoming launches

Notes:

SAMPLE PRESS RELEASE

FOR IMMEDIATE RELEASE

Contact:
Susan Smith
Holistic Health Coach
(212) 555-5654
www.susanhealth.com
susan@healthcoach.com

Killing You Sweetly—How Sugar Is Undermining Your Health

New York, NY—February 22, 20XX—Did you know that Americans consume a whopping average of 526 cans of sugary soda per year? That's 6,000 calories each month (21 pounds each year!) that directly lead to obesity and diabetes. By implementing healthy alternatives, you can avoid becoming a statistic and eliminate your sugar addiction.

In just one hour, you can get unbiased, expert information by signing up for the [Your Title Here] workshop hosted by [Your Name].

Don't waste hundreds of dollars on another weight loss plan or fad diet. Attend this revealing workshop designed to help you break your sugar habit and you'll be well on your way to creating a healthier lifestyle. This technique isn't about depriving you of your favorite snacks or forcing you to eat bland diet foods. Instead, you'll learn top tips for incorporating delicious, satisfying foods in your diet.

The first step to improving your health—and the rest of your life—begins at Healthy Spaces, 334 Main Avenue, New York, on April 5, 20XX, at 7 p.m.

The [Your Title Here] workshop explores the effects of sugar on your body and how you can successfully overcome it. Participants will gain a greater understanding of why we crave sweets, how sugar decreases our energy, and the cycle of sugar addiction. They will learn how to identify the hidden refined sugar in common foods and explore tasty alternatives to stay sugar-free for life.

[Your Name], Health Coach, facilitates the [Your Title Here] workshop. [She/he] practices privately in [Your Location], coaching clients on how to reach their goals for health, weight loss, and stress reduction. Additionally, [she/he] presents workshops and lectures on living a healthy, balanced life. Contact [Your Name] directly for more workshop topics and how [she/he] can provide workshops for your corporation or clients.

www.susanhealth.com
susan@healthcoach.com
(212) 555-5654

Notes:

Take your press kit to meetings with potential corporate clients, referral partners, and workshop venues. Direct potential clients and referral partners to your online press kit, where they can access your most up-to-date information.

Press kits are especially helpful if you feel drawn to becoming an outside contributor or syndicating your articles. This is what you will use to submit to publications for consideration.

Once you have sent your press kit, you must follow up. Contact the person, confirm that they received the packet, and ask if they have any questions about the material. During this call, you should request an in-person meeting to discuss what opportunities exist for you to share your knowledge and expertise with their organization. Use this as an opportunity to build relationships.

YOUR BIOGRAPHY

When you host workshops or present yourself to a corporation, doctor's office, wellness center, or exercise studio, you will often be asked about your background and qualifications. This is the purpose of your biography. It is a portal into your life experience and a condensed version of your career history. It provides your readers with insight into who you are. It can demonstrate your credibility and highlight what sets you apart from others.

You should include your biography in all your marketing materials, including brochures, newsletters, and flyers. In most cases, your biography will only be a few sentences. After all, your marketing materials should be more about meeting your clients' needs than about you. Keep your biography short, relevant, and to the point. Have a friend or colleague proofread it for readability and grammar.

A few things to include in your biography:

- Your education
- Awards you have received
- Something personal about yourself
- Your membership in special associations
- Your mission statement or business philosophy
- Specialized training, certification, or licensing
- Relevant or influential experiences in your life

ADVERTISING

Although some of our graduates find that advertising brings them a few clients each month, we have found that it is not generally effective for Health Coaches. People are more likely to work with someone they have met or been referred to, and consumers are so overwhelmed with advertisements that they often don't pay attention.

Notes:

SAMPLE BIOGRAPHY

BACKGROUND

(Begin your bio with a brief paragraph about why you are a Health Coach. Start with target market, then explain why you focus on that target market. Perhaps add few sentences of your health story or health philosophy.)

[place your picture here]

QUALIFICATIONS

(your name)
Health Coach

TRAINING AND EDUCATION

The Institute for Integrative Nutrition
Health Coach Training Program

(list other education you have here, including complementary therapies, university, certification programs, etc.)

CERTIFICATION AND ACCREDITATION

(list any certifications you have)

OTHER EXPERIENCE

(here you should list any places, organizations, or centers where you have conducted workshops or presentations; or where you do holistic health coaching, health histories, or group programs)

XYZ Community Center, New York
Workshop Presenter

PUBLICATIONS

Holistic Health Articles and Newsletters
Used for distribution to clients and email subscribers

(if you have had any other information published, please insert that here)

Contact Information
Phone: (212) 222-2222
Email: you@you.com
Website: www.you.com

BIOGRAPHY EXAMPLE

Jane Smith is a Health Coach and loving mother of two. She decided to become a Health Coach to fulfill her passion for working with children and parents to improve their health and build vibrant families. Jane received her training at the Institute for Integrative Nutrition. She offers individual health, nutrition, and lifestyle coaching to parents and families, and she is also a group workshop presenter and published author.

Use the space below to brainstorm ideas for your biography. Don't worry about complete sentences or perfect grammar. Just get the ideas flowing!

Where were you born and raised?____________________________

What is your education and special training?

What associations do you belong to?

What awards have you received?

What unusual experiences have influenced you?

What sets you apart from everyone else? What's something fun, unique, interesting, or quirky about you?

What specifically do you provide for your clients?

Notes:

Notes:

If you are computer savvy or are ready to hire support, you can try Internet advertising. You can purchase banners on other people's websites that display a catchphrase and your contact information. You can buy certain words from search engine companies so that your website comes up on the right hand side of the page when people search for those particular words. For example, if you purchased the words "holistic" and "nutrition," your website would come up when someone typed those words into the search engine. Your choice of keywords to purchase is crucial, and you will have to pay the search engine company each time someone clicks on your link. The links that come up on the right are paid for. The ones that come up on the left are not paid for, but are generated from the search engine algorithm that factors in the content on your site and its domain name. To get started, check out www.google.com/ads.

Another specific type of online advertising you can do is Facebook advertising. After creating your Facebook page, consider creating ads and target based on location, demographics, and interests. For more information, check out www.facebook.com/advertising.

Notes:

Notes:

If you light a lamp for somebody,
it will also brighten your path.

—Buddhist saying

CHAPTER 17:

REFERRALS AND TESTIMONIALS

REACHING OUT TO OTHERS

Whether you are reaching out to a wellness center, corporate contact, referral partner, doctor's office, workshop location, or media outlet, it is always best to contact them in an organized and professional way. Your goal is to grab their attention, make an impression, show the benefits of your work, and build relationships that will lead to you finding more clients and growing your business.

STEPS TO REACH OUT

- Make a list of people you already know with whom you'd like to build a working relationship, like doctors, yoga teachers, or corporate contacts.
- Make a list of organizations and people you want to get to know based on your target market and goals.
- Research these organizations to learn more about their work and to see if they have a potential need for your services.
- Attend events (if applicable) at these organizations to learn more about them and to increase your own visibility.
- When you are ready to reach out and inquire about opportunities, think about what you'd like to have happen. For instance, do you want to be a referral partner or a workshop presenter? Be sure you are open to different possibilities.
- Make initial contact in person, by phone, or by email based on how well you know the person. Ask who would be the best person to speak with regarding

Notes:

any of these areas: volunteer opportunities, partnering, referrals, guest speaking engagements, program support, or media.

- Contact the person in charge, introduce yourself, and ask what you can do to learn more and how you can support the organization's clients, patients, or viewers.
- Ask about scheduling a meeting to learn more about the organization (or person) as well as how you can support one another.
- Bring support materials like your press kit. Remember to discuss your benefits.
- Ask questions to figure out how your services will fit the organization's needs.
- Offer a Health History to the person in charge, if appropriate, to let them get comfortable with your work.
- Get your foot in the door. Find your entry point by figuring out what you can offer and when.
- Keep building the relationship and make sure to stay in touch.

REFERRAL SYSTEMS

Clients like to see professionals who come recommended by someone they already know. Not many people pick their doctors, dentists, and massage therapists without a referral. You know how when you go to a doctor and need a test that they can't perform, they send you to a doctor who can? That's an example of a referral system. Almost all health professionals have referral systems because they are an effective way of gaining new clients.

As a Health Coach, you can set up referral systems with doctors, chiropractors, acupuncturists, personal trainers, massage therapists, and anyone else with clients who might be interested in your services. Directly asking for referrals is common practice among healthcare providers, so you need not be shy. We have included a sample letter for you to send to potential referral partners. Please customize this letter for yourself and use it to start reaching out.

The first step to setting up a referral system is to make an appointment with someone who would be a good referral partner, such as a chiropractor, doctor, or yoga instructor. To initiate contact, send the referral letter we have provided. Be sure that you have tailored it to suit your needs. At the meeting, the goal of your conversation should be to talk about how you can support them and their clients or patients. You are not there to "push" your services, but rather to learn more about them. The more you learn about their work, the more clearly you will know how you can be of support.

For your first appointment, bring a list of questions centered around determining how you can offer your services and support. This meeting should focus on establishing common ground and building a relationship with your potential referral partner. As your relationship grows, this can lead to them referring clients to you and vice versa, or to you being invited to teach or lecture with or for them. You could even explore

REFERRAL LETTER

Notes:

Dear (*Person's Name*),

My name is (name) and I am a Health Coach, helping people (state your specialization). I'm very interested to learn more about your practice and your patients' biggest struggles.

I understand you specialize in (list the professional's focus); my program specifically helps clients like yours develop new lifestyle habits to support their doctor's health recommendations. I (know, have read, heard, seen, been told) very positive things about your work and can certainly see that you are committed to health and wellness.

As a busy (doctor, professional, etc.), I'm sure you don't have the time to work with each patient on how to implement your recommendations, but that is the focus on my service. Perhaps my program can complement your recommendations to fully serve your patients.

I would like to learn more about your (work, practice, company) and how I can be of support to both you and your (patients, staff, employees). I am looking for a (chiropractor, physician, acupuncturist—choose the correct title), someone I can trust and partner with for the betterment of our clients and our businesses, to add to my referral network. My clients are sometimes in need of a professional that understands their health goals, and I am approaching you because (list a genuine compliment that draws you to this professional).

I have (a coaching program, workshop, a series of articles) that I am confident would provide much value to your (patients, clients). My business (has already been featured in, also works with, or list some other accomplishments including a successful client story). I'd be happy to discuss my (program, workshop, etc.) with you and to learn even more about how your work could be of value to my clients.

Thank you for your work in the community. Please let me know when you would have time to talk either by phone or in person about how we could support one another. I can be reached by email at (email address) or phone at (phone number). I look forward to learning more about your work, and will follow up with you (one week from now, date) to connect further.

Kind regards,
(Your Name)
(Your Title)

PS. I've attached a (*brochure, article*) to give you a better sense of my work and the benefits I offer, which I think you'll enjoy. You can also visit my website at (*address*).

(You can also include a brochure, business card, or flyer if sending by mail.)

Notes:

writing a relevant article, perhaps for their website or newsletter. They may also simply take your brochures and business cards. Your goal is to find the first entry point and get your name, website, and contact info in front of their client list. Remember not to be pushy, let them talk more than you do, and help them see the value of what you offer as it relates to them and their clients. To that end, share what you can offer based on what they need.

You may want to offer your new referral partner a free initial consultation with you. This will allow them to get a sense of how you work. Remember, building these relationships takes time. People will work with you and refer clients to you when they trust you and understand the value of what you do. Be yourself, be polite, and show genuine interest in their work.

If you already have an established relationship with someone whom you would like to invite to become a referral partner, it may be appropriate to ask that person over for tea or a meal and discuss how you envision helping each other through referrals. You could also send them your press kit with a personalized letter inviting them to create a referral system with you. However, our experience shows that talking face to face is more effective than sending materials in the mail.

It's important that you genuinely like and trust the people who become your referral partners. You will be sending your clients to them, and you want your clients to have a good experience. Once your referral system is set up, stay in contact with your referral partner to continue building the relationship. For example, let's say you have set up a referral system with a chiropractor and a client is looking for one. Give your client your partner's phone number, and then call or send a card to the chiropractor letting them know that your client is coming to see them. Or, after the appointment, send a card thanking them for taking good care of your client and telling them that you look forward to future referrals.

If they send you someone first, send them a small thank-you gift in return. No matter how small the gesture is, it will make a strong impression. An appropriate gift could be the Integrative Nutrition book or a homemade snack, which would give them a deeper understanding of your work.

Take a moment now and make a list of 20 health professionals in your area who you could partner with. Use the Internet, check out the phone book, and ask for ideas from everyone you know:

1. ....

2. ....

3. ....

4. ....

5. ....

6. ....

Notes:

7. ....

8. ....

9. ....

10. ....

11. ....

12. ....

13. ....

14. ....

15. ....

16. ....

17. ....

18. ....

19. ....

20. ....

Start with the first person on the list and work your way down. Make contact by sending them your referral letter (by email or snail mail). It may take a few months to reach everyone on this list, so be patient. Out of 20 people, there should be at least one who will be thrilled to create a referral system with you.

INFORMAL REFERRALS

Word of mouth is one of the best and most cost-effective ways of marketing. Your current clients, friends, and family can become an effective marketing team for you by telling people they know about your services. You may even want to create a referral structure for nonprofessionals.

Spread the word about your new business by talking to the social butterfly in your group of friends, your hairdresser, local real estate agents, restaurant owners, and anyone else that you think may be well-connected. Make sure that all of these people are familiar with what you do so they can spread the word in their circles. A great way to fill them in is to invite them to a complimentary Health History session. At the end of the Health History, they may even want to sign up! If they do, it will likely lead to positive shifts in their lives, which people will inevitably notice and want to know why. Even if they don't sign up, they can still be a good source of referrals. You can tell them that you are taking on new clients and if they know of anyone who might be interested

Notes:

CREATE A REFERRAL NETWORK

Often, Health Coaches will need to refer clients to other practitioners for further treatments. And other practitioners will frequently have the opportunity to tell their clients about your work. You will need to have a few items in place before moving forward:

1. Know what kind of client you are looking for and communicate this to your referral partners. This is mainly about your target market. Your referral partners need to know who to send to you in order to send potential clients to you.
2. Be picky about your partners. Health Coach Christi Collins offers this advice: "You need to trust them, their selection criteria, their intuition, and be comfortable referring them to you."
3. Create a system. Once you or your referral partner realizes there's a referral opportunity, then what? What can you provide your partners with to give to a client that is a perfect fit for you? Postcards, brochures, and business cards all work here. Also, how will you follow up with the client or partner to make sure the connection happens?
4. Always send "Thank-yous." Send at least a handwritten note, but if you have a strong relationship with your partner, consider what else you can send or do to show your gratitude.

in working with you, they should send them your way. At this time, you can tell them about your referral policy.

Your referral policy can involve giving the same gift to everyone who refers clients to you, or you can do it on a case-by-case basis. For instance, you might give them a book or a gift certificate for every person they refer to you who signs up for your 6-month program. If they refer two clients, you may offer them something a bit larger like a massage certificate. If it's a close friend or family member, it might be appropriate for you to treat them to lunch or dinner. Do whatever feels right to you. Everyone likes to be appreciated, and when you give sincere gifts, they will remember you and most likely continue to send clients your way.

Even if you aren't comfortable with promoting your services to your close friends and family, you can invite them for a complimentary Health History session, letting them know you want the practice. Once the Health History is complete, don't be concerned with trying to close the deal. Simply ask them how it was for them. Let them know that you really appreciate their time and that you enjoyed your session. You can casually mention that you are looking for clients and if they know anyone who might be interested in hiring you, they should feel free to send them your way and you will take great care of them.

Notes:

WORKING WITH DOCTORS

Health Coaches can successfully work with doctors as referral partners, once a target market is established. While doctors can diagnose and treat, some may be unaware of nutrition's place in healing or addressing health concerns. Even those doctors that do have awareness may not have the time to work out a plan with a patient, much less time to provide support and accountability. Doctors frequently tell patients to eat better and exercise, but patients still don't do it. This is where the Health Coach comes in!

When partnering with a doctor, you can work with the patient to implement the doctor's orders. Many doctors have no experience with Health Coaches, so you get to educate them on your role with their patients and how you can support their practice.

CLIENT TESTIMONIALS

Client testimonials allow your current and past clients to share their success stories. This helps potential clients relate to you and your work. Hearing about the success that people have had in your 6-month program will motivate potential clients to work with you.

REFERRAL-BUILDING TACTICS

- Attend meetings and seminars to meet new people.
- Schedule office visits. Make a date to visit your potential referral partner.
- Serve on committees. This is a great relationship-building strategy that doubles as a visibility strategy.
- Volunteer or trade services. Offer free Health Histories to all referral partners (you could even barter your 6-month program with some of them).
- Share resources. You can share an office space with other health professionals, such as massage therapists, or share your contacts and email lists with them.
- Collaborate on projects. You can put together a wellness event with people you'd like to add to your referral network.

Adapted from *Get Clients Now: A 28-Day Marketing Program for Professionals, Consultants , and Coaches*, 2nd ed., by C.J. Hayden, New York, NY: AMACOM, 2007.

Notes:

GATHER AND USE TESTIMONIALS

- Who are your best clients? Which clients have had the greatest successes and achieved tangible results? Contact these clients, tell them how much you enjoyed working with them and let them know that you are looking for some testimonials.
- Thank the clients who agree to provide a testimonial and let them know what your deadline is. It is best to give people about a week.
- Ask them to write one to two paragraphs about working with you, the results they achieved, where they were before they met you, and where they are now.
- Edit their text and check for grammar and spelling mistakes.
- Show the client their revised testimonial for their approval.
- Place the testimonial on one page, with the client's name, age, and profession at the top. Include a picture of them if they are comfortable with it, but if they are worried about confidentiality, just use their first name.
- Upload your testimonials to your website.
- Gather as many testimonials as you can and store them electronically.
- Create a binder of your testimonials to show potential clients, organizations, and referral partners.
- Arrange several testimonials on one page to hand out to workshop attendees as a quick reference.
- Ask organizations you worked for or where you held workshops to write testimonials for you.
- Include one or two testimonials on all of your marketing materials, newsletters, brochures, flyers, and press kits.

List people or organizations that could provide testimonials for you:

1. ....

2. ....

3. ....

4. ....

5. ....

REFERENCES

You will find that some potential clients—individuals, corporations, and organizations—want to hear from people who are familiar with your work. They are interested in working with you but want to get another opinion before hiring you as their Health Coach or workshop presenter. This is an instance when it is useful to have references on file.

Notes:

After working with clients and organizations, especially those who expressed enthusiasm for your work, ask them to write a few sentences highlighting your unique qualities and the benefits they received as a result of your work together. Build lasting relationships with these people and organizations, because they will become your professional references. Stay in touch, send them your newsletter, keep them up-to-date on what is happening with your business, and invite them to some of your workshops and seminars. This way if they are called as a reference, they will have had recent communication and know the latest news about your business.

If you lack experience in a certain area that you would like to break into, such as corporate workshops or leading school seminars, donate your services for the first few times. Continue to gain experience, build relationships, and collect references. You can add all of these different references to your biography and press kit.

Create a reference handout that includes client feedback, a list of organizations where you have given workshops, and other relevant education or achievement information. Key references are past clients or clients currently in your 6-month program, referral partners, and organizations where you have led workshops and corporate clients. If you don't have many references at this time, think back to your education, work experience, and achievements. Who could vouch for your skills as a Health Coach? Perhaps an old friend or a family member who is familiar with how much you know about food or a fellow student who knows you well could write your first references. Ideally, you want people who have direct experience with you as a Health Coach to act as your references. Know that these references will come with time, as you build your practice. If you are not ready to include your references' contact information on your handout, you can simply note that your references are available upon request.

List some people or organizations that could be your references:

1. ....

2. ....

3. ....

4. ....

5. ....

Don't let life discourage you; everyone who got where he is had to begin where he was.

—Richard L. Evans

CHAPTER 18:

WORKING WITH CORPORATIONS

Working with corporations is similar to working with individuals. Corporations can be approached many different ways and programs can be customized to specific needs and to your expertise; it simply takes clarity on knowing how you work best. No matter what type of program you create for your corporate clients, corporate wellness programs can serve as a supplement to your practice or become a full focus.

The demand for corporate wellness increases each year. As the statistics around chronic diseases increase, support of preventative measures and insurance rates continue to increase, and companies proactively seek programs to lower their costs and increase employee productivity.

With your experience in health-related goals, you know firsthand the effectiveness of implementing small changes. Imagine the impact of your influence on an entire company!

HOW TO BEGIN

Let's first set an intention to make corporate wellness programs a supplemental activity or a full practice. It may not be right for you at this stage of building your business.

Notes:

Consider the following (1 being lowest; 5 being highest):

How drawn do you feel to work in corporate environments?	1 2 3 4 5
How strong are your corporate contacts?	1 2 3 4 5
What is your comfort level with public speaking?	1 2 3 4 5
How confident are you with your follow-up skills?	1 2 3 4 5
How much of your target market works in the corporate environment? (1 being "not many;" 5 being "all of them")	1 2 3 4 5
What is your interest level in working in group settings?	1 2 3 4 5
How strong is your personal corporate experience?	1 2 3 4 5

SCORE

25–35 Wow! Definitely consider corporate wellness as a full target market and concentrating most of your efforts on corporations as clients.

15–15 Sounds like your main focus lies elsewhere, but your interest is piqued at the idea of corporate programs. Consider supplementing your priority target market with corporate clients.

0–15 Corporate wellness probably isn't your calling right now. Perhaps you can reconsider this option at a later point in your practice. Your energy can be more effective in other areas where you are more comfortable.

Congratulations! Set your intention here:

I intend to pursue corporate programs as ____.

(a supplement to OR a focus of my main practice)

CREATE YOUR CORPORATE PROGRAM

Now that you have set your intention around what part corporate programs will play in your practice, let's get clear on what your programs can look like. Corporations are as unique as individuals and require an equal amount of customization. However, as you do with individual clients, you get to decide how you work best and can search for clients that match your optimal work setting.

1. WORKSHOPS

The most popular "entry" option for corporate wellness programs is workshops. An entry option allows the corporation to taste the program without committing to a major investment.

Proposing two workshops a month on the same topic and scheduling them at different times and days allows more employees to attend and gain exposure to the information. Consider offering a package of six workshops over six months to begin.

Workshop pricing suggestions range from $300–$600 per workshop. We suggest starting at $400 per workshop and offering a package discount for committing to a 6-month workshop program. For instance, you could price individual workshops

Notes:

at $400, which would total $4800 for two workshops a month for six months. The discount for a full 6-month workshop program commitment would bring the rate to $3600 ($300 twice a month for six months).

More tips for presenting workshops:

- Provide a menu of workshops with a brief summary (one to two sentences) of each workshop.
- Suggest one morning and one afternoon workshop for scheduling variety.
- Consider providing healthy snack alternatives during the workshop to support the workshop's topic.
- Always make yourself available for one-on-one conversations after the workshop. Build relationships with the employees for better program feedback and to build their trust as possible individual clients. Be prepared to offer a Health History consultation and/or sign up employees directly to your newsletter.
- Create a marketing plan with the company to give employees at least three exposures to the workshop information. Prepare suggestions of how the workshop can be marketed to employees (e.g., email, a note with their paycheck, flyers in the restrooms) and when marketing for the workshops should begin (three to four weeks prior).

Like with an individual client, consider what else you can include between workshops as an added value.

- Will you invite the employees to bonus monthly teleseminars?
- Can you host monthly "Question and Answer" calls where clients and employees submit questions that you address on the call?
- Can you include healthy lifestyle suggestions and recipes in internal newsletters or company-wide communications?
- Do you have relationships with product vendors or other service providers that can provide discounts to their services?

2. GROUP PROGRAMS

Similar to a workshop, group programs can be scheduled once or twice a month over a 6-month time frame on different days and at different times to accommodate varied schedules. Unlike a workshop, you will incorporate more coaching, more interaction, and less lecturing in a group program. Group programs are covered in more specifics in Chapter 19, but know that a group program structure can utilize the corporation as the source of clients.

When setting a rate for a group program, the corporation can fully fund the cost or they can subsidize the cost for employees (pay for part while the employee pays the

Notes:

other part). In general, group programs are much more affordable for individuals and provide a similarly supportive yet unique experience to individual coaching.

Like the workshop option, consider what you can provide as added value components to a group coaching program. You will also need to create and suggest a marketing plan to increase participation.

3. INDIVIDUAL PROGRAMS

Some companies may be interested in providing one-on-one coaching for employees, although this option is much less likely than the workshop and group program offerings. However, they may consider offering individual coaching to upper-level executives or as incentives for high-performing employees. Like the group program, this option can be subsidized or fully funded by the employer.

4. TIERED PROGRAM OFFERINGS

Providing a menu of options can help motivate a conversation when a client (corporate or individual) doesn't know where to start. Even though you may present tiered programs to a corporate client, suggest one of the programs as an ideal fit for the company.

WORKING WITH INSURANCE COMPANIES

Some companies want to reduce insurance premiums through a wellness program and will require detailed monitoring of individual health statistics throughout a long-term wellness program. Health Coaches that want to include this depth of a service will need to be familiar with multiple chronic diseases (obesity, heart disease, diabetes) and have access to a monitoring service that connects employee doctor visits to an anonymous database for secure observation. This is a very advanced topic, but we bring it up here so you are aware of it in case a company requests this type of information.

CONTINUING YOUR WORKING RELATIONSHIP

Because corporations are businesses, they have to justify benefits expenditures. Be prepared to summarize the results of your impact on employees before the end of your program so you can prepare a recommitment conversation. Use both qualitative (descriptive words) and quantitative (numbers, percentages) measures. This will require surveying the employees. Surveying for a corporate program will be covered later in this chapter.

When surveying, especially in a corporate environment, the safety of anonymity will encourage more feedback. You may also need to provide incentives for participating in the survey. We suggest three check-ins to guarantee crystal clear feedback: beginning, middle, and end.

Notes:

CORPORATE HEALTH COACHING PACKAGES

SAMPLE TIERS

I offer three levels of coaching, ranging from my most comprehensive elite package to my jump-start program. Each package is guaranteed to get results and can be scheduled at your convenience.

Elite Custom Coaching

- Twelve 45-minute group coaching sessions over twelve months
- Monthly one-on-one laser coaching sessions
- Six 1-hour health and wellness teleclasses
- Lunch-and-learn activities tailored specifically for your group
- Unlimited individual email support
- All books, materials, and recipes included
- Discounts to local health and fitness hot spots

Step Up to Success

- Twelve 45-minute group coaching sessions over twelve months
- Three 1-hour health and wellness teleclasses
- Individual email support during open hours
- All books, materials, and recipes included
- Discounts to local health and fitness hot spots

Jump Start to Wellness

- Twelve 45-minute group coaching sessions over twelve months
- Books, recipes, and other great giveaways
- Discounts to local health and fitness hot spots

Before the workshops begin, survey the employees to determine their goals around weight loss, energy level, mental focus, and stress level. Ask for specific numbers, including rating their self-perception on a scale of 1–10 or by percentages.

Ask these same questions in the middle and at the end of the program. Also ask for comments about what is working for them as individuals and what they would like to learn more of. Ask them to share personal victories since the workshops began. Compile the results and present them to your client, including the comments without names. This provides both qualitative and quantitative feedback. Showcasing any improvements and connecting it to employee productivity will encourage the corporation to continue in any program with you.

Note that corporations move very slowly and programs like this may take several months to show any improvements.

Notes:

WHAT TO EXPECT FROM A CORPORATION

Some corporations are very slow to communicate and make decisions. Expect multiple follow-ups in various forms (email, mailings, phone calls, in-person meetings) with multiple people across multiple departments. Maintaining professional contact can increase your chances of completing a partnership, so use the process as an opportunity to showcase your drive and trustworthy conduct. Providing dates or times for them to respond to you or to setting a date or time that you will contact them again gives structure within your communication and allows them to let you know what you can expect from them. It also holds you accountable to do what you say you are going to do and when you say you are going to do it!

Corporations are also slower to pay invoices than individuals. Generally, they cut checks on certain days of the month, usually once or twice a month. Propose services in packages so you can bill once and wait for only one check. Thirty to sixty days is a reasonable time frame to expect payment, but also set payment timeframes as a general practice policy.

Take a moment to reflect on this chapter.

Are you interested in working with corporations? If so, what kind of programs do you want to offer?

....

....

....

....

What are your next steps?

....

....

....

....

Notes:

Notes:

If opportunity doesn't knock,
build a door.

—Milton Berle

CHAPTER 19:

PHONE AND GROUP COACHING

In addition to in-person, one-on-one coaching, there are a few other options. In this chapter we will detail coaching over the phone as well as in groups. Both provide great opportunities to expand your services, reduce overall program cost, and allow you to make more money. You will be able to reach more people and create connections, furthering the ripple effect.

PHONE COACHING

Health coaching is just as effective over the phone or via video calling. Phone coaching is a great way to expand your practice while working from the comfort of your home. It is perfect for clients who are busy, want the convenience of calling from home or the office, travel frequently, want to reduce commuting time, live outside your area, or are working parents who need to be home during evening hours.

Phone coaching works well for Health Coaches who don't have an office space, want to work from home but don't want to see clients there, like to travel, or don't want to be encumbered with an in-person client schedule. If you like to talk on the phone and enjoy the flexibility of being able to do your sessions from anywhere, phone coaching may be a great fit for you.

If you know you want to do phone coaching, be sure to mention it in your marketing materials. Simply call or email potential clients, let them know about this new work you are doing and invite them to do a Health History with you over the phone. Let them know what to expect. Tell them you will email them the Health History form to fill out and send back to you, or you'll fill it out together over the phone. Send them a reminder email or give them a quick phone call the day before your session. Suggest that

Notes:

they put aside an hour of time in a quiet and comfortable space for your phone session. Consider asking them to have a glass of water or cup of tea handy.

Have your clients call you, giving them more responsibility for their session. When they call, ask them a question to create relatedness and connection. You can ask how their day was, or ask what is new and good in their lives. Make sure they are in a comfortable, quiet, private space. Proceed to go over the Health History form as you would in person. By now you have most likely practiced Health Histories over the phone with your classmates. Ask your potential clients questions, listen, and avoid giving advice.

After they've agreed to work with you, take their credit card number over the phone to hold their first official session of their program. Even if you don't have a credit card merchant account, this action will have them take you seriously. If you are able to accept credit cards, bill them immediately for the first month. If you are only accepting checks, tell them you will need to have six post-dated checks (if they are paying in this way and are legal in their state) and the signed Program Agreement at least 24 hours before their first session. Schedule all 12 sessions with them while you have them on the phone. If this is not possible, schedule at least two months in advance. Ask them to get their planner and confirm the dates.

After you get off the phone, email them the Program Agreement, Welcome and Goals forms, and a reminder of when their sessions begin. Encourage them to email or fax the forms back as soon as they can.

A 6-month program over the phone works almost the same way as an in-person program. You meet once every two weeks for 50 minutes and follow the same structure for your sessions. At the end of each session, send them a quick email telling them how great the call went and give them the recommendations for that session. Email them the appropriate handouts. You may want to keep a record of your email exchange in a folder labeled with their name for easy reference.

We recommend that you ship their giveaways in two separate installments—one after they sign up for your program and one halfway through. It's less work for you if you don't have to go to the post office each week, and receiving gifts in the mail allows your client to feel special. After you've received their completed Program Agreement and payments, mail them their first giveaway package, including their binder for the handouts and the recipes that you will email them after each session. You'll also want to include one giveaway for each session through the third month—six giveaways total. Be sure to make a note of which ones you sent so you know what to send in the second package.

PHONE COACHING TIPS

- Invest in a hands-free headset with mute capabilities.
- If possible, meet your client in person at least once during your 6-month program.

Notes:

- If you cannot meet in person, exchange photos via email.
- Start and end on time.
- Give the client a warm welcome and check in at the beginning of the session.
- Remind them to find a private, quiet, and comfortable space that is free of distractions.
- Begin each session with a simple breathing/grounding exercise to slow their pace and be present with you.
- Do not multitask while on the phone.
- Be conscious of the tone of your voice, and don't speak too quickly.
- Make sure the client knows you are listening.
- Ask questions and be interested.
- Don't be afraid of silences.
- Take notes.
- Direct them to the mailed giveaway that corresponds with each session.
- Email them a copy of the session notes page, along with the action steps you've outlined, once you complete the session.
- If you send follow-up emails to check in with the clients, do so on a regular day and time. This adds consistency to the process.
- At each session, ask if they tried your recommendations from the previous session.
- Send a reminder email before each session.

VIDEO CALLING

While phone coaching is convenient, many coaches like to see the client's face and body language. There is a solution that offers the best of both worlds—video calling!

Video calling allows a Health Coach to communicate with a client through live-streaming video chat. Not only will you be able to hear your client, but you'll be able to see them too! There are various video calling options, but we recommend Skype, which is the most popular software and is free of charge.

There are many benefits of video calling, including:

- It's a virtual face-to-face client session in the comfort of your own home.
- You can expand your business by working with clients beyond your geographic area.
- You can see your client, read their body language, facial expressions, and other non-verbal cues. This is especially helpful with quiet clients.
- You can demonstrate a technique and show your client tangible examples of healthy foods and other products.

Notes:

What you'll need:

- A webcam
- A computer
- High-speed Internet service
- An account—create your account with Skype at www.skype.com
- Software—available on the Skype website

Have a back-up plan. When working with technology, remember to prepare for technical difficulties. Have a back-up plan in place and communicate it with your client.

Make sure you prepare for video delays or malfunctions, scratchy audio or no audio, slow Internet or no Internet, and computer and hardware glitches. Let your client know that should any of these mishaps occur, you will call them at a specified number to continue the session. Even though you may want to try and work out the technical glitches right away, it is more helpful to stay on track with the session over the phone.

GROUP COACHING

Group coaching is a highly efficient technique to expand your practice and reach more people. The group setting creates a community of support and facilitates connections. It is also an opportunity for you to work with people who can't afford your individual program fees. Group programs typically range from $75 to $150 per person, per month. A good strategy is to charge half of your individual program fee. For example, if your individual coaching program is $250 per month, it is fair to charge $125 for your group coaching program.

You can conduct the group in person, or by phone using a conference call line. If you would like to start a group program, it is helpful to first determine your target market. Is it the same target as your regular practice? Once you have decided, pick a time and location that best suits the needs of your target market. It is important to choose a start date and session time before you begin to market the program. For example, one of our graduates runs an extremely successful group program for young corporate women at 7:00 a.m. on Wednesday mornings in NYC. They meet at her convenient midtown office, have breakfast, and participate in group coaching for an hour and a half before work.

MARKETING YOUR GROUP

A group program is only successful if you have members in the group. The first step is to market the group. Begin your marketing efforts about five to six weeks before the start date. You can promote your group just as you promote your other services: with email offers, newsletters, your website, workshops, networking events, and through referral

Notes:

partners and clients. Use the How to Promote Your Programs—Email Template found in Chapter 20 and adapt it for the group program. Remember, a golden rule of marketing is to give people what they want. Always discuss the benefits that the participants will receive from working with the group. As an incentive, you may want to offer a deadline to enroll and an early enrollment discount; for example, "Enroll by X date, and you save $100 off the total cost of the group!" or, "Space is limited—there are only 5 spots left!"

When promoting a group in your newsletter or in an email, remember that your contacts need to hear from you multiple times. People are busy and they need to be reminded that you are offering an exciting new program. A general rule for promoting a group is to send four emails total. Send one to officially announce the group, about three to five weeks before you start. Then, send another email two weeks before your start date. Send the third email a week before the start date, and the fourth email one day before the event. Use these emails to remind people of the benefits that they will receive from working with the group. Also include the location and dates of your program. If you are conducting the group by phone or teleconference, mention the kick-off date and the dates of the calls. Always remember to state how they can sign up, for example, "Secure your spot now by (clicking here)," "Send an email to (your email address)," or "call (your phone number)." Make sure people know how to take the next step to join you.

Other marketing efforts may include teleclasses, article writing, and guest blogging. Alex Jamieson, author of *The Great American Detox Diet,* suggests starting these marketing pieces three months in advance. She also suggests focusing the articles or blog topics on pieces of the program content. At the end of each blog or article, provide a strong call to action to sign up for the group program that directly addresses the issue you just presented. Alex says, "One of my biggest success tips is really to share. Share as much as you can. Share 90 percent of what you're going to give them in the program."

Nisha Moodley, Health Coach and creator of freedom-focused programs and retreats, used a teleclass to launch her first group program. Relating it to the program theme, Nisha announced the program at the end of the teleclass, directed callers to the web page, and incentivized signing up quickly with a deep discount. She then followed up with another teleclass, surveying her list about what they wanted to know.

Additionally, have your contacts and referral partners spread the word about your services. Alex recommends offering 50 percent of your program fee to referral partners, especially if they are promoting your program consistently through their own newsletter or blog. Using referral partners increases your exposure to people you otherwise would not have access to. When you have people market for you, always be sure to send them the exact text you'd like them to use. This makes it easier for them to help you. Include emails, tweets, Facebook posts, and the link necessary for signing up.

Another marketing method to consider is providing a scholarship to someone who could help promote your services. Nisha gave a scholarship to what she calls a "high-leverage person" and chose a Pilates studio owner.

Notes:

WHAT A 6-MONTH GROUP PROGRAM LOOKS LIKE

- Choose a specific date, time, and location.
- Hold individual Health Histories or one group orientation for everyone who is interested. You can adapt the template for the Sugar Blues lecture to use for your group program.
- To save time, you can skip the Health History session and simply have them send you a completed form as part of their enrollment to reserve their spot.
- Have everyone sign a Program Agreement as part of the registration process.
- Be sure to collect payment from each participant before you begin. Consider offering an online payment method so you can direct all participants there.
- Hand out the schedule for the meetings. Typical group programs run every other week for six months.
- Follow the session outlines, located in the Specialty Coaching Resources, and adapt them appropriately for the group. An ideal group size is six to ten people. Generally, your group size should be no less than four and no more than 30 participants. This ensures that each individual will get enough personalized attention and that you'll be compensated fairly for your time and energy. Running a group program is similar to individual coaching: you use the same paperwork, give individual recommendations, and provide giveaways at the end of each session.

Each session should run from 75 minutes to two hours, depending on the size of the group. You can host your groups in your home, at a wellness center, at the office of a referral partner, in a rented space, or by teleconference. Meet with the group at the same time and day every two weeks, and have this schedule set before the group begins.

Customize your group programs as you see fit. For example, some coaches choose to host monthly seminars on special topics in addition to their group coaching sessions.

MANAGING A GROUP PROGRAM

When running a group meeting, it is helpful to have the room arranged before people arrive. Place the chairs in a circle for smaller groups. For larger groups, rows of semicircles may work better. Encourage the participants to sit next to different people each time.

Group members will feel more comfortable sharing if they know that they will not be judged and that their confidentiality will be respected. The group trust may take some time to develop. Remind them that this is a safe space, and that they are welcome to be who they are. This can help them open up and reach their goals more quickly.

Call on quiet people and encourage them to share. Remind them that sharing can encourage their personal growth and help them move through blocks. Everyone in the

Notes:

group should receive your individual attention at some point during the program. This may be during their group shares, a Q&A period, or a one-on-one coaching session. You should make sure that all participants feel recognized as individuals. Send personal and group emails to check in, letting people know you are with them and are interested in their growth.

Often, the more vocal members of the group dominate the conversation. When this happens, thank them for sharing, and say you would be happy to talk with them after the session but that you are on a schedule and have a lot of information to cover. You must be clear with your boundaries. Look out for those who are overly talkative, needy, show up late, or are disrespectful. They are not supporting the group dynamic. Be proactive in handling these situations, but do so with compassion and understanding. At the end of your group program, you can offer individual programs and maintenance programs to the group participants.

CONDUCTING GROUP PROGRAMS BY PHONE

Similar to one-on-one phone consultations, you can also conduct group programs over the phone. We have outlined some simple steps:

1. Review the group program outlines. You will use the same session content by phone as you would in person. Remember, the outlines are meant to serve as a guide. You do not need to follow them step-by-step. Adapt the outlines to work for your group and your target market.
2. Decide on a specific time and date that you would like to start. Evenings tend to work well for many people, especially those who have day jobs. Keep the same time and day for all 12 sessions. Schedule the sessions to occur every two weeks.
3. Market your group program. You can do this much like you would your regular work (email, newsletter, lectures, referral partners, flyers, etc.). Offer "early enrollment" discounts as an incentive to join and mention the benefits of the group calls. You can also expand your marketing to several different states because it's over the phone.
4. A phone group works well with four to 30 or more people. Decide what number you are comfortable with.
5. Price the program the same as you would an in-person group.
6. Enroll participants as you would an in-person group (Health Histories, group orientation, etc.). Accept credit card payments via PayPal, or have them send you checks (either the entire amount or post-dated). Provide payment deadlines, and be sure you receive payment before the start date.
7. Have each participant complete the group Program Agreement form and send it to you before the start of your group.

Notes:

8. Once a member has enrolled and paid, send them a welcome email with the following information:
    - Welcome form
    - Goals form
    - Program Schedule
    - Phone number and access code
    - Program policies (missed sessions, etc.)
    - Gratitude for their participation
    - What to expect from the program
9. Set up your group conference calls. You can use a service like www.instantteleseminar.com or www.freeconference.com. You will need to create a user account on either of these systems, and the service will provide you with a phone number linked to your account. You will then need to schedule all 12 of the group program calls. The system will ask you for the number of participants. You will create a PIN (access code) to give to your participants in the welcome email. Again, it's best to schedule all of the calls at once. If you need assistance setting up your account, you can contact technical support for either of these services.
10. Begin your group calls. Call in for your sessions a few minutes ahead of time and follow the outlines. It's best to have a headset and use a landline.

You can find additional tips and resources for running group programs in the curriculum and Specialty Coaching Resources.

Make a list of topics you would like to offer in a group coaching session:

1. ....
2. ....
3. ....
4. ....
5. ....

Make a list of all of the people you know who might be interested in a group coaching session:

1. ....
2. ....
3. ....
4. ....
5. ....

Notes:

PROGRAM COMPLETION RENEWAL OPTIONS

Many clients do extremely well during group programs because a lot is covered in a short amount of time. When this is the case, some might choose to work with you one-on-one in order to continue this work in greater depth.

Offer the individual program to:

- Clients who enjoy a slower and more relaxed pace and want continued support for another six months
- Clients who have achieved amazing results in a short amount of time and want to continue with a deeper focus on their main health concerns
- Clients who would like to work on a different goal than the one they focused on during the group program
- Clients who simply appreciate the value of your support and services

You can send these clients a letter when they've finished your program. Here is an example to use as a template.

> Dear (name),
>
> I've created a few options for graduates of my group program who are interested in continuing to work with me:
>
> - Sign up for an individual program for six months. Your program cost will be a discounted rate of $____________ per month.
> - Create a customized program. You and I can agree upon a program that is best for you. Price to be determined.
> - Participate in a maintenance program. See me once a month to continue receiving support and working toward your goals. Price to be determined.
>
> I have enjoyed working with you and welcome the opportunity to continue our work together. If you have any questions, I am happy to help.
>
> Warmly,
> Health Coach Name
> Health Coach Contact Info

Do not let what you cannot do interfere with what you can do.

—John Wooden

CHAPTER 20:

ADDITIONAL PROGRAM OPTIONS

There are several other career options for Health Coaches other than personal or group coaching sessions. A few of these include leading workshops, teleclasses, public speaking engagements, cooking classes, health food store tours, and monthly seminars. You also have the option of working with a younger population—children or teenagers. We provide you with resources for whichever option you choose. This chapter details some of the suggested steps to take and suggestions to help support you. If you are ever feeling overwhelmed when planning a workshop or teleclass, please refer to this section. And as always, keep referring back to the Golden Path for continual guidance.

WORKSHOPS

Leading workshops is an excellent way to get clients. It is also a great opportunity for you to strengthen your presentation skills. Teaching topics related to health and nutrition can help you increase your confidence, learn more about interesting topics, and be perceived as an expert in the field of health and wellness.

In the beginning, aim for getting five to ten people to your workshop. As you build your public speaking skills and expand your business, you can lead workshops for increasingly more people. The idea is to attract the types of people who you want as clients. You can present at community centers, libraries, health food stores, women's groups, schools, universities, health centers, wellness centers, gyms, and even your own home.

When you approach a new location about doing a workshop, it is always helpful to visit the location in person, introduce yourself, and ask who is in charge of programs

Notes:

or scheduling. Indicate that you are looking to volunteer to do workshops to help the organization. Give them your elevator speech and ask, "I really love/appreciate the work you're doing here. How can I help support you by bringing in more people to this location and offering my expertise to the community you serve?" Play the role of a Health Coach. Make the workshop a win-win situation for both you and the location.

We suggest that you bring your press kit with you when visiting potential workshop spaces. You can include an outline of your proposed workshop in the press kit, along with a full page of positive feedback you have collected from participants at past workshops (if you have this).

WORKSHOP MARKETING

You don't have a workshop unless you have participants, so marketing your workshop is essential. The following are ways to promote your workshop:

- Post flyers at key locations: health food stores, community centers, bookstores, and other locations where your potential target market spends time.
- Tell everyone you know about the workshop—clients, friends, family, and colleagues. Have them tell people and offer them a referral incentive. You could have them send out the invitation to their entire mailing list. An important point to keep in mind is to touch base with as many people as possible who are connected to your target market. Find those who already have a pre-existing contact list of qualified candidates.
- Send an email announcement to your contact list.
- Promote the workshop in your newsletter.
- Invite people from the organization where you are giving the workshop. Encourage them to post the event on their announcement board or in their newsletter.
- Have your referral partners send out information about your event to their contacts. You can send them a pre-written version of the Direct Sales Email Template, so it's easy for them to help you out.
- Go to other events and make yourself known. Hand out flyers at expositions, social gatherings, health fairs, and similar events.
- Post on websites—your website, your referral partners' websites, and community or event websites frequented by your target market.
- Send out invitations using social media.
- Take out an ad in a publication that your target market reads.
- Place an announcement in the events listing section of local newspapers or newsletters.

Ask people to sign up for your workshop in advance so that you know who is coming. You can do this by having them RSVP to you or the location that is hosting your workshop.

Notes:

How to Promote Your Programs—Email Template: Use this template to help craft your email to promote an upcoming program or product. Be sure to tweak the language so that it sounds natural and your own voice shines through. Making it your own will more accurately represent you and your brand.

Subject:

Subject Line

Make sure to create a catchy subject line that will grab attention, so that people actually open the email.

Examples:

Are you tired of always being tired?

Reducing your stress is just a moment away!

This program is going to change your life!

Email Body

The following formula will help you present engaging content, allowing the reader to connect with you and know that you understand his/her problems. This will encourage them to take the next steps.

1. Greeting.

Use the person's first name if possible.

Example: Dear (name),

2. Ask a question.

Have the person think about something in their life that relates to what you are promoting in your email.

Example: Are you tired of always feeling tired? Do you wish you had more energy than you can handle?

3. State the benefits.

Make a bulleted list of what people will get from your special offer.

Example: Are you ready to:

- Have more energy than you can handle?
- Understand why you crave sugar?
- Learn to sleep soundly all night?

4. State the program/offering.

Showcase how you want the person to take action. You may want them to attend a course, sign up for a session, or purchase a product.

Example: My upcoming course, "Permanently Re-energize Your Life," is going to permanently change how much energy you have every day. In this course you'll learn . . . It all starts on December 7th, at 8:00 p.m. ET, at (location).

Continued

Notes:

How to Promote Your Programs—Email Template (Continued)

Subject:

5. Ask for commitment.

It's important to tell the person how they can take you up on the offer. Be clear and offer some incentives. You could offer a discount if they sign up by X date, mention that there are only X spots left, or they get a free bonus if they register by X date.

> Example: Are you ready to have more energy than you can handle? If so, you don't want to miss out. You can register for the course at (email, website address, phone number). Your investment is only $97 if you register by November 19 (then the price goes up to $147). Don't miss this opportunity!

6. Make a bold statement.

Remind them again that this is a chance they don't want to miss and remind them again how they can participate.

> Example: Remember, this class will teach you all that you need to know to stop feeling tired, eat foods you actually enjoy, and feel great in your body. Permanently. Don't miss out! There are only 10 spaces available. Are you ready? Please (visit this link, email me here).

7. Closing.

Offer your commitment and encouragement.

> Example: I look forward to working with you in this (course, class, consultation, program) and am completely committed to all of the positive results you'll accomplish.

To your success,
(Your name)

If you have people RSVP to the location, be sure to give the location a sign-up sheet that they can use to keep track of your participants, including names, telephone numbers, and email addresses, as well as how they heard about your workshop. This is helpful for future marketing efforts.

WORKSHOP & TELECLASS PROMOTION SUCCESS STRATEGIES

When promoting your workshops and teleclasses by email, it's important to realize that your contacts need to hear from you multiple times. Since most people are busy with their daily lives, you need to be in touch repeatedly to have them take notice and see

Notes:

the benefit of coming to your event. Here is a quick and easy timeline for promoting your events:

Email # 1: Send three to five weeks before your event. You can use the How to Promote Your Programs—Email Template we provide in this chapter.

Email # 2: Send two weeks before your event. Keep the excitement going, and let people know what they can look forward to and how to register.

Email # 3: Send one week before your event. Talk about how many people have registered, how excited everyone is, and that you hope they can join you because they will get so much out of it.

Email # 4: Send one day before the event. Let them know this is the last chance to register. You can even say things like "there are only three spaces left" or if you are charging, "this is the last day to receive the $(amount) savings." Always remind them how they will benefit and how to register.

Email # 5: Send this email the day before the event to people who signed up to remind them of the event details.

You may have some concerns about being "pushy" and wonder if this is too many emails to send. People are busy and need to be reminded and motivated to attend. You may want to post reminders on Facebook, Twitter, and any other social networking site you use. If you don't do this consistently, it will be more difficult to fill your events Please trust that this works, and follow our recommendations.

PRESENTING THE WORKSHOP

The workshop begins long before the actual start time. Familiarize yourself with the outlines and handouts for giving workshops. If you are creating your own topic, you can use our format to design your new workshop.

When preparing for your workshop, make sure you have everything you need, including:

- Workshop outline: You may want to print this out in a large font size so that it is easy for you to read.
- An assistant who will provide support, distribute handouts, and help schedule participants for Health History consultations.
- Your business cards.
- A sign-in sheet for everyone at the workshop.
- A sign-up sheet for Health History consultations with time/day slots that you are available—prepare this before the workshop by referencing your calendar to find times when you can do the sessions.
- Handouts related to your talk.
- Snacks/food to give out (fruit, trail mix, simple treats).
- A watch, clock, or cell phone to keep track of time.

Notes:

WORKSHOP CLOSING

This is the time to bring it all together and invite attendees to a consultation. You should save plenty of time for this important section.

Before you start the final paired/group share, say something like: "Before we close the workshop, I have a special gift for all of you. And before I talk about that I'd like you to turn to your partner and share something that you learned or found helpful in this workshop."

After the group share, say the following types of things:

- I appreciate you for taking action to be here tonight, because making changes in life comes from taking action.
- I love my work as a Health Coach, because I support my clients to reach their individual goals such as weight loss, having more energy, less stress, better relationships, etc.
- I not only support them with their food choices, but also with their lifestyle choices to make sure we address the whole picture so they can be successful long term.
- I help them make step-by-step, individualized, easily integrated changes, so that they stay on track and reach their goals permanently.
- We have lots of fun in my programs, and I work with both individuals and groups.

Then share the "call to action":

- I again appreciate you for coming tonight, and I know I can't possibly cover everything in one (evening, afternoon) that you need to know to work on (workshop topic). So as a special gift for each of you to stay on track, and not just think about what we discussed here, but to finally take steps and do something about it, I am inviting all of you to a free initial consultation with me.
- During this consultation, we will discuss your goals and the things you'd like to accomplish and have always imagined for your life. We'll also talk about how you are possibly getting in your own way.
- In addition, you'll have the opportunity to learn about how I can support you in one of my programs to permanently reach your goals.
- Who is interested in scheduling a consultation with me?

Then, direct them to your assistant who has your schedule. Or, if doing a teleclass, give them the link to your online scheduling system or tell them your email and phone number so they can reach you to schedule the session. Give them a deadline by which they should contact you.

Notes:

OTHER WORKSHOP TIPS

1. Share information about yourself and your challenges, so they can relate to you. Be sure not to talk about yourself the whole time; share stories as appropriate.
2. Use humor and make it fun. This helps the audience relax and feel safe.
3. Bring props—for example, you can bring an empty Snapple bottle, filled up with the equivalent amount of sugar. You could also do the same with a yogurt container or a bottle of soda. Every 4 sugar grams on the nutrition label equals 1 teaspoon of sugar. For example, if there are 24 grams of sugar per serving, that equals 6 teaspoons of sugar per serving (24g divided by 4g = 6 tsp). Remember that a 16-oz. bottle would be two serving sizes, so that would equal 12 tsp of sugar in this example! You could even bring in a cookie box to show them the hidden sugars on the ingredient list. Or bring a box of sugar, and ask the participants how many pounds they think the average person consumes each year (some estimate the amount to be over 160 lbs per person per year!).
4. Don't give it all away; the point of the workshop is to get them in touch with their challenges and the negative way their food choices are affecting their lives.
5. Make the workshop interactive; do some writing exercises about goals or other pertinent topics.
6. Make references to your work. For example, "This is the kind of thing I support my clients with in my 6-month program."
7. Share client success stories and examples that relate to the topic at hand. This helps them realize you've helped others, so you can help them too.
8. Do some group shares; ask them, "How do you relate to this?"
9. Stop for a stand and stretch break; let them loosen up their tension.
10. Remember that the workshop/teleclass is a prelude to a Health History or other program you are promoting. Make sure you collect their emails when they sign up and put everyone on your newsletter list.

FOLLOW-UP

- Send thank-you emails to participants; appreciate them for their time.
- Add everyone's contact information to your mailing list.
- Send a confirmation email to Health History registrants to remind them of their session time.
- Email a handout related to the content of your workshop to each participant. When you give something extra after the workshop, participants see you as a valuable and knowledgeable support person.

Notes:

TOP 10 WAYS TO GET CLIENTS FROM YOUR LECTURES

1. **Make sure the audience knows what you do.** Talk about your program during the talk. Offer Health Histories. Often people do not sign up for a consultation because they have never been asked. Leave time at the end to mingle and answer questions.
2. **Bring an assistant.** Your assistant can sign people in, collect contact information, and schedule Health Histories, so you can interact with participants in a professional manner. Consider bringing a client who's willing to share the benefits of working with you.
3. **Collect useful contact information.** Have participants sign in and add their email address. Invite them to sign up for your newsletter, so that you stay on their radar. When they think of nutrition and wellness, they will think of you.
4. **Make sure attendees know how to contact you after the lecture.** Put a flyer, business card, and/or your contact sheet/bio on each person's chair. It gives them something to read when they arrive and will help them learn more about your work. Get used to giving out your flyers and business cards like hotcakes.
5. **Make your talk interactive.** Don't talk at your audience; talk to your audience. Encourage interactive elements such as paired shares, group shares, and group exercises. People love to talk and should be included in the workshop process.
6. **Tell client success stories.** For example, "When one of my clients, a busy mother of three, came to me, she was totally hooked on sugar. These days, after adding some of the tools I described, she is much more energized." Clarify what the problem was and describe how you helped that person. This presents you as a credible problem solver. If you do not have clients, share how you've helped yourself overcome your own health concerns.
7. **Do a mini-coaching demo in front of the class.** This establishes your credibility and expertise and gives participants an idea of your coaching style. If they like what they see, they will be inspired to sign up with you.
8. **Invite attendees to a Health History.** After you give them details about your program and services, be sure to invite them to a free one-hour consultation with you. We know we've mentioned this already, but it is so important that we're saying it again!
9. **Provide a valuable giveaway.** Share a useful tip that attendees can refer to often. Give away a favorite recipe that's related to your talk, a tip sheet, special report, or article. Perhaps they will pass it on to someone who is interested or simply think of you when they use it. Include your contact information at the bottom.
10. **Circulate an evaluation form (optional).** This will allow you to get feedback on your talk. Ask what attendees liked/learned and what future topics they would like to explore. Ask if they would like to learn more about one-on-one health coaching, and include space for a phone number and an email address.

Notes:

PUBLIC SPEAKING

OVERCOMING NERVOUSNESS

You might be nervous about giving a workshop. That's completely normal. Public speaking often requires you to "feel the fear and do it anyway." Many of our students become comfortable and confident public speakers, and for some it becomes their favorite aspect of this work. You will also find that your confidence grows in other areas of your life through public speaking. A whole range of tasks and situations that you once found intimidating will no longer create the same level of fear. Here are some helpful tips on overcoming the fear of public speaking.

Prepare: The more you prepare, the more comfortable you will be with your workshop. Write an agenda of what you intend to talk about. Consider the objectives of your workshop. What do you want your audience to get out of it? For example, you may want them to leave your workshop with an ability to identify hidden sugars in foods. You will likely want them to sign up for a Health History consultation with you. Once you know your objectives, you can create an agenda to meet those objectives. Your agenda becomes a road map. When you create your agenda, think about how much time you will allot to each topic, as well as how you will conduct that part of the workshop (e.g., a lecture versus a paired share or group activity), and any materials or handouts you will need.

Here is a template that you can use to create a workshop agenda:

WORKSHOP AGENDA

What you will cover	How	Timing	Materials needed

Notes:

Breathe: One of the best things you can do to stay grounded and focused when leading a workshop is to breathe. Use the paired shares and group shares as a time for you to check in with yourself and make sure you are breathing and relaxed.

Start small: If you are very nervous about leading a workshop, you may want to start small. You can invite three or four friends over for a workshop in your home. You can practice with them and ask them for feedback, what you did well and what you could improve. Realize that everyone wants you to be successful. Everyone who comes to your workshop is there because they want to learn from you and have a positive experience. They are on your side and want the workshop to go well just as much as you do. Understanding this (and believing it!) will go a long way toward helping you relax into your role as the workshop facilitator.

TELECLASSES

If many of your clients are phone clients, you may want to offer your monthly seminars as teleclasses. You can schedule an hour-long teleclass each month. Topics can range from cooking tips to Sugar Blues to Eating for Energy. Almost anything that can be taught in person can also be taught on the phone. Record your call and make it available for people to listen to afterward.

Even if your clients are local and you hold in-person seminars, teleclasses are a low-cost, convenient way to expand your business and spread the word about your company. There are many free or low-cost companies you can use to set up a teleclass. You may schedule your teleclass on www.instantteleseminar.com or www.freeconference.com. They each have services to record your call.

We recommend doing teleclasses for free at first while getting a sense of what does and doesn't work. Once you feel comfortable, you may charge. Typically, coaches charge anywhere from $19 to $29 per class. Keep in mind that you may raise your rates as you gain more experience. You will need to be set up to accept credit cards in order to receive payments for teleclasses.

You can use sites like www.paypal.com or www.directpayinc.com to collect fees. In the future, you may also want to use a shopping cart system such as www.cartville.com. This automates the process, and helps to create consistent systems as you grow your business. All you need is a phone, headset, and a computer.

REASONS TO LEAD A TELECLASS

- Access to potential clients from the comfort of your home, with no travel time required.
- Access people who can refer you to potential clients.

Notes:

- Build credibility with potential clients.
- Deepen relationships with existing clients.
- Reduce your marketing budget (no costs for space or materials).
- Get known for being an expert.
- Talk with people who want to hear what you have to say.
- Get more participation since shy people can speak up.
- Test new material and ideas.

WAYS TO PROMOTE YOUR TELECLASS

- Send an invitation to every contact on your mailing list.
- Mention your upcoming teleclass to in-person participants at your workshops.
- Promote in your newsletter: list the topic description and how to register for the class.
- Have referral partners and colleagues mention the teleclass to their contact groups and/or list the class in their newsletter.
- Promote your class on websites that your target market visits.
- Post your class on Facebook, Twitter, your blog, and any other social networking sites you use.
- Place a classified listing (free or low-cost) in a periodical that your target market frequently reads.
- Begin your marketing at least three to five weeks before the actual date, to make sure you have as many callers as possible.
- Mention the benefits of the class in your promotions, and be clear about what the participants will get out of it. Also tell them how to register for the class (email or link on your website), and give them a deadline to do so.

HOW TO DEVELOP A TELECLASS

- Brainstorm topics and decide on the content you want to deliver.
- Design your outline and stages of your talk.
- Decide whom you would like to invite to your teleclass.
- Determine how you will market the teleclass.
- Pick a day and time.
- Schedule the class.
- Decide if you would like to charge for the class (we recommend doing no-fee classes at first, to build your contacts and experience).
- Set up the conference call line.
- Invite participants. Include the day and time of the talk, as well as a class description.

Notes:

- Send the call-in number and access code to enrolled participants. They can enroll by sending you an email confirming their interest, or you can have them register through a platform like Instant Teleseminar. If you are charging a fee, send them the link for payment.
- Send out reminders one or two days before the talk.
- Practice your talk beforehand.
- You can use a professional service to record your teleclass. This allows participants to revisit your class and gives you the option to make the recording available for those who were unable to attend the live session. You may even decide to offer a link to your class recording on your website.

STAGES OF TELECLASS CURRICULUM

- Introduction: warmly welcome everyone to your talk.
- Share your excitement and a personal story about you, and relate that story to your talk.
- Tell them what to expect from the call, reviewing the bullet points of your outline.
- Remind them of the class protocol: pay attention, mute phone when not speaking, limit potential distractions.
- Start your talk, following the outline you created.
- Do a group share in the middle of the talk to check in around topic content or to see if there are questions.
- Summarize what you talked about in the call.
- Near the end, thank them for their attention.
- Allow a Q&A session, depending on the time remaining.
- Offer an invitation to a Health History consultation. Tell the participants that you are offering this as a special bonus to call participants. If they would like to set up a time, tell them they can call or email you. You can also say that you will send everyone an email after the call to clarify what the Health History is and how to schedule one.
- You can also use your teleclass to promote any other services, including a group program or other items unique to your practice.
- Send them a special handout, article, or other gift after the class.
- Follow up with the email Health History invitation, including your website, contact information, and a client testimonial or case study.
- Respond to those who contact you.

Take some time to sit down and think about setting up a workshop or teleclass. What topics are of interest to you? Where would you be able to conduct a workshop? Who would you invite to attend? Feel free to map out these thoughts by answering the

Notes:

following questions. This should help you get started and motivate you to expand your skills and build your practice.

List five topics you feel comfortable talking about in public:

1. ....
2. ....
3. ....
4. ....
5. ....

List five places in your area you could conduct a workshop at (e.g., YMCA, local gym, school, coworking office, etc.):

1. ....
2. ....
3. ....
4. ....
5. ....

COOKING CLASSES

Depending on your level of comfort in the kitchen, you may decide to offer monthly cooking classes. Teaching your clients that cooking healthy meals is easy and fun can improve people's lives dramatically. Many people think that cooking takes hours of hard work. They don't realize that it can be a simple and rewarding activity. Please note that even if you do not have a lot of experience cooking, you can still teach a successful cooking class. It's okay to show your clients that you are not an expert, but that cooking wholesome and nutritious food can be easy. An outline and guidelines for conducting a cooking class are located in the Teaching Classes Resources.

HEALTH FOOD STORE TOUR

Many people are intimidated by the various products that appear on the shelves of a health food store, so they buy organic or healthier versions of the packaged food sold in the regular grocery store. Some of your clients may have never stepped foot in a health food store. Scout out the best one in your area and introduce yourself to the manager. Give the manager your business card, explain that you are a Health Coach and that part of your program involves giving your clients a tour of a health food store. Let the manager know how many people you would like to bring on the tour, and that you intend

Notes:

it to last about 90 minutes. Explain that you will be encouraging your clients to buy products after the tour and to come back to do their shopping in the future. Most stores will be very welcoming. See if the manager can agree to offer your clients discounts on the day of the tour. Agree on a date and time with the manager and thank them.

Some of your clients may want a private tour. If this is the case, you can always substitute a health food store tour for one of their sessions. An outline and guidelines for conducting a tour are available in the Teaching Classes Resources.

MONTHLY SEMINARS

You can also offer monthly seminars on other health-related topics, such as a Sugar Blues or an Eating for Energy talk for your current clients. You can customize seminars to fit the needs of your target market. For example, if you work with corporate clients, you may want to do a stress reduction seminar. If most of your clients are busy moms, you can do a seminar on fun snacks for kids. The options are endless. These seminars are your opportunity to explore topics that are interesting to you, while also providing your clients with additional education and inspiration.

ADDITIONAL MONTHLY SEMINAR IDEAS

- **Create abundance**
  –Identify limiting beliefs about moneymaking
  –Collage about what participants want to create in their lives
  –Set new intentions about money
- **Create a healthy home environment**
  –Clear clutter
  –Learn organizational tips
  –Clear negative energy (incense/smudging/salt/music)
- **Fast/cleanse**
  –Healthy ways to cleanse
  –Different forms of cleanses and fasts
  –What time of year to cleanse (usually springtime)
- **Natural beauty**
  –Make-your-own face scrubs
  –Eat for healthy nails, skin, and hair
  –Learn anti-aging information
- **Slow down for good digestion**
  –Benefits of stress-free mealtimes
  –Create a positive eating environment
  –Chewing practice or chewing meditation

Notes:

- **Stay healthy through the holidays**
  - –Manage family stress
  - –Gift exemption
  - –Importance of exercise
- **Time management**
  - –Identify goals, desires, and priorities
  - –Work smarter, not harder (to-do lists/scheduling tips/delegating)
  - –Set boundaries for time management
- **Dietary theories: Ayurveda, Blood Type Diet, etc.**
  - –Quizzes to identify type
  - –Food and lifestyle recommendations
  - –Choose three components of this theory to incorporate into diet or lifestyle

You can also offer seminars that address common health concerns. Your clients are probably hearing about these and could use some education and support. Health seminar topics could include:

- IBS
- Allergies
- Diabetes
- Heart disease
- Cold and flu season
- Men's health issues
- Women's health issues

GUEST SPEAKERS

A great way to add benefit to your program while reducing your own workload is to invite guest speakers to your seminars. Do you know someone with their own business who can offer expert advice and demonstrate their services for your clients? They would probably be happy to speak in front of a new audience, and your clients would be thrilled to hear them. Guests will often speak for free in exchange for being allowed to give their marketing materials to your clients. Possible guest speakers include:

- Chiropractors
- Acupuncturists
- Personal trainers
- Natural foods chefs
- Massage therapists
- Skin care consultants
- Meditation instructors
- Personal finance experts

Notes:

- Yoga or Pilates instructors
- Vitamin and supplement experts

Start by creating an outline for your seminar. Figure out what you want to say. Then use the outline for Sugar Blues or Eating for Energy to help you organize your information. Leave at least 20 minutes at the end for your clients to ask questions and get support to make specific changes based on what they just learned. Practice helping your clients support one another. You can have them do paired shares or assign buddies to check each other's progress.

SCHEDULING YOUR MONTHLY SEMINARS

Scheduling can become the most complex component of your monthly seminars. When you have only two or three clients, you may try to work around their schedules, but as your client base grows this will likely be impossible. We recommend that you pick a day of the week that works best for you, and tell your clients when they sign up that your monthly seminars are always on that day, for example, "My monthly seminars are always held on the first Monday of the month. I hope you will be able to take advantage of them!"

WORKING WITH CHILDREN

Working with young people can be extremely rewarding. Getting five-year-olds to eat kale on a regular basis is an incredible accomplishment because their lives will turn out completely different than if they were to grow up eating McDonald's and Doritos. If you enjoy the company of children and you would like to incorporate them into your client base, go for it! You can work with them just as you would with any other client. Simply use the Children's Health History form provided by the school to get started.

Don't underestimate children. They are often more open to change and new foods than adults give them credit for. Because they have not been alive as long, children do not have as many habits built up as adults do. Also, they are often more in touch with their bodies and surroundings than adults. With the right support, children have strong instincts about how to get themselves well. Spend a good amount of time at the start of your program building rapport and connection. This is critical because it makes your child client feel safe enough to open up to you. Ask great questions, lead them gently, and allow them to trust you. Be encouraging and show them you understand their situation. Treat them with respect, make them feel special, and let them know that you are truly listening.

Children are spontaneous. You may need to shorten your sessions or incorporate movement and stretch breaks in order to keep their attention and focus. You don't want their time with you to feel too serious.

IDEAS FOR ADDING FUN TO YOUR SESSIONS

- Lead them on a kid-friendly health food store tour.
- Let them come up with their own recommendations.
- Make kid-friendly food together, such as ice pops or "ants on a log."
- Meet somewhere unexpected, such as a playground, or sit on pillows on your office floor.
- Bring in food, giveaways, and other props for them to touch, look at, taste, and discover.
- Give them stickers and different-colored pens to use in their food journal and notebook.

Keep in mind that it often takes children three tries to like a new food. The first time it is usually too new, the second time they still don't like it, and the third try their taste buds usually come around. So be patient with them.

Depending on the age of your child client, the parent may play a major role in the program. In some cases a parent may sit in on sessions. During the Health History, determine how involved the parent will be and make sure everyone is on the same page. When working with children ages 12 and under, you will want the parents to be involved. They should sign the Program Agreement form before you begin working with the child. Give parents copies of all the handouts so they understand the work their child is doing with you. It's also good if you provide the parents with recipes and bring them along on the health food store tour, which will help them to become more aware of how to incorporate healthier foods into the household.

Some graduates who work with children have every other session with the parent and every other session with the child. This way they get to work with the parent on how to balance their life while raising a child. They teach the parent better cooking techniques and support the parent in setting a healthy example. In the sessions with the child, the coach introduces healthy snack foods, talks about the food-mood connection, and discusses primary food.

TEENAGE CLIENTS

Teenagers usually respond very well to working with Health Coaches. Most seek adults who they can confide in and look up to. If you are interested in working with teenagers, you can begin by offering workshops at high schools and teen camps. If your goal is to sign up clients for a 6-month program, we recommend you also invite the parents to the workshops because they are the ones who are going to pay for and probably drive the teenager to see you. You want to show the parents your professionalism and the potential health benefits for their child. Having parental support and encouragement will greatly increase your teen clients' satisfaction and success in your program.

Notes:

CHILDREN'S HEALTH HISTORY

PLEASE WRITE OR PRINT CLEARLY

Name: ....

Address: ....

Telephone: .... Email: ....

Age: .... Birthday: .... Place of Birth: ....

Height: .... Weight: .... Grade: ....

Why did you come for this Health History? ....

....

Do you enjoy school? Please explain: ....

....

Do you have a large or small group of friends? ....

Who is your best friend? ....

....

What do you do for fun? ....

....

What is your favorite sport or activity? ....

....

What are fun things you do with family? ....

....

What are your favorite things to do when you are alone? ....

....

What chores do you do around the house? ....

....

When is bedtime? .... When do you wake up? ....

Do you ever wake up at night? .... Do you ever have nightmares? ....

Do you get bellyaches? .... Do you get headaches or earaches? ....

Is it hard to see or read? .... Do you get itchy? ....

Do you have allergies or sensitivities? ....

....

Does anything else hurt? ....

....

What do you eat for breakfast? ....

What do you eat for lunch? ....

What do you eat for dinner? ....

What do you eat for snacks? ....

What do you drink? ....

What foods do you wish you could eat more often? ....

....

What food do you wish you never had to eat again? ....

....

What do you want to learn about your body and about food? ....

....

Anything else you want to say? ....

....

Teens react well to being granted greater responsibility and being treated like adults, so the parents of your teenage clients often don't need to be closely involved in the 6-month program. When signing the Program Agreement, make it clear that your sessions will be between you and the teenager only. As a bonus, you could invite the parent to attend the monthly seminars as a guest of your teenage client. You can find a Health History form for teens in the Health History Resources.

If the teenager shares information with you that could affect their safety or the safety of others, it is imperative that you support your client by telling their parents. Examples of this include drug use, suicidal comments, violent tendencies, and eating disorders. If your client refuses to tell their parents, you must inform them yourself. Telling their parents the truth will ultimately help your clients to overcome their struggles.

Have any of these program options intrigued you? Workshops, teleclasses, cooking classes, health food store tours, monthly seminars, working with children or teenagers?

....

....

If so, which one(s)?

....

....

What are your next steps?

....

....

....

Choose a job you love, and you will never have to work a day in your life.

—Confucius

CHAPTER 21:

BEYOND HEALTH COACHING

GETTING OUT OF YOUR OWN WAY

Often it is very easy for us to think about how we are "not good enough," and we wonder if we have what it takes to be successful in business. Our inner critic likes to tell us that we have faults or that other people know more than we do. It's important to recognize this inner voice, and take steps to lessen its potential effect on you. If you listen to your doubts, or if you let your fears get in the way, you may not take the steps needed to attain the success you truly desire. If you are able to catch the negative thought patterns and then recognize that they truly have no power over you, you can move forward more easily.

When you stop to think about it, you will understand that you have a lot to offer your friends, family, clients, and yourself, by being a Health Coach. Use these steps to help you minimize any limiting beliefs before they sabotage your efforts:

- When a fear or negative thought comes up, stop and recognize that the thought is there. Take a deep breath, and notice how you feel.
- Check in with yourself, and notice that the thought only has power over you if you allow it to.
- Ask yourself, "Do I know for sure that this thought is true?" or "What is the worst that can happen if I take this action?"
- Focus on turning your negative thought around and choose a different thought that causes you less anxiety or fear.
- Figure out how to believe in yourself and keep your mind focused on your goals.

Notes:

- Take step-by-step actions toward your goals and don't let your fears hold you back.
- Keep practicing, continue this process, and trust yourself.

CREATING A BUSINESS MIND

As you learn the skills needed to build your practice, it's important to cultivate your mindset. Believe it or not, once you begin this work, you own a business, whether you end up doing health coaching full-time or part-time or launching a product or program. As such, you'll need to start thinking like a business owner. Consider what it will take for you to be successful, how you will talk about your work, how you will project confidence, how you will structure your time, and how you will present a professional image to the world.

Start practicing what it is like to be more professional and concise in your emails and in conversations, especially when you talk about your training at the school. Ask yourself, "How would a successful businessperson behave in this situation?" Focus on building your confidence and trust that you know enough to try the marketing tips you'll learn in this book and through the other curriculum components. And most importantly, take action every week toward building your business.

CAREER OPTIONS BEYOND HEALTH COACHING

Students come to the school with a variety of intentions. Most of you want to practice as a Health Coach, but some of you have other ambitions. There may even be a few of you that aren't sure how you will use your training. That's okay—we will help you clarify how to best use your education and natural skills. While searching your soul for the answer, use these questions to guide your exploration:

What are some areas you are interested in?

....

....

....

What is your dream job?

....

....

....

Notes:

What is your previous professional experience?

....

....

....

How comfortable are you working with people?

....

....

....

Can you combine your holistic training with your current profession?

....

....

....

We encourage you to take a deep look at your interests, strengths, personality type, previous experience, and goals to determine what career is best for you. We can support you in careers beyond health coaching and offer a few suggestions of popular careers here.

WRITING AND PUBLISHING A BOOK

Do you want to combine your passion for writing and health and become a published author? Or maybe you have a great story, solution, or healthy recipes to share. Writing a book can be a great way to get your message to the masses. Writing a book can also build more credibility so you can generate income in other ways like public speaking, workshops, and your coaching services.

According to Michael Ellsberg, author and book proposal writer, "nothing in the world increases your credibility as an expert as having a book to your name . . . and you will be able to leverage that indirectly to increase your income enormously."

A published book can also serve as a brochure. Traditional brochures can still serve a purpose in any business, but consumers have become overwhelmed with information. Stand out to them by offering a book you authored on a topic in your field.

Michael explains, "If you demonstrate that you are the greatest expert in your field by showing your knowledge and your insight and giving case studies and histories and anecdotes and all the rest that goes into creating a great book, people are naturally going

Notes:

to draw that conclusion." Becoming a resource to your audience allows them to get to know you and build trust in you.

HOW TO GET PUBLISHED

There are two main ways to get published:

1. Traditional publishing
2. Self-publishing

Traditional Publishing

Using a traditional publishing route requires an agent and a publisher. A typical relationship with a publisher supplies an advance to the author against future royalties. Royalties are generally around 10 percent to the author, 40 percent to the retailer, and 50 percent to the publisher. The publisher takes care of production costs, editing, cover design, interior layout, copyediting, PR, distribution, and listing with an ISBN identifier.

Even if you have a fantastic book idea, it can be difficult to get the attention of an agent, representation by a publisher, and get an advance. Competition is so fierce that publishers no longer accept unsolicited manuscripts submissions, which is a direct submission from the author. This responsibility is now outsourced to literary agents. Literary agents take 15 percent of any money you receive from a project. Literary agents are very particular about the projects they take on since they invest their own energy and time into a project.

To get noticed by an agent, you will need a unique angle on your topic. It also helps to have a large platform or following already, like public speaking notoriety, a massive email list, or have an established celebrity presence. To develop a unique angle, Ellsberg suggests these two questions:

"What group is there out there that doesn't have a book yet focused on health and wellness for them or what angle? What aspect of health and wellness has yet to be written about?"

To begin the process, you'll need to write a book proposal. For more information, please refer to the Reference Library class, *Get Published Now*.

Self-Publishing

New print-on-demand technology has made self-publishing much more accessible to authors and for the product to look as credible as a book from a major publisher. Now, instead of investing thousands of dollars for an advanced print run of 3,000 or 5,000 books, you can print smaller batches at the same printing quality.

Self-publishing works well in two circumstances, according to Ellsberg:

1. You are unable to attract an agent or publisher.
2. You have a strong platform already established and can sell your books at events or online.

Notes:

When approaching a company for print-on-demand services, you can choose to design your own cover and the interior layout, or hire a professional graphic designer. With either option, you will submit the files to the printer for a set-up fee, but then the book is ready quickly! (Adapted from Michael Ellsberg, www.ellsberg.com)

Digital Publishing

In addition to hard copy publishing, digital publishing is now a convenient option. Sites like Amazon's Kindle Direct Publishing (https://kdp.amazon.com/self-publishing/signin) allow authors of all levels to quickly and efficiently make their works available to the public. Technology changes frequently, so thoroughly research your options for the programs that work best for you.

While there are many techniques to support every writing style, the most important piece of writing, according to Michael Ellsberg, is to write a little every day. He suggests setting a goal of a number of words or a number of pages, but to strive to commit to writing something each day.

WRITING ARTICLES

Writing articles is a fantastic way to build exposure to your target market and to offer yourself as a resource, rather than only marketing your product or service. Being a knowledge resource allows your target market to build trust in you as an expert. Articles can be written for traditional print publications or online publications.

To make your articles as effective as possible, keep the topic geared to your target market. Solve some of their problems. You don't want to give away all your secrets, but you want to provide resourceful tips. Write about things you enjoy and that provide value to your reader.

Research your target market's needs. Get a feel for what's of interest to your target market. What are people reading about? Where are they struggling? You can find this combing through Facebook, online forums specific to your target market, or just talking to them.

To get started, think about what you will want to write about along with an introduction to a solution. This is called brainstorming. Write down all the things you could talk about in an article, in no particular order, with no restrictions on topics.

Then arrange what you know about each topic into a logical order. Most topics addressing a problem and solution will follow this order:

1. Present the problem. Draw in the reader by identifying with their problem. Ask them questions they can relate to.
2. Set the stage and get them in touch with the fact that they have a concern. Give a little detail about the physiology of the problem. Let them know they aren't alone. Perhaps present statistics if it's appropriate.

Notes:

3. Provide tips to implement. You don't have to give every single solution. Provide three to four main points that can add value. People won't do everything at once, so give them just a little.
4. Summarize the information presented and include a final piece about getting support to make the goal happen.

At the end of each article, include a few lines for your bio explaining that you are a Health Coach and then describe your target market. Within your bio, also include a call to action like signing up for your newsletter or joining a group program or individual program.

Remember to keep your article simple. For instance, "how to" articles are very popular because they are usually very simple and quick to read. In general, keep your articles to a couple of paragraphs with a few bullet points or a list of key points. People frequently skim articles and, most of the time, don't read it word-for-word.

Generally, 500 to 700 words total is the standard length for an article, especially online. If you are writing for a publication, ask them what their standard article length is. Make sure you know their guidelines so that you are in line with what they are looking for.

Articles are usually very informal, so write in a conversational tone and avoid becoming too technical. Remember to spell-check and proofread your work. Consider having someone else proofread your work for grammar and spelling, too.

Titles are usually written after the article is written. Catchy titles get read more than boring ones. Popular techniques to create catchy titles include "How to ______," "10 Ways to Reduce/Increase ________," etc.

Consistency is part of getting your articles read, so keep writing and keep putting them out there. Utilize your newsletters and your blog. Look into online or printed publications that target the same market you want to work with and approach them to use your articles. Writing articles is easy to do and is a great way to get exposure, especially if you are an introverted personality. Articles are mainly a time investment, but can lead to more clients, greater credibility, and a growing practice! (Adapted from Robert Notter, www.bookclientsnow.com)

CREATING A PRODUCT

Many of you will feel called to create a product, whether it's a healthy food product, a new line of green cleaning products, or a cool piece of technology. There is a great need for more healthy products on the market—they just need to be created!

If you want to look into creating a product, the best place to start is by talking with people who have already developed and marketed their own creation. No matter what the product is, there are some basic elements to have in place before rolling it out to the market:

Notes:

1. **Business plan.** Consider funding, legal structure, partners, investors, distribution, and pricing. A business plan can be complex, so reach out for support around this.
2. **Certifications or licenses.** S.C.O.R.E. and the Small Business Administration have resources to guide you in determining what you need to apply for to remain within U.S. legal guidelines.

There are many steps involved in creating a food product that goes far beyond the scope of this workbook. Products are large-scale projects and may require capital from investors or a bank loan. We strongly recommend getting a solid support team of professionals around you to properly guide your decisions throughout the process.

If this is an area you feel a strong calling to get involved in, research your favorite products. What other product would you like your product to be like? Whose business philosophy do you admire? What type of stores would you like to carry your product? We encourage you to start talking to people in the industry. Start networking. Research and interview other entrepreneurs. Utilize tools from local governments for small businesses and like-minded communities.

Do you want a business partner? What are your strengths and weaknesses? Where is your experience? What type of person do you need to fill in where you're less experienced? How many partners do you need? Again, talk to people who have traveled that road and can give seasoned advice on victories, regrets, and "I wish I had known . . ."

The end product can be extremely satisfying, but requires patience, stamina, and consistency. Prepare to spend at least a couple years testing, researching, and budgeting. This is where a structured goals plan and time management system become necessary. This may seem like a lot of information, but do not get overwhelmed. If this is where your passion lies, set an intention and stick to it. Imagine the gratification of seeing your product on store shelves and in the hands of people all around the world!

GETTING INVOLVED IN SCHOOL FOOD

One area that many of our graduates are involved with is school food. Today people are more aware than ever that sugar, low-quality meals, and junk foods are hurting our children. Parents and community groups are starting to press for more nutritious foods in schools so that our children can be healthier and have a brighter future.

There is a lot of work to do. Schools and parent groups need active support to learn what foods are healthy for their children and how to get nourishing foods into school cafeterias.

WAYS YOU CAN HELP IMPROVE SCHOOL FOOD

- Offer free wellness workshops directly to kids.
- Ask the head of the PTA what is already being done to improve school food.

Notes:

- Offer free wellness workshops to PTA members, school administrators, or concerned parents.
- Find out what your state and local government says about school food and organize a letter-writing campaign.

RESOURCES FOR SUPPORTING THE HEALTHY SCHOOL FOOD MOVEMENT

- www.ecoliteracy.org
- www.healthyschoollunches.org
- www.angrymoms.org (by Integrative Nutrition graduates)

Giving generously to people and organizations that need support can be an important part of fulfilling your vision. The more you understand that the universe supports you to achieve your dreams and to always have enough, the easier it is to share your time, energy, and expertise with others.

EXPAND YOUR CAREER

These are just a few options that have become popular among our graduates in addition to health coaching. There are many unique niches available. We have listed a few specialties to spark the creativity within you!

- Run retreats
- Start a radio show
- Develop a cooking show
- Own a wellness center
- Publish a magazine
- Work in a healthcare setting, such as a hospital or doctor's office
- Consult on corporate wellness
- Be a school food expert or activist
- Partner with sports organizations as a wellness coordinator
- Become a cooking instructor
- Train as a professional chef
- Be a wardrobe therapist/stylist
- Develop a wellness app
- Provide holistic animal maintenance
- Create green products for children
- Provide pre- and postnatal care
- Develop food products
- Manage a holistic business
- Coordinate holistic travel packages
- Create holistic beauty/hair care products and services

Notes:

- Offer holistic dry cleaning services
- Develop green cleaning products
- Produce holistic events
- Write recipes
- Manage a holistic beverage service
- Distribute holistic food
- Own a health food store
- Open an organic restaurant
- Become a food critic
- Manage a nonprofit CSA
- Farm organic food or animals
- Create sustainable food development
- Create multimedia classes
- Provide grocery shopping services

Some of these may sound off-the-wall and some are obvious. The point of the list is to show you the many ways of incorporating your training into a fulfilling career that supports your family, your goals, and your desire to change the world through better health. If becoming a Health Coach does not seem like a good fit for you, spend some time looking at what you can offer instead. There's a perfect career out there waiting for you!

Are you intrigued by the idea of creating a business beyond health coaching? If so, which avenue would you like to pursue?

....

....

....

What do you have to offer your friends, family, colleagues, and community?

....

....

....

What are your next steps?

....

....

....

Only those who risk going too far
can possibly find out how far they can go.
—T.S. Eliot

CHAPTER 22:

ADVANCED COACHING TIPS

You are beginning to know what it feels like to be a Health Coach. You are most likely discovering that health coaching is a highly rewarding undertaking and a lot more interesting than watching television or working at your computer!

The core of our work as Health Coaches is to support our clients on their journey to health and wellness. We are a source of loving encouragement, we share helpful tips, and we guide them to move forward with their goals. There are certain practice parameters that Health Coaches must follow. It is important to follow these parameters in order to successfully practice and make a lasting difference. If you have any questions about these parameters or when to refer someone who needs professional support beyond your abilities, please check in with your Coaching Circle classmates or alert someone at IIN.

In your work with clients, you are going to have some who are gems and some who are more difficult. In this chapter, we provide you with some ideas on how to work successfully with your challenging clients. Even if you enhance your coaching and foster successful relationships with your clients, you may still come across difficult clients, no-shows, or those who want to withdraw mid-program. If any of these situations occur please consult the guidelines in this chapter and reach out for support from your Coaching Circle classmates and Accountability Coach. Step back, take a deep breath, and rely on your intuition to get you through challenging situations.

TIPS FOR SUCCESSFUL CLIENT-COACH RELATIONSHIPS

INCREASE FOODS THAT SUPPORT HEALTH

If you can get your clients to eat more greens, vegetables, whole grains, sweet vegetables, and healthy fats and proteins, you will dramatically change their lives for the better. The

Notes:

food we eat creates our blood and our cells, and it also feeds our thoughts. By supporting your clients to increase their consumption of healthier foods, they will see and feel the improvements. Eventually, unhealthy foods will get crowded out and your clients will be motivated to take their health to the next level.

REDUCE FOODS THAT DON'T SUPPORT HEALTH

As you know, most health conditions will improve with the reduction of meat, milk, sugar, caffeine, and artificial or chemicalized junk food. Work slowly to add healthier options to your clients' diets so that, over time, they can reduce foods that don't support health and energy.

START WITH SECONDARY FOOD, THEN INCORPORATE PRIMARY FOOD

Many Health Coaches have their food figured out. They know what works for them, and how to eat to get the most energy. Sometimes they automatically think everyone else has this figured out as well. These coaches often jump right into primary food issues with their clients, skipping over the incremental education around secondary food. This is not an effective strategy. If you want your clients to experience change in their lives and improved health, the best thing you can do is target their secondary food first. Have them incorporate more leafy greens, whole grains, high-quality protein, and home-cooked food first. Once these foods become part of their regular diet, you can begin to look at the primary food issues that are out of balance and need changing. Without first changing the food that people eat, it is difficult to change their lifestyle choices.

LOVE YOUR CLIENTS

Offer unending encouragement and support, and compliment them often on their progress. You may even want to send them a card or letter in the mail acknowledging how far they have progressed in your program. Remember important details about their lives, such as their pets' and family members' names. Let them know you are happy to be working with them.

LISTEN TO YOUR CLIENTS

Provide your clients with a safe space to talk and be heard. When you are present with clients and are actively listening, you will find that your intuition will guide you during your sessions. Often, the client just wants to talk. Remember, you don't have to solve their problems, but by simply having someone to listen to them, your client will often figure out the answers to their issues.

Notes:

DEFINE CLIENT GOALS

When you begin a health coaching program, it is important to have the client fill out the Goals form, where they clearly define their goals for the program. Clients must first be aware of their present situation and define what they would like to accomplish through working with you. It is also valuable to continually check in with the client around their progress toward these goals. As their program continues, you can create new goals or redefine existing goals.

FOLLOW THE SESSION OUTLINE

We provide you with an outline to use for your sessions. You do not need to follow it word for word, but the outline provides effective direction for you and the client. Review the outline and practice with your Accountability Coach so you are familiar with it, but remember, let the client lead the session.

FOCUS ON THE POSITIVES

Always start your sessions by asking the client what is new and good. Often, people tend to focus only on what is not going well. As you help clients focus on the positive things they are doing and what is good in their lives, they create a space for more good to enter.

HANDOUTS AND GIVEAWAYS

Provide the client with handouts and giveaways (like food samples, books, self-care items, and so on) at each session. We provide you with various handouts that you can use in the Client Handout Library.

TWO OR THREE RECOMMENDATIONS PER SESSION

End your sessions with two or three simple recommendations that the client can work on until your next session. Remember, it is important not to overwhelm the client with too much work, and you should always go at a pace that is comfortable for the client.

ASK QUESTIONS

Ask clients high mileage questions to get them thinking. You don't need to come up with all of the answers to your clients' problems. After all, they know more about their lives than you do. Presented with the appropriate questions, clients will figure out so much on their own. After you ask the question, give them time to respond and come up with their own conclusions. Here are some sample questions you might ask:

Notes:

- "How is that working for you?"
- "What do you think you should do?"
- "What do you think you should eat?"
- "Who can you turn to for more support?"
- "Why do you think you are feeling this way?"

HELP YOUR CLIENT GET SUPPORT

Encourage your clients to get support outside of your sessions from family, friends, spiritual groups, and other people and activities that encourage connection and community.

PERSONALIZE THE PROGRAM

If you have expertise in other areas related to health, such as yoga, Pilates, or massage, you can incorporate these into your program. Chances are, if there is something that you enjoy doing that has helped to improve your own health and happiness, your clients could benefit from it as well. This could also include things like meditation, art, music, writing, or any other type of creative outlet. Add your personal touches and complement the program with topics specific to each client and their goals.

KEEP TRACK OF CLIENT PROGRESS

Keep track of your clients' progress between each session on the Client Progress form. Remind your clients frequently of what they are accomplishing through working with you.

RESPONSIBILITY

Let your clients take ownership of their health by having them commit to it and be willing to do the work. They will thank you for it.

CREATE A PARTNERSHIP

People usually relate to hired professionals as experts or authority figures, and your clients will most likely relate to you in this way too. Keep in mind that you are working together with your client and that collaboration works best when there are no traditional roles. Get out of the need to claim all the credit or have all the answers.

BE A COMPASSIONATE GUIDE

You don't need to tell your clients everything they should do. Ask them what they want to do or not do in the program. While you are guiding them, you are not healing

Notes:

them but rather they are healing themselves. You should be honored to be a part of the process. You actually help the client more when you are less attached to getting results, which can lead you to get tense and stop breathing deeply. Take deep breaths often during sessions to release attachment.

DEDICATION

Put your focus on the client, what the client wants, and how to help them achieve it. Be committed to clients' goals, outcomes, growth, learning, experimentation, integrity, discovery, and evolution. Try offering new food options and new ideas, and help them understand how to make your suggestions a priority. Remind them that you will support them and hold them accountable, but that they need to be motivated to do the work.

BE GENTLE BUT DEMANDING

Being too soft or nice will not help your clients. Not confronting an issue because it makes you uncomfortable is unfair to the client.

RESPECT DIFFERENCES

Remember your client is not you. Meet your client where they are and do not impose your views on what is nutritionally right. You are probably highly advanced in your own habits because you have been interested in nutrition for quite some time, but not everyone is as in tune with their diet. Let the client set a pace that is comfortable for them. You can give them an extra push, but you need to set them up for success. Go slowly and give them recommendations you know they will follow.

COURTESY

Insist that you are both on time, prepared for sessions, and show up feeling 100 percent committed to the session. Have the client pay on time, don't reschedule appointments, clarify your rescheduling protocol for yourself, and go over your policies with the client, especially if they miss or arrive late to a session.

CLIENT RETENTION

You will want to focus on two aspects of client retention. One is keeping your clients satisfied with the 6-month program, so they don't want to withdraw. The other is resigning clients for another 6-month or maintenance program when their first program is up.

You want each and every one of your clients to be a raving fan of you and your program. You want your clients to be so thrilled about working with you that they tell

Notes:

everyone they know about you and maybe even sign up for a second 6-month program. The happier your clients are with you, the more enjoyable it will be for you to work with them.

The best way to create raving fans is to support your clients on achieving the goals they set forth in the beginning of their program. Be in constant communication about what their goals are and how you can support them to attain these aspirations. To keep your clients happy, it is extremely important that you maintain a high level of professionalism. You should be on time and prepared, stick to your word, send them reminders before each session, and send them notes after each session. You do not want to let your clients down in any way. They depend on you to be their support system, and if you are a day late in doing something that you promised (such as sending an email, an article, or the address of a yoga studio), they will take your lateness to mean that they were not a priority.

As we've mentioned, you need to get the payment from your clients at the beginning of their program. Once the money is out of the way, the sessions have already been paid for in clients' minds. If they have to write you a new check every month or pay you in cash every month, they may question the purchase every time. Getting full payment in advance is crucial to retaining clients.

Make sure your clients feel that their program is customized specifically for them. Provide giveaways that relate to what you've talked about during your sessions. Make recommendations based on their individual circumstances. Send clients notes in the mail to let them know how well they are doing. You may also want to incorporate personalized welcome letters or birthday cards. When the time comes for the giveaway at the end of each session, let them know how it will be helpful for them. Even if it's a tongue cleaner and they have not talked about their dental health, let them know that using a tongue cleaner is a great way to reduce cravings. They will appreciate your thoughtfulness.

These extra touches do not take a lot of your time and will add tremendously to your clients' satisfaction. Take into account that the higher your clients' satisfaction is, the more enjoyable your job will be. If your clients are happy to see you, tell you about how much they love working with you, and spread the word to others, your confidence will grow along with the size of your business and your personal fulfillment.

IDEAL CLIENTS

In the beginning of your career as a Health Coach you will take on different types of clients from various age groups, income levels, and genders. Working with a variety of people will help you discover what type of clients you enjoy most. It will soon become clear which clients energize and inspire you. It is this group of people that you should declare as your ideal clients and build your marketing strategy around.

The clearer you are about the clients with whom you want to work, the easier it will be for you to find them and for them to find you. It is possible to have a thriving

Notes:

Must Have	Preferably Has	Preferably Does Not Have	Must Not Have

part-time or full-time practice working with clients you truly enjoy. You do not need to suffer through working with clients who make your life miserable simply for a paycheck or experience. We encourage you to only take on clients with whom you find pleasure in working.

MY IDEAL CLIENT

In order to attract your ideal client, first identify what that client would be like. Use this chart to get clear about the characteristics and personality traits that you would prefer your clients to have or not have. If you already have one ideal client, you can use that person's qualities as a guide.

Take a moment to look at your ideal client chart every day. As you become more mindful of exactly the client you are looking for, you will notice that type of person showing up more frequently in your life.

DIFFICULT CLIENTS

Working with clients who are difficult will drain your energy and stifle the progress of your practice. Your program is an intimate relationship that is shared for six months. Being in such a relationship with even one client who creates complications can ruin your exhilaration and motivation around being a Health Coach.

Try to identify potentially difficult clients during the Health History, and do not sign them up for your program.

TYPES OF CLIENTS YOU MAY NOT WANT TO WORK WITH

- People who don't show up or come late and make excuses. If they do this from the beginning, they will most likely continue through the entire program.

Notes:

- People who complain over every detail of the program or the Program Agreement. An ideal client is ready and willing to sign up and enjoy your program, but a difficult client has many hesitations.
- People who challenge you and question your abilities. If someone isn't sure they want to work with you, it most likely means they will not be successful in your program.
- People who try to negotiate fees. People who take an inch will often try to take a mile down the road.
- People who don't do the work, resist your guidance, make excuses, or lie.
- People who, for whatever reason, get on your nerves and are difficult to be around. Some people will not be a good fit for you, so let them walk out the door and save yourself the agony.

If someone who fits any of these descriptions comes to an initial Health History, simply complete the Health History form and thank them for coming. Escort them out without explaining your program or the fees. If they ask you about it, you can honestly say that you don't think the two of you would work well together or that your program probably isn't designed to fit their particular needs. You don't need to go into detail about why, just politely send them on their way. You could also refer them to someone else.

If you already have difficult clients, you may choose to discontinue your work with them. You can explain to them that your skill set is not suited to meet their specific needs. Let them know you can provide a referral to another practitioner who is better suited to helping them achieve their goals. While it may be difficult, remain positive and professional as you have this conversation. You can refund their money, prorated for the number of months you worked together, or give them back their post-dated checks. Let them go, and focus your energy on getting more ideal clients.

PREVENTING NO-SHOWS

The absolute best way to prevent no-shows at scheduled sessions is to have your clients pay up-front and to be clear from the beginning about your tardiness and attendance policies. If you do not get paid, either in full with post-dated checks (if they are legal in your state) or with a credit card number up-front, you will send the message to your clients that they do not have to be committed. Let them know that if they don't give you 24-hours cancellation notice, they cannot make up the session.

You should also send a reminder email, or call or text them the day before each session. Confirm the time and place of your appointment and let them know that you look forward to seeing them.

Notes:

WHEN A CLIENT WANTS TO WITHDRAW

There are a few reasons why clients may want to withdraw from your program. The most common grounds include fear, not achieving their expected results, thinking they already know everything, and financial issues.

In most cases, this could happen halfway through your 6-month program. If and when this happens, share with your client that these thoughts are not uncommon. Tell them that many people go through this at the halfway point. Remind them how far they have come. Explain why the program is six months long. Give them the space to express their concerns. Ask them if there is anything that they would like to see happen as you move forward.

You can mention a few things that you see them accomplishing over the next three months, and tell them you look forward to supporting them in making those positive changes. Most people who contemplate withdrawing from your program are really seeking more support.

In special circumstances, you may want to let your client withdraw. If they lost their job and genuinely cannot afford it, if they were diagnosed with a serious illness, or if they are an extremely difficult client, it may be in your best interest to discontinue the program and refund their money for the sessions that have not yet occurred. To prevent withdrawals, stay in constant communication with your clients about their goals and what they hope to achieve through your work together.

FRAUD FACTOR

At this point some of you still might not be seeing clients. Maybe you aren't even telling people that you are a Health Coach. For one reason or another, you may feel you are not equipped to coach others. Maybe you are waiting until you graduate, until you've read all the books, until you've heard all the guest speakers or until your own health is "perfect."

You may be thinking, "Who am I to tell other people what to do around their health?" You may feel like a fraud when you label yourself a professional Health Coach. We call this feeling the "Fraud Factor."

List all the reasons why you feel unequipped to coach people:

1. ....

2. ....

3. ....

4. ....

5. ....

Notes:

Where do these beliefs come from?

1. ....

2. ....

3. ....

4. ....

5. ....

How can you let go of these self-limitations and create new thought patterns centered on your incredible skills and intuition as a Health Coach?

1. ....

2. ....

3. ....

4. ....

5. ....

We are here to tell you that you are not a fraud. You have learned more about health than most of the people on this planet. Your knowledge, along with the tools we provide for you, is enough to help people increase their health and happiness. You do not need to be 100 percent healthy and perfect to be an effective Health Coach. Listen, ask questions, give recommendations, and use the resources available to you.

Now is the time to start seeing clients! Identify what is keeping you from getting out there and sharing what you know and who you are. Is it your busy schedule or low self-esteem? Do you think you don't know enough about nutrition? Use your Coaching Circle classmates and the school to help you overcome these obstacles. This is the time when you will have the most support. This is the year to begin. You have something very valuable to share with people, so get out there and start sharing it!

MAGIC OF MIRRORING

Often, the people who seek your coaching are going through a lot of the same life circumstances you are. We call this the magic of mirroring.

If you are trying to lose 10 pounds, chances are most of your clients will be as well. This phenomenon is especially true when it comes to money. If you are struggling with money, you will attract people who are also struggling with money. This is one of the beautiful aspects of being a Health Coach. It is through coaching others that we heal our own wounds and move forward with our lives. If you find yourself attracting lots of clients who cannot afford your program, the best thing for you to do is examine your own relationship with money. How can you open up to receiving?

Notes:

List five life circumstances you are currently going through or most recently went through:

1. ....

2. ....

3. ....

4. ....

5. ....

How did you overcome these? Have you had any clients with these same concerns?

....

....

....

....

Don't be afraid to use your personal experiences and struggles to help others. They may end up helping you in return!

HEALTH COACHING PARAMETERS

Health Coaches do not heal anyone. Clients do the work and are responsible for their own life and health. We are their "guide on the side." It is important not to work with clients who have major health concerns or who are taking multiple prescription drugs. Their concerns are often too complex and are best supported through other means.

When working with clients who have minor health concerns, you may wish to inform them of potential complementary and alternative ways of addressing these concerns. Research continues to support the use of more holistic and integrative treatment modalities involving diet and exercise for conditions such as migraine headaches, constipation, arthritis, and numerous other ailments.

Always use a credible reference guide to assist in suggestions. For example, the *Natural Medicines Comprehensive Database* includes summaries on uses, safety, effectiveness, and interactions of numerous foods, herbs, and supplements. The National Center for Complementary and Alternative Medicines (NCCAM) offers an online A to Z guide on a wide range of nutrition and health topics as well as summaries for the use of specific herbs and up-to-date research from ongoing clinical trials. Visit the website at http://nccam.nih.gov. *The Physician's Desk Reference* (PDR) can be used to investigate the possible side effects and contraindications (food or otherwise) associated with certain medications.

Notes:

You should never tell a client to stop taking medications or to stop seeing their doctor or medical practitioner. You should always recommend a client consult with their medical practitioner before using these methods in place of a medically prescribed regimen or medication. Furthermore, you should never encourage clients to make radical life changes (such as quitting a job, leaving a relationship, or moving out of town). Clients will come up with their own solutions to their problems and when they do, you can support them with the decisions they make.

Clients are in charge of their lives, and they are ultimately responsible for the outcomes of their decisions. In order to help protect yourself against any possible liability, be sure to always have your clients fill out the Program Agreement and explain to them that they are responsible for their own decisions.

WHEN TO REFER CLIENTS

As a new Health Coach, you should seek out clients who are in good overall health. Avoid working with clients on multiple medications or with advanced, chronic, critical, or complex health conditions, such as cancer, degenerative illnesses, or life-threatening eating disorders. It is usually fine to work with people who have autoimmune disorders like diabetes, thyroid issues, and metabolic syndromes. In these cases, it is also important that the client be under the care of a medical practitioner. We recommend the client alert their practitioner that they are in your program. This way, you can help support the efforts and recommendations of the medical care provider.

If you are unsure about working with any particular client, refer to the Additional Coaching Support section of the 6-Month Program Resources, or seek the advice of your Coaching Circle classmates or a trusted healthcare professional, and always err on the side of caution. Sometimes a client may not reveal this information until they are already enrolled in the program with you. In this case, it is imperative that the client is already working with a healthcare professional and that the professional knows the client is working with you.

If the client has cancer, a life-threatening illness, or a serious chronic condition and refuses to work with a medical care professional, we strongly urge you to stop working with that client to protect both parties involved. You can refer these clients to a medical doctor, osteopath, naturopath, or nurse practitioner. Health coaching is not a substitute for seeing a medical professional.

It is helpful for beginning Health Coaches to be aware of certain distinctions in order to determine if a client needs additional support from a mental health professional. Developing active listening is the best way to be aware of whether or not you should refer your client to another professional to check for underlying or complex medical or emotional issues.

Listen to your intuition. If you think you might be in over your head, you most likely are. Set and trust your boundaries. Don't let your desire to be helpful or your fears of rejecting someone allow you to be drawn into an inappropriate situation. Depending

Notes:

on the extent of your client's condition, you may still be able to work with the client while they are seeking professional health treatment.

If your client shows signs of depression, mania, mental instability, or suicidal tendencies, you should refer them immediately to a mental health professional.

Signs of depression include:

- Decreased energy, fatigue
- Feelings of hopelessness or pessimism
- Persistent sad, anxious, or "empty" mood
- Feelings of guilt, worthlessness, or helplessness
- Thoughts of death or suicide, or suicide attempts
- Appetite and/or weight loss, overeating, or weight gain
- Insomnia, early morning awakening, or oversleeping
- Difficulty concentrating, remembering, or making decisions
- Loss of interest in pleasure or hobbies that were once enjoyable, including sex

Signs of mania include:

- Poor judgment
- Racing thoughts
- Increased talking
- Suicidal thoughts
- Grandiose notions
- Unusual irritability
- Increased sexual desire
- Decreased need for sleep
- Markedly increased energy
- Inappropriate social behavior
- Abnormal or excessive elation

Signs of mental instability include:

- Client is out of touch with reality, fixated on events of the past
- Client is emotionally unable to cope or follow through on basic strategies or excessively anxious, emotional, or angry
- Client is suffering from a recent trauma, domestic violence, or grief/loss
- Client is dealing with a substance abuse issue or other serious addiction

A client's reference to suicidal thoughts or tendencies should be taken very seriously. Handle them in the following ways:

- When talking about thoughts of suicide with a client, do not swear to secrecy.
- Ask the client if they are currently having thoughts of suicide or have a suicide plan. Be aware that the more detailed the plan and the greater their access to the means to carry out their plan, the greater the risk of suicide.

Notes:

- Ask them if they are working with a mental health professional. If they are not, have them contact their doctor or the suicide hotline in your area to get a referral. They can also go to the local hospital.
- Have them make a plan to meet with a professional either on the spot or within the next few hours. If there will be an interval of time before this meeting, ask them to agree not to take any actions to hurt themselves at least until they meet with the professional. Help them to identify and call a support person that can come and be with them until their appointment in order to help them stay safe and reduce their feelings of isolation.
- If the client is a minor, talk to their parent or guardian about how to keep the client safe and emphasize the importance of professional help.

Remind parents that anytime alcohol or drug use is involved, suicide risk increases. Refer depressed and suicidal clients to:

- Medical doctor, osteopath, or naturopath
- Therapist
- Psychiatrist
- Psychologist
- Rehabilitation program
- Licensed social worker
- Mental health professional

Making a professional connection with a mental health professional is a good idea. You can refer clients to them if the need arises, and they can act as a resource on matters related to mental health.

ADDITIONAL ISSUES TO CONSIDER FOR REFERRALS

Child abuse and maltreatment is defined as:

- Sexual abuse
- Malnourishment
- Use of drugs or alcohol
- Extreme emotional abuse
- Improper/inadequate supervision
- Substantial risk for physical injury
- Physical abuse, injury, or excessive corporal punishment
- Inadequate shelter, clothing, education, medical, or surgical care

In the event that you witness or learn that a minor is being abused or neglected in some way, we advise you to file a report with the child welfare agency or hotline in your area as soon as possible.

Notes:

If it is an emergency situation, the police should be called. If the person who revealed the instance of child abuse to you is a direct witness, encourage the witness to call and make a report. However, if you believe a child is truly in danger, we suggest you make the call. If you are not in a profession in which you are legally mandated to report these issues, you may do so anonymously.

If a client reveals that they were the victim of a relatively recent crime, such as rape or domestic violence, encourage them to report the incident to the local police department. In addition, encourage them to meet with a therapist or visit an intervention agency that deals with the posttraumatic issues of such events. This is also relevant in cases where the incident occurred in the not-so-recent past. If a client still feels threatened by the perpetrator of a past crime, they should be encouraged to seek legal support or work with an appropriate intervention agency.

Always be on the lookout for ways to nurture your dream.

—Lao Tzu

CHAPTER 23:

BEYOND THE 6-MONTH PROGRAM

Some of you may be approaching the end of a 6-month program with your first clients. If so, you are probably wondering, what's next?

For some clients, six months is the perfect amount of time. For others, it is just the beginning. As you start to work closely with clients and develop trusting relationships, you will find that many clients will crave your support beyond their original six-month commitment. The key to client retention is to provide an exceptional health coaching experience that motivates them to keep working and reach new goals.

When speaking with clients about signing up for additional services, be sure to focus on the benefits of additional coaching. This is very similar to the Health History consultation. Suggest new goals or ways to boost their current goals. Have a conversation about what continued coaching would look like. The idea is to continue to provide support and guidance to your client to help them reach even higher goals!

RE-SIGNING CLIENTS

As you come to the end of a 6-month program, you can offer your client the opportunity to work with you for another six months. It's best to offer this to clients with whom you truly enjoy working and that you think would benefit from more of your support. It might feel scary to ask clients to keep seeing you, but you have nothing to lose. Simply let them know that you are interested and available for further support. Chances are, they are wondering how they are going to manage without seeing you anymore!

A second 6-month program can be enormously significant for clients. They already have established a trusting relationship with you, and they are healthier and thinking

Notes:

more clearly than they were six months earlier. In their second program, they will be able to work very deeply on creating a life they love even more.

To re-sign clients, talk to them at the end of session 10 or 11 and mention that you have a special offer for people who sign up for a second program. Let them know they have come a long way through their work with you and can continue to grow and thrive even more over the next six months. This gives them some time to think about what they want their life to look like after their program ends.

You can also offer them a maintenance program, which would mean seeing them once a month for six months or every other week for three months. A maintenance program is a lower-cost, lower-commitment arrangement that may appeal to clients who crave more support but don't have the time or resources to do another 6-month program. If your client is having difficulty deciding what's best for them, use your closing-the-deal skills to walk them through the process. If they decide to work with you again, have them re-sign the appropriate Program Agreement, get their new full payment, set up their new appointments, and congratulate them on making such a powerful commitment to themselves and their well-being.

Some clients may want to continue with health-related goals, but others will be eager to take on other parts of their life. As a Health Coach, you can be their sounding board and safe space to explore primary food–related sectors of their lives. If the client doesn't have anything specific in mind, the Clean Sweep exercise is a strong activity to show areas that need improvement. The full exercise is at the end of this chapter and in the 6-Month Program Resources.

For more coaching content, use these resources to begin exploring:

- Michael Arloski, *Wellness Coaching for Lasting Lifestyle Change*
- Jennifer J. Britton, *Effective Group Coaching: Tried and Tested Tools and Resources for Optimum Coaching Results*
- Byron Katie, www.thework.com
- Danielle LaPorte, *The Fire Starter Sessions*
- Thomas Leonard, *How to Coach Anyone*
- Gladeana McMahon and Anne Archer, *101 Coaching Strategies and Techniques*
- Laura Whitworth, Karen Kimsey-House, et al., *Co-Active Coaching: Changing Business, Transforming Lives*

CUSTOMIZED PROGRAMS

If you are already a licensed professional, such as a chiropractor, massage therapist, personal trainer, or yoga instructor, you can certainly combine your previous career with health coaching. You can add one or two massages, yoga classes, or training sessions to your 6-month program and increase the price accordingly. If you are interested in combining health coaching with other practices, consider offering various tiers of service.

Notes:

Create a handout that outlines your different program offerings. Explain your basic 6-month health coaching program and list the fee. Then list a medium-priced program that combines health coaching with one extra service each month, such as one massage or private yoga session. Your deluxe program can include two extra services each month. Make sure you give your clients a cost incentive to want to buy the more expensive programs, and let them know that they are getting a discount when they buy more. For example, if your regular program is $195 per month, you can have your medium program cost $245 per month and your deluxe program cost $295 per month.

Throughout your career as a Health Coach, you can continue to add special offerings to your basic program and see which ones your clients respond to. Other services that graduates have successfully added to their programs include: monthly food shopping, private monthly cooking classes, Pilates sessions, polarity therapy, and fashion consulting. Again, we recommend that you stick with the standard 6-month, every-two-week format.

At some point, you may come across a client who wants extra support and asks to meet with you once a week. One week is usually not enough time for a client to try out and fully integrate the recommendations from the previous session. If you do 24 sessions you may find yourself doing more work by creating new content for the extra sessions. Additionally, you may find yourself giving an unbalanced amount of energy to this one client. Sticking to your every-other-week coaching schedule allows you to keep your own life in balance and be the best Health Coach possible. You can explain to your client that the 6-month program has proven to be very effective and that they are much more likely to have success in meeting their health goals if they try this format. However, it is entirely up to you how you work with that person. Experiment and see what works best. You can find some sample tiers below.

ELITE CUSTOM COACHING

- Twelve 45-minute group coaching sessions over twelve months
- Monthly one-on-one laser coaching sessions
- Six one-hour health and wellness teleclasses
- Lunch-and-learn activities (offered to a group)
- Unlimited individual email support
- All books, materials, and recipes included
- Discounts to local health and fitness hot spots

STEP UP TO SUCCESS

- Twelve 45-minute group coaching sessions over twelve months
- Three one-hour health and wellness teleclasses
- Individual email support during open hours

Notes:

- All books, materials, and recipes included
- Discounts to local health and fitness hot spots

JUMP START TO WELLNESS

- Twelve 45-minute group coaching sessions over twelve months
- Books, recipes, and other great giveaways
- Discounts to local health and fitness hot spots

Throughout your career as a Health Coach, you can continue to add special offerings to your basic program and see which ones your clients respond to. Other services that graduates have successfully added to their programs include: monthly food shopping, private monthly cooking classes, Pilates sessions, polarity therapy, and fashion consulting. Again, we recommend that you stick with the standard 6-month, every-two-week format.

STILL LOOKING FOR CLIENTS

This is a great place to be because your business can only grow from here. You are at the beginning of creating a career you love, and you have so much to look forward to. Your task now is to fill your pipeline with potential clients by networking in person and sharing with people that you are a Health Coach. Network at business groups and parties. Give talks. Invite people to Health Histories and do as many as you can. The more Health Histories you do, the sooner you will have paying clients. Figure out who you know who is connected to your target market and build those relationships so that you have a consistent stream of people sending you clients.

Brainstorm and list five places where you can meet new potential clients:

1. ....

2. ....

3. ....

4. ....

5. ....

CLEAN SWEEP

You have more natural energy when you are complete with your environment, well-being, money, and relationships. The Clean Sweep Program, created by Thomas Leonard, consists of 100 items which when completed, give you the vitality and strength that you want. This program can be completed in less than one year, and it is a great tool to use with clients and yourself.

Notes:

Instructions

1. Answer each question. Be rigorous with yourself. If the statement is "sometimes" or "usually true," please do not check the YES line until the statement is virtually always true for you. If the statement does not apply to you, or will never be true for you, then check the YES line. You get credit because it doesn't apply or won't ever happen.
2. Revisit this exercise every few months to gauge your progress.

ENVIRONMENT

YES	NO	
____	____	1. My personal files, papers, and receipts are neatly filed away.
____	____	2. My car is in excellent condition (doesn't need mechanical work, repairs, cleaning or replacing).
____	____	3. My home is neat and clean (vacuumed, closets clean, desks and tables clear, furniture in good repair, windows clean).
____	____	4. My appliances, machinery and equipment work well (refrigerator, toaster, snow-blower, water heater, toys).
____	____	5. My clothes are all pressed, clean, and make me look great (no wrinkles, baskets of laundry, torn, out of date or ill-fitting clothes).
____	____	6. My plants and animals are healthy (fed, watered, getting light and love).
____	____	7. My bed/bedroom lets me have the best sleep possible (firm bed, light, air).
____	____	8. I live in a home/apartment that I love.
____	____	9. I surround myself with beautiful things.
____	____	10. I live in the geographic area of my choice.
____	____	11. There is ample and healthy lighting around me.
____	____	12. I consistently have adequate time, space, and freedom in my life.
____	____	13. I am not damaged by my environment.
____	____	14. I am not tolerating anything about my home or work environment.
____	____	15. My work environment is productive and inspiring (synergistic, ample tools, and resources, no undue pressure).
____	____	16. I recycle.
____	____	17. I use non-ozone-depleting products.
____	____	18. My hair is the way that I want it.
____	____	19. I surround myself with music that makes my life more enjoyable.
____	____	20. My bed is made daily.
____	____	21. I don't injure myself, fall, or bump into things.
____	____	22. People feel comfortable in my home.
____	____	23. I drink purified water.
____	____	24. I have nothing around the house or in storage that I do not need.
____	____	25. I am consistently early or easily on time.
____________		SECTION TOTAL

Notes:

WELL-BEING

YES	NO	
____	____	26. I use caffeine (chocolate, coffee, colas, tea) fewer than 3 times per week, total.
____	____	27. I rarely eat sugar (fewer than 3 times per week).
____	____	28. I rarely watch television (fewer than 5 hours per week).
____	____	29. I rarely drink alcohol. (Less than 2 drinks per week)
____	____	30. My teeth and gums are healthy (have seen a dentist in last six months).
____	____	31. My cholesterol count is healthful.
____	____	32. My blood pressure is healthful.
____	____	33. I have had a complete physical exam in the past three years.
____	____	34. I do not smoke tobacco or other substances.
____	____	35. I do not use illegal drugs or misuse prescribed medications.
____	____	36. I have had a complete eye exam within the past two years (glaucoma check, vision test).
____	____	37. My weight is within my ideal range.
____	____	38. My nails are healthy and look good.
____	____	39. I don't rush or use adrenaline to get the job done.
____	____	40. I have a rewarding life beyond my work or profession.
____	____	41. I have something to look forward to virtually every day.
____	____	42. I have no habits that I find to be unacceptable.
____	____	43. I am aware of the physical or emotional problems or conditions I have, and I am now fully taking care of all of them.
____	____	44. I consistently take evenings, weekends, and holidays off and take at least two weeks of vacation each year.
____	____	45. I have been tested for the AIDS antibody.
____	____	46. I use well-made sunglasses.
____	____	47. I do not suffer.
____	____	48. I floss daily.
____	____	49. I walk or exercise at least three times per week.
____	____	50. I hear well.
__________		SECTION TOTAL

MONEY

YES	NO	
____	____	51. I currently save at least 10% of my income.
____	____	52. I pay my bills on time, virtually always.
____	____	53. My income source/revenue base is stable and predictable.
____	____	54. I know how much I must have to be minimally financially independent and I have a plan to get there.
____	____	55. I have returned or made good on any money I have borrowed.
____	____	56. I have written agreements and am current with payments to individuals or companies to whom I owe money.
____	____	57. I have six months' living expenses in a money market-type account.
____	____	58. I live on a weekly budget that allows me to save and not suffer.
____	____	59. All my tax returns have been filed and all my taxes have been paid.
____	____	60. I currently live well within my means.
____	____	61. I have excellent medical insurance.
____	____	62. My assets (car, home, possessions, treasures) are well-insured.
____	____	63. I have a financial plan for the next year.
____	____	64. I have no legal clouds hanging over me.
____	____	65. My will is up-to-date and accurate.
____	____	66. Any parking tickets, alimony, or child support are paid and current.
____	____	67. My investments do not keep me awake at night.
____	____	68. I know how much I am worth.
____	____	69. I am on a career/professional/business track that is or will soon be financially and personally rewarding.
____	____	70. My earnings are commensurate with the effort I put into my job.
____	____	71. I have no "loose ends" at work.
____	____	72. I am in relationships with people who can assist in my career/professional development.
____	____	73. I rarely miss work due to illness.
____	____	74. I am putting aside enough money each month to reach financial independence.
____	____	75. My earnings outpace inflation, consistently.
__________		SECTION TOTAL

Notes:

Notes:

RELATIONSHIPS

YES	NO	
____	____	76. I have told my parents, in the last three months, that I love them.
____	____	77. I get along well with my sibling(s).
____	____	78. I get along well with my co-workers/clients.
____	____	79. I get along well with my manager/staff.
____	____	80. There is no one who I would dread or feel uncomfortable "running across" (in the street, at an airport or party).
____	____	81. I put people first and results second.
____	____	82. I have let go of the relationships that drag me down or damage me ("let go" means to end, walk away from, declare complete, no longer be attached to).
____	____	83. I have communicated or attempted to communicate with everyone who I have damaged, injured, or seriously upset, even if it wasn't fully my fault.
____	____	84. I do not gossip or talk about others.
____	____	85. I have a circle of friends/family who love and appreciate me for who I am, more than just what I do for them.
____	____	86. I tell people how they can satisfy me.
____	____	87. I am fully caught up with letters and calls.
____	____	88. I always tell the truth, no matter what.
____	____	89. I receive enough love from people around me to feel good.
____	____	90. I have fully forgiven those people who have hurt/damaged me, intentionally or not.
____	____	91. I am a person of his/her word; people can count on me.
____	____	92. I quickly correct miscommunications and misunderstandings when they do occur.
____	____	93. I live life on my terms, not by the rules or preferences of others.
____	____	94. I am complete with past loves or spouses.
____	____	95. I am in tune with my wants and needs and get them taken care of.
____	____	96. I do not judge or criticize others.
____	____	97. I do not "take personally" the things that people say to me.
____	____	98. I have a best friend or soul mate.
____	____	99. I make requests rather than complain.
____	____	100. I spend time with people who don't try to change me.
__________		SECTION TOTAL
__________		GRAND TOTAL

Adapted from the Clean Sweep Program, created by COACH U founder, Thomas Leonard.

Notes:

Notes:

The great aim of education is not knowledge, but action.

—Herbert Spence

CHAPTER 24:

FUTURE BUILDING

As you get further into the program you may begin to think more and more about your future and what it holds. You may want to receive more education or certifications, or you may be ready to build upon your current career. Whatever your thoughts, it's important to clearly create your future and reflect on the accomplishments you have and the ones you wish to attain. In this chapter we will go through some exercises to help you identify your future so you can take the necessary steps to achieve all of your dreams!

FURTHERING YOUR EDUCATION

As a student at Integrative Nutrition, you already know enough to be a Health Coach and to have a positive effect on many people who come your way. You do not need to know every little detail about nutrition and health in order to help your clients. With that said, furthering your education can be exciting and energizing. Through reading books and attending classes, workshops, or retreats on topics related to health, nutrition and lifestyle, you can re-inspire yourself about your career.

List five topics related to your work as a Health Coach that you would like to learn more about:

1. ....

2. ....

3. ....

4. ....

5. ....

Notes:

How much money can you allocate in the next six months to furthering your education? Even if you have little money to spend, you can still learn so much. You can barter with a teacher, attend free seminars, or borrow books from the library. The Open Center in New York City; the Omega Institute in New York; the Esalen Institute in California; and the Heartwood Institute in California all offer weekend, weeklong, and month-long classes on topics related to health and wellness. Check them out along with other resources in your area.

What are some classes, workshops, or books that are within your budget and related to your areas of interest?

1. ....

2. ....

3. ....

4. ....

5. ....

A gentle warning about getting addicted to workshops and brain candy: you already know so much more than the average person. Your listening skills and natural intelligence, not how many books you've read or degrees you have, are what make you a powerful Health Coach. Further your education for your own interest and fun, not because you think you don't know enough.

CAREER FUTURE BUILDING

What would you like to accomplish in your career by the end of the week?

....

....

....

What would you like to accomplish in your career by the end of the month?

....

....

....

Notes:

What would you like to accomplish in your career in the next year?

What would you like to accomplish in your career in the next two years?

What would you like to accomplish in your career in the next five years?

What would you like to accomplish in your career in the next 10 years?

What would you like to accomplish in your career in the next 20 years and beyond?

The principal motivating factors in life are goals. If you do not have them, you won't know what you are working toward. Regardless of where your passions lie—either in health coaching or another career—setting goals for your future provides motivation. Then you must do the work to turn these dreams into your reality.

CREATE YOUR FUTURE

There is a direct correlation between your thoughts and the future you create for yourself. The more confidently you move forward with your practice, the more success will come to you.

Notes:

Whatever your goals are, act as if you have already accomplished them. Carry yourself as if you have the number of clients you want. Talk to potential clients as if you know that they are going to sign up for your program and it is going to be one of the best things that ever happened to them.

Every time you catch yourself thinking that this might not work out, change your thought to something more positive. When an opportunity to expand your business comes your way, jump on it! Don't let potential clients, referral partners, or leads slip past you. Trust your instincts when it comes to people. When your gut tells you that there is an opportunity coming your way, take it and then give gratitude. Gratitude is a way of thanking the universe and inviting more opportunities.

List three things you feel confident and positive about right now.

1. ....

2. ....

3. ....

REFLECTING ON YOUR ACCOMPLISHMENTS

Building your business is a journey, not a destination. It is not a problem that has to be solved, but rather a process through which you will learn what being successful means and looks like to you. If you can develop the habit of recognizing your accomplishments along this journey, you will have the added bonus of experiencing joy.

When you stop to recognize how well you are doing, you put focus on your own prosperity and invite even more. One way to appreciate your progress is to do an inventory before going to bed each night and appreciate everything you did well that day. Another way is to post your to-do list or Big Rocks somewhere in your office and when you have accomplished something, check it off the list. By doing this you will see exactly how much you have done. Consistently remind yourself that you are an amazing person and you are doing the best that you can.

What are you most proud of regarding your health coaching practice or other business?

....

....

....

What has been your greatest accomplishment in the past six months?

....

....

....

Notes:

FOCUS ON OPPORTUNITIES NOT OBSTACLES

Successful people focus on opportunities, not obstacles. They see potential growth, not potential loss. It comes down to the age-old question, "Is the glass half empty or half full?" We're not talking about positive thinking here; we're talking about your habitual perspective on the world.

You don't want to make choices out of fear, to constantly be thinking of what could go wrong in any situation. Successful people expect to succeed. Try to be optimistic. Act using the mindset, "It will work because I'll make it work." Have confidence in both your abilities and creativity and believe that if things get messy, you will be able to find another way to succeed.

If you want to experience success, focus on the opportunities in everything. If you focus on opportunities, they will come to you. If you focus on obstacles, they will be all around you. Your field of focus determines what you find in life.

Try this as your motto: action beats inaction. Successful people get started. They trust that once they get in the game, they can make intelligent decisions in the present moment and adjust their skills along the way.

Adapted from *Secrets of the Millionaire Mind: Mastering the Inner Game of Wealth* by T. Harv Eker, New York, NY: Harper Business, 2005.

What obstacles have you overcome to be where you are today?

....

....

....

What concrete benefits have you brought to your clients, friends, family, and to yourself as a result of committing to IIN and health coaching?

....

....

....

List 10 things you love about yourself:

1. ....

2. ....

Notes:

3. ....

4. ....

5. ....

6. ....

7. ....

8. ....

9. ....

10. ....

Notes:

Notes:

Be brave. Take risks. Nothing can substitute for experience.

—Paulo Coelho

CHAPTER 25:

STRENGTHEN YOUR BUSINESS

As you near the end of the program, you are probably making some decisions about where to take your health coaching practice. Will this be a part-time adventure to make supplemental income on top of your current career? Will you use health coaching only with your family and community without earning money from it? Or will you make health coaching your full-time job, providing income and fulfillment for years to come? This chapter provides helpful information regardless of where you are on your health coaching path or whichever vocational option you choose.

BUSINESS-OWNER MENTALITY

If you enjoy helping clients and can see yourself doing this work full-time, you will eventually have to shift from having a private practice, with up to 15 clients at a time to being a business owner. People with a private practice focus on the clients they have, do their own marketing and networking to maintain their desired number of clients, and invest minimally in business growth.

By becoming a business owner, you are saying to yourself and the world, "This is what I want to do with my life." You make health coaching your career and commit to doing this work for an extended period of time. You work to grow, enhance, and stabilize your business over the long term.

One way to measure your readiness to become a full-time Health Coach is to look at your finances. Have you been able to easily pay your bills with the money you've made from health coaching? If so, you are definitely ready to move forward, knowing it's only going to get better from here. If you haven't been able to easily pay your bills, it's probably best to focus on getting more clients before jumping into heavy-duty business

Notes:

building. Be sure to make a budget and financial projection plan, and assess when the right time would be for you to transition to full-time.

Taking on the mentality of a business owner can actually decrease stress. This may seem counterintuitive, but think about it. Almost all businesses take a few years to build. You can approach your business slowly and methodically and should expect your business' growth to ebb and flow. Every corporation and business expert knows that you can't implement all your ideas for change immediately. They strategize to decide the best moves to make, measure the success of those moves, and then decide what their next move will be. Approach your health coaching practice in the same way.

Once you decide to pursue this work full-time, pick one area you want to focus on and stay on top of it. For example, if you want to increase your visibility, you may book workshops and put more effort into your PR. Do this for a month or two and measure your results. Is your phone ringing more often? Do you have more Health Histories this month? What worked and what didn't work? Once you evaluate the effectiveness of this strategy, you will be better prepared to decide what your next move will be. Keep in mind that your business is a constant work in progress and you don't have to do everything all at once.

RAISING YOUR RATES

Graduation is a perfect time to raise your rates. You can raise them by a little or a lot, depending on your comfort level and what you are already charging. Remember when you were little and learning to ride a bike? First you rode with training wheels and eventually someone took the wheels off. When you rode without them for the first time, you probably realized that you could have taken them off much sooner. Your body already knew how to balance perfectly on the bike, and it was actually your mind that needed longer to develop confidence. Raising your rates is like taking off your training wheels. It's like saying to yourself and the world, "I can do it!"

It's time to take the training wheels off your business. Now that you have developed your confidence, you are ready to openly own your value and charge what you are worth.

In our experience, $195 to $250 per month is a good amount to charge as a newly graduated Health Coach. You may be comfortable charging more or less than that; wherever you are is okay, just be careful not to undersell yourself. Many students and graduates have shared that when they charged $150 per month it was harder to get clients than when they increased their rates to $250. This is because $250 per month is a better indicator of the true value of the program. When people hear that it costs that amount, they understand that it must be really valuable.

What do you charge for your program now?

....

....

What services do your clients get for that cost?

List some of the results your clients have received from working with you so far. List some of the benefits your friends and family gain simply by having your presence in their lives. What would you pay a professional for these benefits and results?

List everything that has gone into making you the professional Health Coach you are today. Include natural talents, unique skills, career experience, travel, personal growth and development, books you've read, workshops you've attended, formal education, and anything else that's relevant. How much would you pay a professional with this level of experience to be your support person?

SETTING FINANCIAL GOALS

As a business owner, you no longer have a boss setting your salary. You get to decide how much money you want or need to make, and then make it happen. Your financial plan helps you determine how many clients you need to see at a given time, which helps you to organize your marketing plan. Financial planning can be fun and empowering as you learn to take charge of your money in a new way.

Notes:

Notes:

KEYS FOR ACHIEVEMENT

- Focus on your goals. Use the time management tools to ensure that you are using your time to work toward your top priorities.
- Evaluate how you are doing. Be honest with yourself. Are you working too hard or not hard enough? Have you accomplished enough this week, and are you able to take a day off without guilt? Constantly measure your level of effort and compare it to your results. This will help you refine your tactics and make smarter decisions.
- Complete your Big Rocks and include scheduling workshops, networking events, and marketing steps each week. If you complete everything on your Big Rocks, you should see results.
- Set up reward systems to keep yourself motivated. These should probably not involve food. Maybe you treat yourself to a massage for every new client you sign, or you buy yourself a new outfit if you reach your target for new clients at the end of the month. Remind yourself why you are doing this work, and set future goals for yourself.
- Have someone in your life who will hold you accountable for completing certain tasks and keep you on track to achieve your future goals. This person could be your buddy, your Health Coach, or a member of your board of directors.
- Get a different point of view on your progress or challenges. Just hearing your problem restated by another person can give you helpful insight. When you are feeling low, it's also great to have someone be your personal cheerleader.
- No matter where you are in your business development, having a mentor and a support team is essential to your success. You can use friends, spouses, or family members for this purpose, but if you are determined to do this work full-time, having a business coach is extremely beneficial. There are many experienced graduates available to help you navigate through your journey.
- A lot of opportunities will come your way as a Health Coach. It is important to stay focused on what you want to achieve and prioritize the action steps that will help you reach your goals more quickly. A rule of thumb employed by many successful graduates is to prioritize the business building steps that bring in clients.
- Whenever your work seems stressful or dull, remember that you are the boss and can reinvent yourself and your business, so add fun activities to your routine. Take a class on something you always wanted to learn. Try a new food or recipe and then share it with your clients. This work never has to be monotonous. At the end of each day, appreciate yourself for your efforts to do your best.

Adapted from *Get Clients Now!: A 28-Day Marketing Program for Professionals, Consultants and Coaches,* 2nd ed., by C.J. Hayden, New York, NY: AMACOM, 2007.

Notes:

List your monthly personal expenses:

Rent/mortgage: $

Food: $

Clothing: $

Entertainment: $

Health insurance: $

Self-care: $

Other household expenses: $

$

$

$

$

$

$

List your monthly business expenses:

Phones: $

Internet: $

Office supplies: $

Client giveaways: $

Cooking class materials: $

Other event expenses: $

Taxes: $

Other: $

$

$

$

$

$

$

How much would you like to save or invest per month? $

Add up all these expenses. This is how much you want to make per month: $

Notes:

Multiply by 12. This is your desired yearly income: $..........

How much of this will come from your health coaching business? $..........

How much will come from other ventures? $..........

How many clients will you need? ....

1. List the amount that will come from coaching each month: $..........

2. List your monthly program fee: $..........

3. Divide line 1 by line 2: ....

This is the number of clients you need to see each month in order to reach your desired income.

For example, if you want to make $6,500 from health coaching this month and you charge $295 per month, you will need to see 22 clients this month to have your desired income. Revisit your marketing strategy to see how your actions can help you meet your goal in an efficient and effective way.

HEALTH INSURANCE

As a self-employed person, you will need to purchase health insurance if you live in the US. As today's workforce becomes more mobile and flexible, new options are being created all the time. Plans often vary by state and region, so research the options and requirements in your area. If you live in the US, visit healthcare.gov for more information.

COVERAGE THROUGH ANOTHER EMPLOYER

If you have a spouse or close relative with a good insurance plan at their job, you may be able to be covered under their plan. This could cost the same or more than paying for your own basic insurance, but you might get more benefits or more flexible options. Also, if you are health coaching part-time and working somewhere else part-time, your employer may be able to cover your health insurance needs.

HIRING HELP

To run a thriving practice, you are going to need support. Help can come from your family, friends, and support team. It should also come from paid professionals. It pays off to invest in yourself so that you can have a great life and accomplish your agenda. Your paid employees and support people are there to help you do just that.

Notes:

HIRING AN ASSISTANT

If you have a solid practice and are consistently making $75 to $100 per hour, you can hire an assistant. This person will take care of basic tasks, such as typing and filing, for $10 to $15 per hour, leaving you much more time to market your business and sign new clients. You should set up the hours that work best for you, and you probably will not need your assistant to work full-time. They could come in for one full day every week or for a few hours each day. Delegate those tasks that take time away from signing clients and that you don't need to do in person. Depending on your needs, your assistant could organize your papers, order supplies, book appointments, buy your groceries, or research new places for you to give workshops. Your assistant could also work remotely and support you with some of your marketing efforts, including posting on your social media networks, doing research for articles and blog posts, and organizing logistics for your workshops and events.

HIRING ADDITIONAL HEALTH COACHES

Signing up too many clients is a good problem to have. If you want to keep a high number of clients in your business but can't handle seeing all of them, hire another Health Coach.

Here's how this can work. You can continue to do Health Histories and close deals with clients, letting them know that you will assign them to a Health Coach in your business who will best suit their needs. Then pay another Health Coach to work with some clients. Negotiate an agreement with your colleague about how much they will be paid. Will you pay them hourly or give them a percentage of the fee? These arrangements are completely up to you.

If and when you hire other coaches, you may want to incorporate education into their benefits. You can take them to time management or personal growth and development conferences to help them improve their coaching and business skills. You can also provide self-care benefits like organic meals in the office, weekly yoga classes, or monthly massages. Having other Health Coaches in your business can be very rewarding. Your team can have lunch together, discuss client health concerns, share laughs and disappointments, and generally support one another.

HIRING OTHER PROFESSIONALS

In what other areas of your life could you save time, money, and energy by paying someone to help you? For example, is it worth it to spend five hours cleaning your home this week, or could you use that time to sign more clients and pay someone $100 to clean your house? Is it worth it to spend extra time commuting across town for your yoga class, or could you hire a yoga instructor to come right to your door?

Notes:

Professionals you could hire include:

- Accountant
- Bookkeeper
- Business coach
- Cook
- Cleaning person
- Massage therapist
- Private yoga instructor
- Writer or writing coach

If you are a new business owner, you might feel uncomfortable being "the boss" and paying others to do what you ask. This is actually a great way to practice knowing your own worth and being "on top of the food chain." Recognize that you are involved in exciting work of which others will want to be a part. Many people would love to work for a passionate, committed business owner who runs their practice with love and integrity and who is making the world a better place. Over time, you will figure out a management style that works well for you. Build your confidence by leading your team and noticing that other people are happy to support you.

STARTING WHERE YOU ARE

Whether you have zero or 30 clients, accept where you are and move forward from there. You do not want to be ahead of yourself or behind yourself in any way. For example, if you want to be a full-time Health Coach and you haven't signed any clients yet, you shouldn't focus on building a website or writing a book. Instead, focus your efforts on setting up and conducting more Health Histories. Likewise, if you already have a full practice and can't handle any more clients, you don't need to spend hours booking a workshop; your energy is probably better spent on managing your time and developing your coaching skills.

Here are some recommended action steps to take, depending on where you are in your business.

IF YOU ARE COACHING PART-TIME

Continue to focus on marketing yourself in person. Stay visible and in demand so that you are continually meeting potential clients who may be ready to sign up with you. This way, when a client finishes a program, you can enroll a new client to fill that slot right away. Give talks, network, and make special offers to clients who refer people that sign up with you.

Notes:

Evaluate how many clients are ideal for you. Are you happy coaching part-time? Do you want to eventually go full-time? If so, when? Some people are happy coaching only five clients at a time. Others want to coach 10, 20, or 30 clients. Some new coaches think that if their number of clients plateaus along the way, they won't be able to do this work full-time. This isn't true. You can grow your business if you want to. Decide for yourself what your ideal number of clients is, then adjust your marketing hours or change your action steps in order to get your ideal number.

IF YOU ARE COACHING FULL-TIME

At this point, you have completed a lot of the basic marketing work it takes to attract clients. You are probably managing a lot of paperwork, people, and opportunities. The time you spend on marketing should be limited and focused. Do one powerful marketing activity every day, or set aside one day a week and do five to seven marketing actions on that day.

Put energy into building a sustainable business structure. Manage your time well and increase your level of self-care to ensure you don't burn out. Hire an assistant at $10 to $15 per hour to help you with administrative details. Enlist PR or media relations support so that you can get your practice out there without having to do all the footwork yourself.

You can also take advantage of passive marketing techniques in which other people find clients for you. Build referral networks with other practitioners so that they send potential clients your way. Under-promise and over-deliver for all your clients so that they become raving fans and spread the word about how fabulous you are.

In Chapter 4 we asked you to set goals for what you want your health coaching business to look like.

Have you achieved your goals?

....

If so, what led to your success?

....

How do you feel?

....

Notes:

If not, that's okay. Take an honest look at why not.

What is one obstacle you are committed to overcoming?

Have your goals changed, and if so, how?

What can you do differently in the future to meet your goals?

HAVING FUN

If you want your career as a Health Coach to be satisfying, you must find a way to incorporate having fun into your business. Being an overly serious workaholic who is adamantly attached to changing the world will get old soon enough. Take a step back, enjoy your precious life, and find a way to create balance between work and play. Remember, no one wants a burned out Health Coach!

Notice what parts of health coaching bring you the most energy and excitement. Do you absolutely love giving talks? Sending out your newsletter? Leading health food store tours? Whatever you enjoy most, do more of it. Similarly, notice what components of health coaching drain your energy and do less of those!

What are three components of health coaching that get you excited?

1.
2.
3.

What are three components of health coaching that drain your energy?

1.
2.
3.

How can you do fewer of the tasks that drain your energy and more of what you truly enjoy?

1. ....

2. ....

3. ....

4. ....

5. ....

Notes:

IDEAS FOR INCORPORATING FUN INTO YOUR PRACTICE

- Create arts and crafts projects to do in your client sessions or in your seminars, such as collages, finger painting, candle making, pottery painting, or making your own holiday cards.
- Take clients out dancing, to karaoke, or for a picnic instead of a regular monthly seminar.
- Hold client sessions outside in a beautiful location.
- Invite exciting guest speakers to your monthly seminars, such as belly dancers, palm readers, fashion experts, feng shui practitioners, or creative writing teachers.
- Offer to help your clients de-clutter their home or kitchen. Hold a session at their place and give them tips on how to clean up clutter.
- Make it a goal to laugh at least once during each session. If this is difficult for you, find something that makes you laugh and keep it in your office at all times.

Do not go where the path may lead,
go instead where there is no path
and leave a trail.

—Ralph Waldo Emerson

CHAPTER 26:

STAYING CONNECTED

MAINTAINING MOMENTUM

It takes a few years and hard work to build a solid practice. Don't expect it all to happen overnight. It may seem to you that some of your classmates or some of our alumni had clients fall into their laps. This is not the case. Building a business takes focus, determination, and a lot of energy. If you are consistently putting yourself out there and building your visibility in your community and target market, you will succeed. Please remember to focus on what is working for you and put your time, energy, and effort into solutions and methods to grow your practice. Use the Golden Path to guide your efforts. Don't focus on your mistakes but rather learn from them, as those are lessons that will guide you to do even better as you move forward.

Everyone has times when they doubt their ability to do this work. It is the nature of being in business for yourself. What's important is that you push yourself through those times and continue moving forward. You will need self-motivation to stay inspired by your work and progress toward your goals. Keep reminding yourself why you wanted to be a Health Coach in the first place. Take constant inventory of the positive influences you have had on your clients, family, and friends. You can be a huge source of inspiration for your community with all you have to offer!

MACRO-VISION

We've been asking you to think about your intentions and vision throughout the program. Having a deep, clear vision is a step of the Golden Path. In Chapter 1, we talked

Notes:

about your vision for your practice. Please revisit this vision. It's helpful to break this down into a macro-vision and a micro-vision. A macro-vision is similar to a mission statement. It is the ultimate goal of your business and maybe even your life. Your macro-vision drives all the choices you make. It answers the questions of why you were born and what impact you want to have on the world. Your macro-vision is bigger than you are.

Here's an example: The macro-vision for Integrative Nutrition is to play a crucial role in improving health and happiness, and through that process, create a ripple effect that transforms the world. Take a moment now to write out the macro-vision of your business.

Use the vision exercise from Chapter 1 and the mission statement exercise from Chapter 8 to help you.

....

....

....

....

....

Now refine your macro-vision. Express it in just two or three sentences.

....

....

....

....

....

MICRO-VISION

Your micro-vision is what you will focus on in the coming months to make your macro-vision a reality. It answers the question of what you are going to do today to support your macro-vision. For example, if your macro-vision is to improve the quality of life for children in your community, your micro-vision may be to get involved in local schools and create a plan to upgrade school lunches.

As a Health Coach, many projects and opportunities will come your way. Your micro-vision helps you make day-to-day choices about where to get involved. Gauge each opportunity that comes your way, so that you're only taking on projects that are a

Notes:

good match for you. Know that it is okay to turn down opportunities if they are not in alignment with your vision. In some cases, you may be offered projects that are in line with your macro-vision but not your current micro-vision. It is okay to postpone those projects until a later date.

Your macro-vision will stay more or less constant throughout your life and practice. Your micro-vision will shift every few months as you complete projects, expand your horizons, and discover new ways to meet your goals. Revisit your micro-vision often to make sure it is still relevant and helping you to fulfill your overall vision.

Write down your micro-vision for your practice in the next six months.

....

....

....

....

....

ADVANCED BUSINESS AND COACHING PROGRAM

One of the most effective ways to build and maintain your business is to stay connected to the Integrative Nutrition community. We encourage you to stay active in your Facebook group and continue to learn and grow with your classmates. Keep meeting regularly with your Accountability Coach.

Another great way to stay connected to the school is through our advanced business and coaching program. This program offers unparalleled training and support for students who want to take their life and practice to the next level. In the program you will have the following opportunities:

- Set goals for your business to work toward throughout the program.
- Learn from experts in the fields of coaching and business.
- Incorporate advanced coaching techniques to maximize your client sessions and build relationships.
- Learn advanced business practices to become a top entrepreneur.
- Consistently sign on clients with accountability and support.
- Develop your confidence and self-esteem.
- Create a life you love with purpose and clarity.

Graduates register for the program after they have applied everything they have learned in the Health Coach Training Program and have experience working with clients. You will receive information about this program and other continuing education opportunities during your course.

Notes:

Integrative Nutrition is a community of people working together to affect great change in the world. We strongly recommend that you surround yourself and get to know your fellow graduates. Your Health Coach friends are invaluable. They will be able to listen to you and offer you business and personal advice that only other Health Coaches can give. Please stay connected to the people and resources that you need to continue to learn and grow.

ADDITIONAL SUPPORT

In Chapter 5 we addressed the need to set yourself up with the right kinds of support people. As you grow your practice, we recommend setting up a board of directors and/or a mastermind group to give you even more support and accountability. Other support people include business coaches and mentors.

BOARD OF DIRECTORS

A board of directors allows you to receive expert advice from supportive people who have additional knowledge and experience. Corporations, schools, and nonprofit foundations use a board of directors to advise them on their business decisions and goal planning. A board of directors will share their knowledge, help you make important decisions, give you support, hold you accountable, and help you reach new levels of success.

HOW TO CREATE A BOARD OF DIRECTORS

1. Decide whom to invite. You will need between four and six people on your board. Who are your peers and mentors with valuable insight to share? Do you know any accountants, lawyers, or business professionals? A friend who works in marketing? Another successful Health Coach or an experienced person in a healing profession?
2. Invite each person to participate in your business as an advisor. Share with them how committed you are to the success of your business and how much you value their wisdom and support.
3. Let each person know up front what their time commitment will be: one conference call each month for 30 to 60 minutes. If they're okay with that, ask them for three possible days and times they could meet every month (e.g., every third Tuesday at 5:00 p.m.). Use these days to choose a schedule that works for everyone on your board.

Notes:

4. Send an email to your entire board introducing everyone and asking them to mark the meeting schedule on their calendars. It should be the same week, day, and time every month.
5. You can use a service such as www.freeconference.com, www.instantteleseminar.com, or www.nocostconference.com to schedule the calls. Be sure to send your board the phone number and necessary access codes.
6. Before each call, choose two or three areas of your business where you need the most support. You could also prepare a summary of your business before each meeting to keep your board up to date on your progress. Make sure you leave time for group brainstorming.
7. Keep meetings regular. The consistent support you'll get from your board is crucial to your success. If members need to leave the group, find others to replace them.
8. Appreciate your board and let them know how much you value their support. Send thank-you cards, emails, or small gifts.
9. Give back. Offer to be on their boards of directors in return.

Write down the names of five people you want to have on your board of directors:

1. ....

2. ....

3. ....

4. ....

5. ....

Your board does not have to be arranged in any formal way. The goal is to have regular contact with knowledgeable people who actively support you and your business growth. Set this up in whatever way works best for you.

MASTERMIND GROUP

A mastermind group is a select group of people that bring their energy, commitment, and excitement to a regular meeting. It is similar to a board of directors, but more geared toward the whole group's success versus a board, which is there just for you. Participants in a mastermind group raise the bar by challenging each other to create and implement goals, brainstorm ideas, and support each other with honesty, respect, and compassion. Mastermind participants act as catalysts for growth, devil's advocates, and supportive colleagues.

Notes:

The agenda belongs to the group and each person's participation is key. Your peers offer feedback, brainstorm new possibilities, set up accountability structures, and create community. This provides you with a valuable support network!

A group should ideally consist of people who have a similar interest, have a similar skill and/or success level, want to exceed their goals, want a supportive team, are ready for their passion to overcome their fear, and have the desire to make their lives extraordinary. Mastermind groups can meet in person, on the phone, or online. Groups typically schedule a required once-a-month meeting. Look for highly motivated people.

You can join an existing group or start your own. Decide in advance how many people should be in your group (five to eight is recommended), and only accept new members with unanimous consent. Consider asking these questions:

- Do you have a personal or business mission or vision statement?
- What are your goals for the coming year, and for the next five years?
- How will you find time to participate in the mastermind group?
- What is your commitment to moving forward in your business and personal life?
- Why should you be chosen to participate in this group?

Even with a screening process, your group is likely to run across people who say they're committed but then don't follow through. Be prepared to ask people to leave the group who are not rising up to the group standard, and do it quickly once the poor behavior becomes evident. A "slacking" member will bring down the energy level for the whole group. (Excerpted from "How to Create and Run a Mastermind Group" by Karyn Greenstreet. http://www.passionforbusiness.com/articles/mastermind-group.htm)

Write down the names of five people you want to contact to start a mastermind group:

1. ....

2. ....

3. ....

4. ....

5. ....

Do you want to have a board of directors and a mastermind group, or start with just one?

....

....

....

What support tools do you feel will work best for you?

Notes:

HIRING A BUSINESS COACH

If you know that you want your business to grow but need more guidance on how to make that happen, you might want to hire a business coach. When your sessions end with your Coaching Circle, your coach may offer his or her services to you at a discounted rate. You may choose to take your coach up on this offer if you think it would be helpful.

Another option would be to hire a different person as your coach. We have graduates who have been practicing successfully for years and offer business coaching to current students and alumni. They would be delighted to hear from you and tell you about the business coaching that they offer.

MENTORS

Anyone who has ever had a mentor or been a mentor knows that the mentor-mentee relationship is a strong bond. To guide a person through something that you have already experienced—to encourage them, warn them of the roadblocks, and tell them they can do it—is an extremely rewarding experience. Likewise, having someone show you the ropes, someone you can confide in and trust, is priceless. Know that there are many people in the Integrative Nutrition community and in the world who would be honored to share their expertise with you.

Ask yourself if you know someone whose business expertise you admire. Who is someone you aspire to be like? Pick up the phone or turn on your computer and reach out to this person. Invite them to lunch, let them know that you have just started a new business and you would love to share some ideas. Emphasize how much you value their expert opinion.

List three people who you would like to have as your mentor:

1.

2.

3.

Now devise a plan for making these people a part of your life. It might be appropriate to hire a person if they are a business coach or maybe you could simply work toward building a friendly relationship. Know that you become like the people you associate

Notes:

with, so surrounding yourself with accomplished, first-rate people is a sure way to invite success into your life.

GIVING BACK

Chances are your life is pretty good, but sometimes you may only be aware of what is not working for you. In reality, many people in our world are hungry, sick, poor, and without a home or a family. When you realize how the less fortunate are living and compare it to how you are living, you will see that most people in the world would love to have your life.

We encourage you to find ways to give freely to those who have less than you. In your local community, there may be senior citizens, children, people with illnesses, or underprivileged families who would benefit greatly from your services and cannot afford them. Sharing your expertise with those who are less fortunate can be hugely rewarding for you, and your new clients will benefit from access to priceless information they would not have without your services.

WAYS YOU CAN GIVE BACK

- Work with a school to offer an inexpensive group program to teens.
- Donate free sessions, cooking classes, or workshops to a benefit auction.
- Organize a group of volunteers to cook a healthy meal for a soup kitchen.
- Work with a YMCA or community center to offer a group program for free or at reduced rates.
- Ask your local church, school, or retirement home if they would like you to give a free talk about wellness.
- Give to community organizations that are working on important health issues.
- Share your time, expertise, or a donation with grassroots organizations, which are often volunteer-run and under-funded.

WAYS TO SUPPORT MOVEMENTS FOR SOCIAL RESPONSIBILITY

- Advocate for clean air and water.
- Protect the quality of organic foods.
- Raise public awareness about the dangers of sugar and junk foods.
- Fight the influence of the food industry on the government and media.

CONSISTENT GOAL SETTING

The more you plan your future, the more likely it is to happen. Remember that pursuing goals is a step-by-step process. You will likely shift and refine your goals over time. It's important to always know why you do this work, and know what you want to do.

Notes:

What are three goals you have for the next week?

1. ....
2. ....
3. ....

What are three goals you have for the next month?

1. ....
2. ....
3. ....

What are three goals you have for the next six months?

1. ....
2. ....
3. ....

What are three goals you have for the next year?

1. ....
2. ....
3. ....

What are three goals you have for the next two years?

1. ....
2. ....
3. ....

What are three goals you have for the next five years?

1. ....
2. ....
3. ....

Notes:

WE APPRECIATE YOU

We know that people reprioritize aspects of their lives when they choose to study with Integrative Nutrition. Some people let go of personal fears and limitations. We truly appreciate you for dedicating yourself to making this world a happier, healthier place to live. Thank you for all the hard work that you put into being a student and for being a part of our community. We are proud to have you as a graduate of our program and hope that you will stay connected and continue to work with us to make our vision a reality. We wish you a happy, healthy future filled with great success.

Notes:

Notes:

INDEX

D

E

F

O

P

Q

R

S

T

U

V

W